THE ALL NEW ATOM

The Hunt For Ray Palmer!

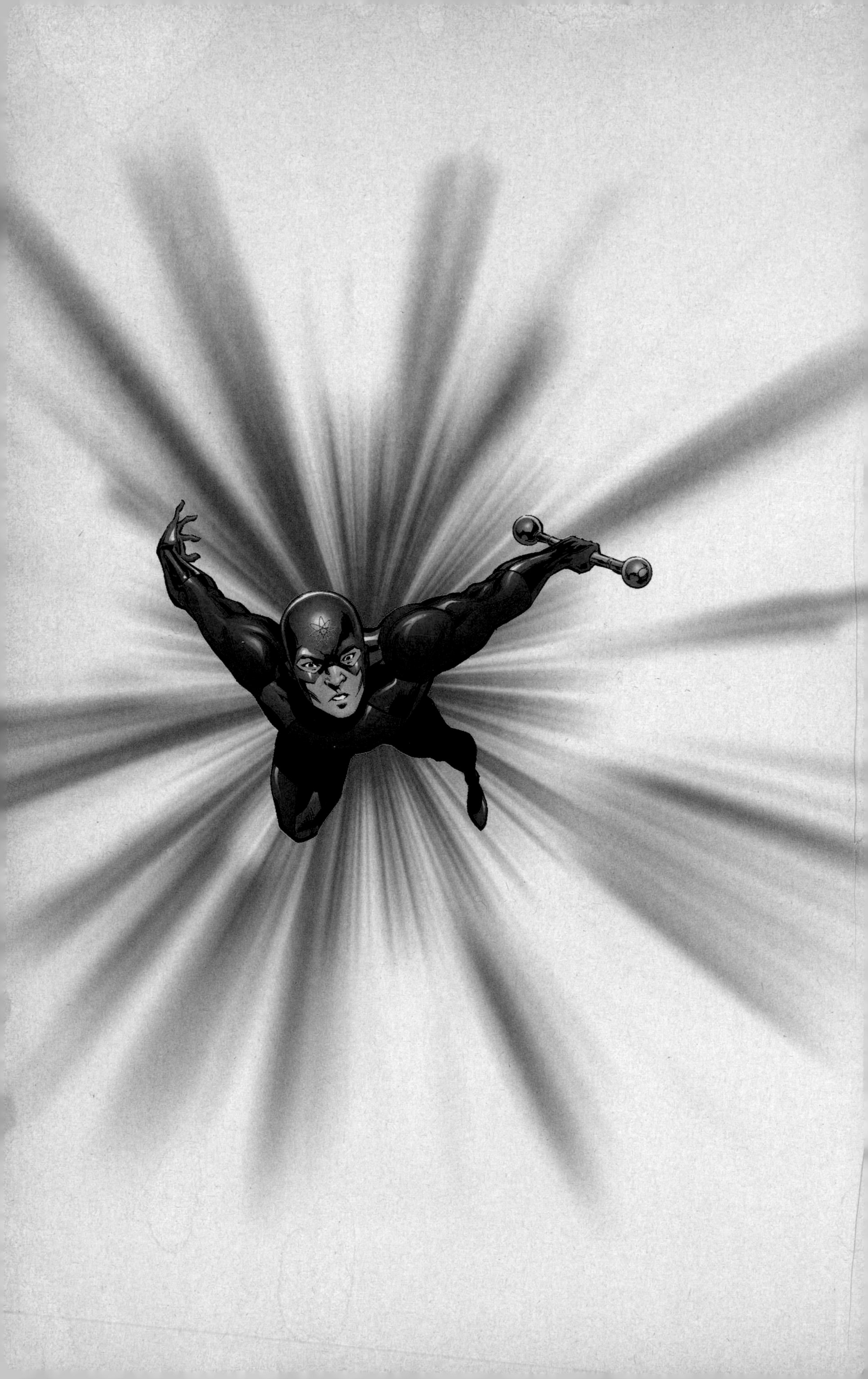

The Hunt For Ray Palmer!

Gail Simone Writer

Mike Norton Penciller

Dan Green Trevor Scott Inkers

Pat Brosseau Travis Lanham John J. Hill Letterers

Alex Bleyaert Colorist

Bonus story: Forward! Into the Past!
Roger Stern Writer

Original Covers by **Ladrönn**

Dan DiDio
Senior VP-Executive Editor

Mike Carlin
Editor-original series

Tom Palmer Jr.
Associate Editor-original series

Bob Joy
Editor-collected edition

Robbin Brosterman
Senior Art Director

Paul Levitz
President & Publisher

Georg Brewer
VP-Design & DC Direct Creative

Richard Bruning
Senior VP-Creative Director

Patrick Caldon
Executive VP-Finance & Operations

Chris Caramalis
VP-Finance

John Cunningham
VP-Marketing

Terri Cunningham
VP-Managing Editor

Alison Gill
VP-Manufacturing

David Hyde
VP-Publicity

Hank Kanalz
VP-General Manager, WildStorm

Jim Lee
Editorial Director-WildStorm

Paula Lowitt
Senior VP-Business & Legal Affairs

MaryEllen McLaughlin
VP-Advertising & Custom Publishing

John Nee
Senior VP-Business Development

Gregory Noveck
Senior VP-Creative Affairs

Sue Pohja
VP-Book Trade Sales

Steve Rotterdam
Senior VP-Sales & Marketing

Cheryl Rubin
Senior VP-Brand Management

Jeff Trojan
VP-Business Development, DC Direct

Bob Wayne
VP-Sales

Cover art by Ladrönn
Logo design by Rian Hughes

**THE ALL NEW ATOM:
THE HUNT FOR RAY PALMER!**

DC Comics, 1700 Broadway,
New York, NY 10019
A Warner Bros. Entertainment Company
Printed in Canada. First Printing.

ISBN: 978-1-4012-1782-2

Welcome to IVY TOWN!

PRESENTED by the Ivy Town Chamber of Commerce

WHO ARE THE PEOPLE IN YOUR NEIGHBORHOOD?

The all new Atom – **Dr. Ryan Choi** – Professor of Nuclear Physics at Ivy University and former pen pal and protégé of the original Atom, Ray Palmer. Ryan moved into Ray's house, took his old job and assumed his costumed identity when Palmer went missing.

Head   Former member of the warrior race the Waiting, Head was cut off from his planet after their attempt to take over Earth. Now a houseguest of Ryan Choi, he enjoys drinking beer, eating EZ Cheeze and watching television. Basically he is now a couch potato-head.

Dr. "Panda" Potter   A professor of Nuclear Physics at Ivy University, Panda has been by Ryan's side ever since he joined the staff. The clingy best friend sponsored Ryan's membership in the "Lighter than Air Society," a group of physicists who regularly meet to play poker, drink beer and debate unsolvable scientific problems.

Dean Mayland   The head of Ivy University made it clear to Ryan he did not want him to take up the mantle of the Atom. Mayland blames Ray Palmer for the temporal mess that Ivy Town has become and wants the legacy of the Atom to end. Choi views him as an ally… but he shouldn't…

Dwarfstar   Sylbert Rundine, Ivytown's first (and only) serial killer, was given a size-changing belt by the university dean, Mayland. In return, the dean wanted Sylbert to kill the new Atom. The battle ended with Dwarfstar being stuck at a subatomic size, and neither Choi nor Mayland was willing to save him from his diminutive destiny.

MISSING:

Raymond Palmer A.K.A. The Atom
After suffering a major identity crisis over a year ago, the Atom shrank into the abyss… his whereabouts are still unknown.

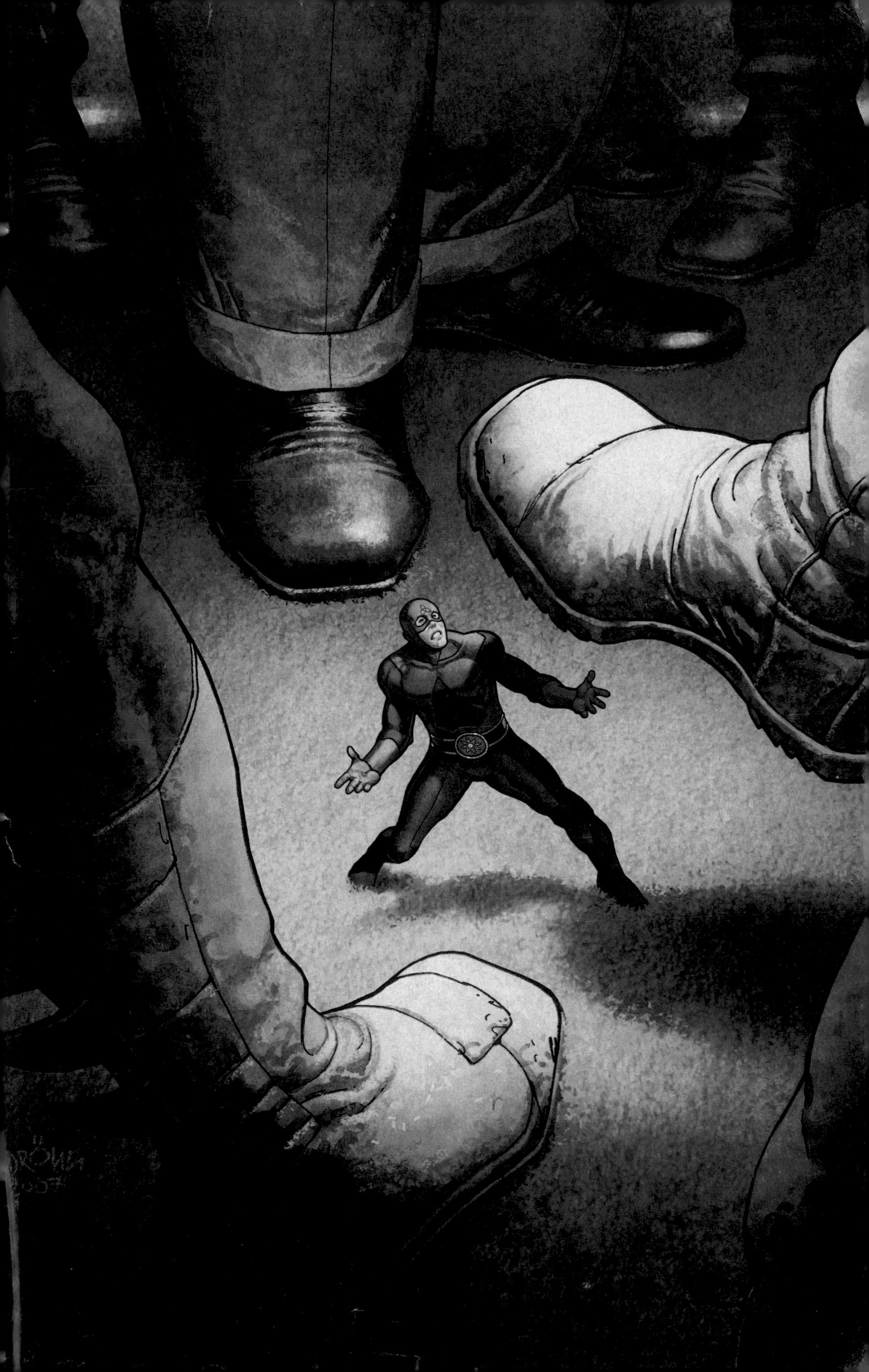

HUNT FOR RAY PALMER: PART ONE
NEVER TOO SMALL TO HIT THE BIG TIME

from **THE ALL NEW ATOM #12**

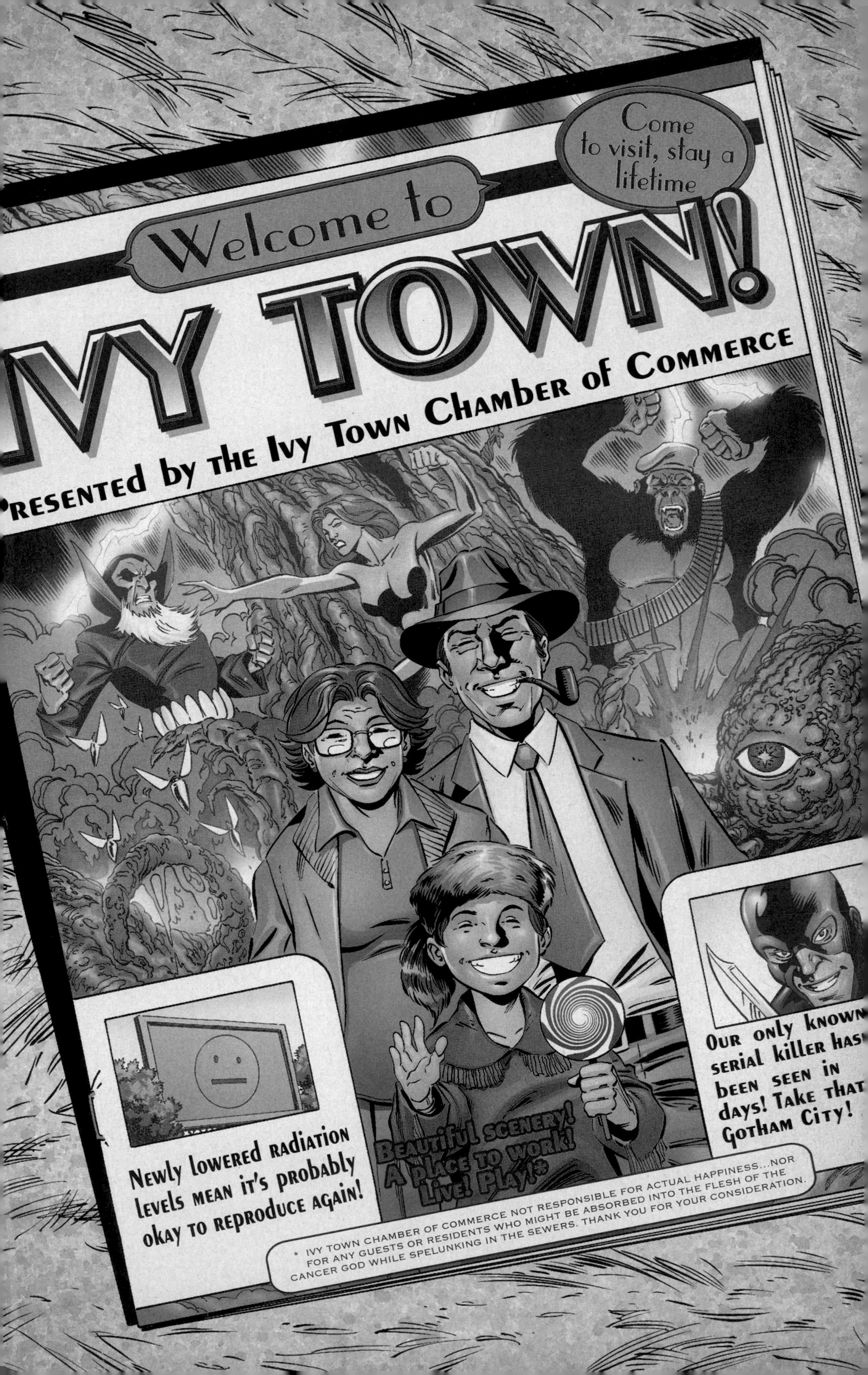
Come to visit, stay a lifetime
Welcome to
IVY TOWN!
PRESENTED by THE Ivy TOWN CHAMBER of COMMERCE
Newly lowered RADIATION levels MEAN it's probably okay TO REPRODUCE AGAIN!
BEAUTIFUL SCENERY! A PLACE TO WORK! LIVE! PLAY!*
OUR ONLY KNOWN SERIAL KILLER HAS BEEN SEEN IN DAYS! TAKE THAT GOTHAM CITY!
* IVY TOWN CHAMBER OF COMMERCE NOT RESPONSIBLE FOR ACTUAL HAPPINESS...NOR FOR ANY GUESTS OR RESIDENTS WHO MIGHT BE ABSORBED INTO THE FLESH OF THE CANCER GOD WHILE SPELUNKING IN THE SEWERS. THANK YOU FOR YOUR CONSIDERATION.

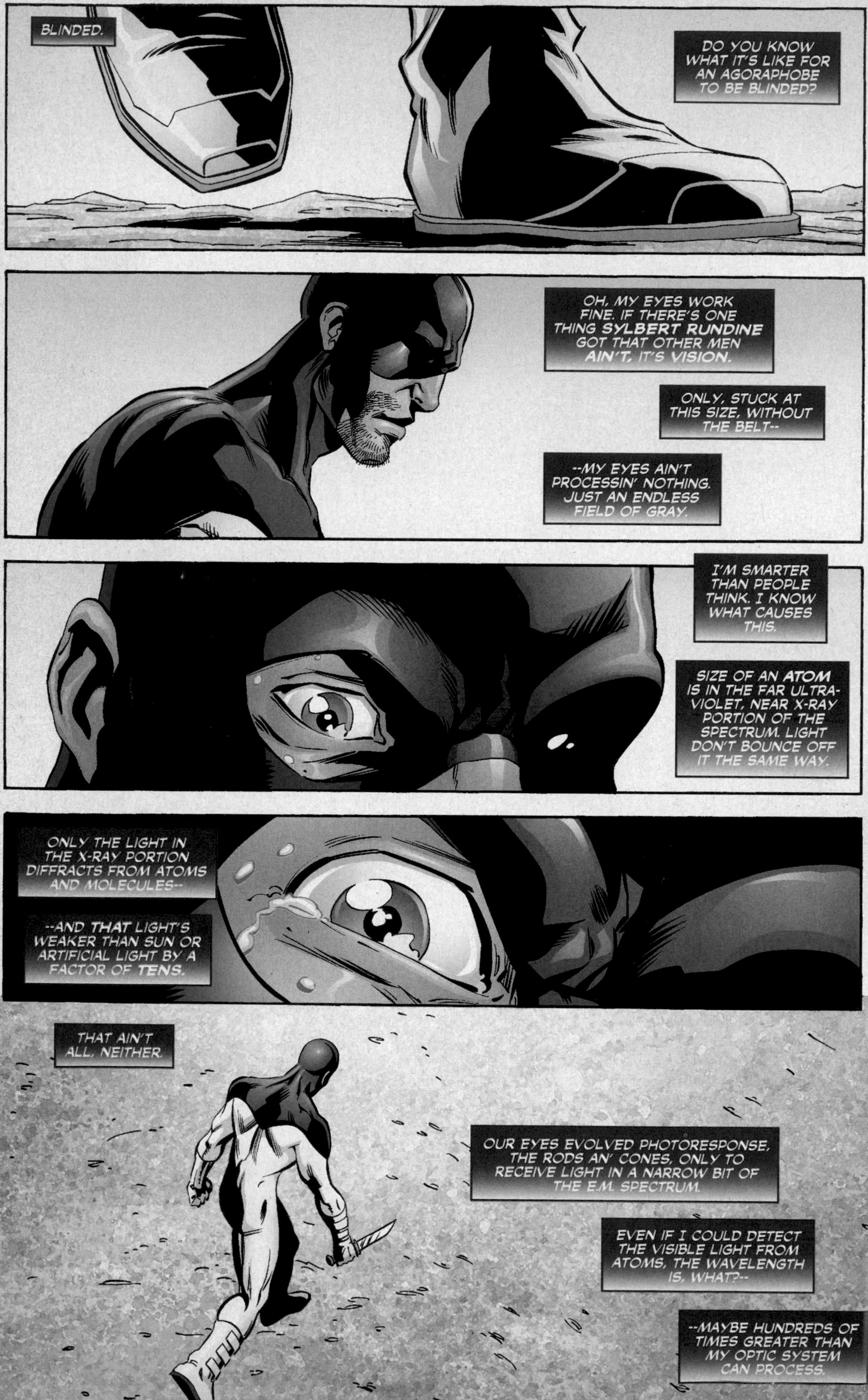
BLINDED.
DO YOU KNOW WHAT IT'S LIKE FOR AN AGORAPHOBE TO BE BLINDED?
OH, MY EYES WORK FINE. IF THERE'S ONE THING SYLBERT RUNDINE GOT THAT OTHER MEN AIN'T, IT'S VISION.
ONLY, STUCK AT THIS SIZE, WITHOUT THE BELT--
--MY EYES AIN'T PROCESSIN' NOTHING. JUST AN ENDLESS FIELD OF GRAY.
I'M SMARTER THAN PEOPLE THINK. I KNOW WHAT CAUSES THIS.
SIZE OF AN ATOM IS IN THE FAR ULTRA-VIOLET, NEAR X-RAY PORTION OF THE SPECTRUM. LIGHT DON'T BOUNCE OFF IT THE SAME WAY.
ONLY THE LIGHT IN THE X-RAY PORTION DIFFRACTS FROM ATOMS AND MOLECULES--
--AND THAT LIGHT'S WEAKER THAN SUN OR ARTIFICIAL LIGHT BY A FACTOR OF TENS.
THAT AIN'T ALL, NEITHER.
OUR EYES EVOLVED PHOTORESPONSE, THE RODS AN' CONES, ONLY TO RECEIVE LIGHT IN A NARROW BIT OF THE E.M. SPECTRUM.
EVEN IF I COULD DETECT THE VISIBLE LIGHT FROM ATOMS, THE WAVELENGTH IS, WHAT?--
--MAYBE HUNDREDS OF TIMES GREATER THAN MY OPTIC SYSTEM CAN PROCESS.

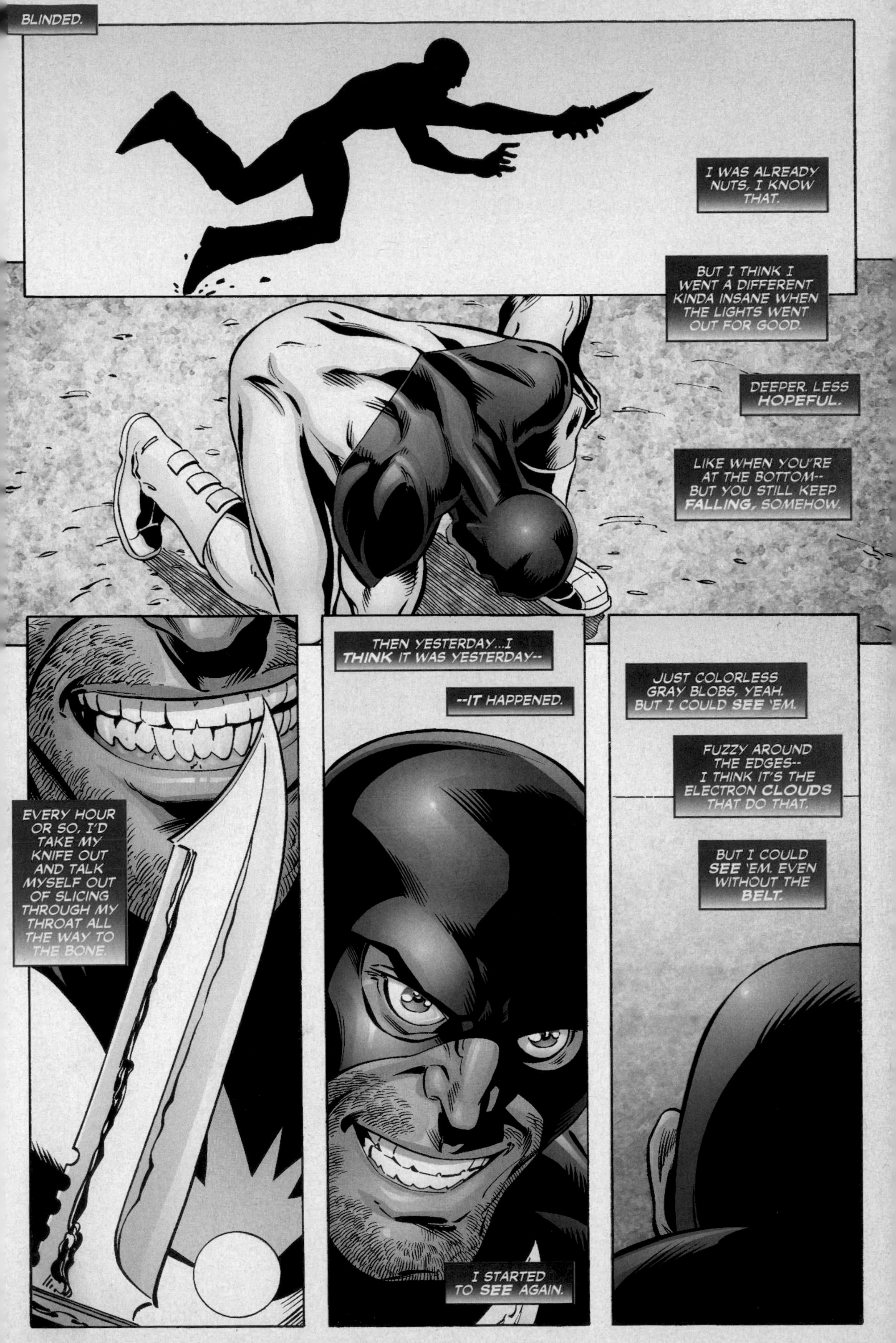

BLINDED.
I WAS ALREADY NUTS, I KNOW THAT.
BUT I THINK I WENT A DIFFERENT KINDA INSANE WHEN THE LIGHTS WENT OUT FOR GOOD.
DEEPER. LESS HOPEFUL.
LIKE WHEN YOU'RE AT THE BOTTOM-- BUT YOU STILL KEEP FALLING, SOMEHOW.
EVERY HOUR OR SO, I'D TAKE MY KNIFE OUT AND TALK MYSELF OUT OF SLICING THROUGH MY THROAT ALL THE WAY TO THE BONE.
THEN YESTERDAY...I THINK IT WAS YESTERDAY--
--IT HAPPENED.
I STARTED TO SEE AGAIN.
JUST COLORLESS GRAY BLOBS, YEAH. BUT I COULD SEE 'EM.
FUZZY AROUND THE EDGES-- I THINK IT'S THE ELECTRON CLOUDS THAT DO THAT.
BUT I COULD SEE 'EM. EVEN WITHOUT THE BELT.

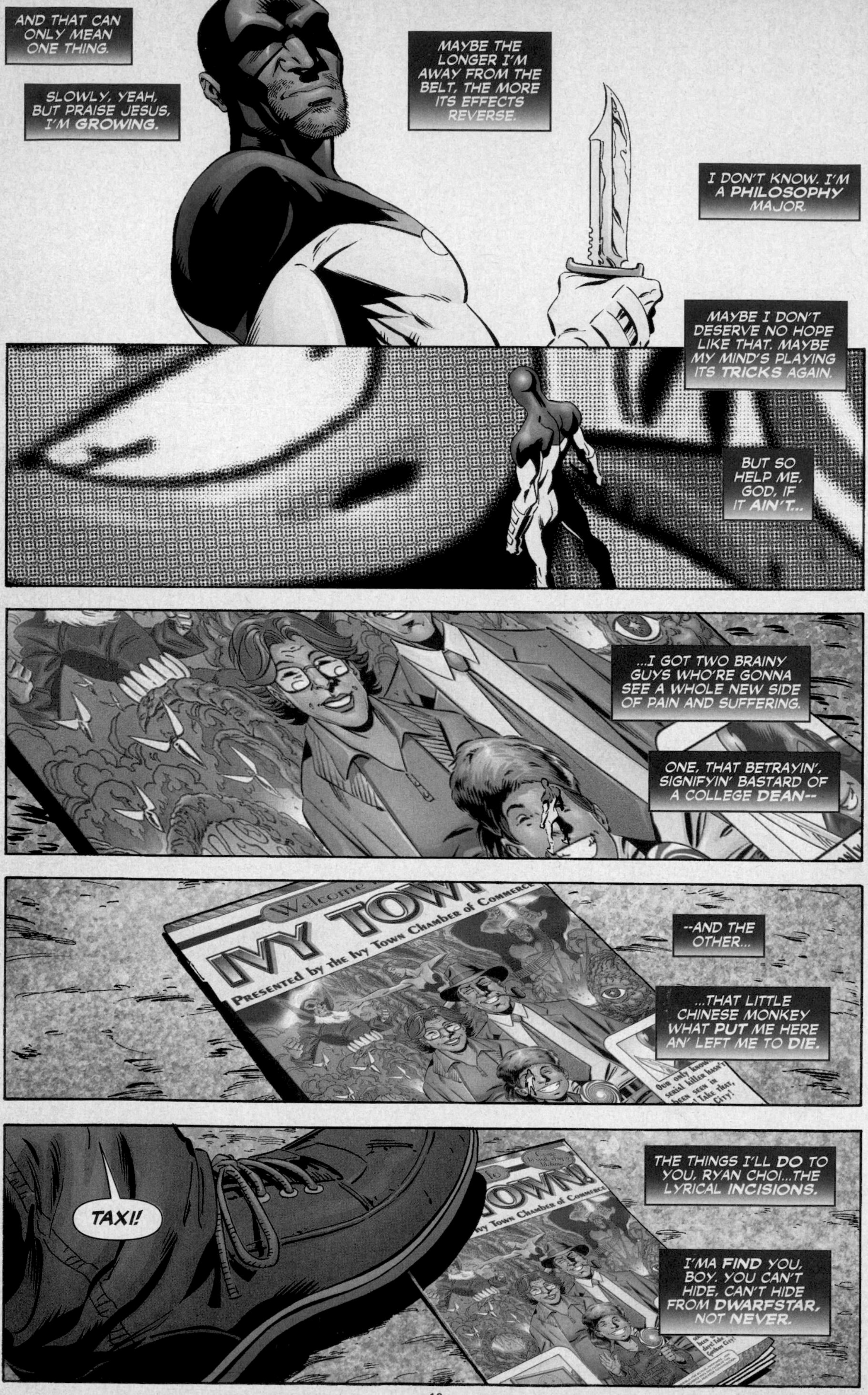
AND THAT CAN ONLY MEAN ONE THING.
SLOWLY, YEAH, BUT PRAISE JESUS, I'M **GROWING.**
MAYBE THE LONGER I'M AWAY FROM THE BELT, THE MORE ITS EFFECTS REVERSE.
I DON'T KNOW. I'M A **PHILOSOPHY** MAJOR.
MAYBE I DON'T DESERVE NO HOPE LIKE THAT. MAYBE MY MIND'S PLAYING ITS **TRICKS** AGAIN.
BUT SO HELP ME, GOD, IF IT **AIN'T...**
...I GOT TWO BRAINY GUYS WHO'RE GONNA SEE A WHOLE NEW SIDE OF PAIN AND SUFFERING.
ONE, THAT BETRAYIN', SIGNIFYIN' BASTARD OF A COLLEGE **DEAN--**
IVY TOWN
Presented by the Ivy Town Chamber of Commerce
--AND THE OTHER...
...THAT LITTLE CHINESE MONKEY WHAT **PUT** ME HERE AN' LEFT ME TO **DIE.**
THE THINGS I'LL **DO** TO YOU, RYAN CHOI...THE LYRICAL **INCISIONS.**
TAXI!
I'MA **FIND** YOU, BOY. YOU CAN'T HIDE, CAN'T HIDE FROM **DWARFSTAR,** NOT **NEVER.**

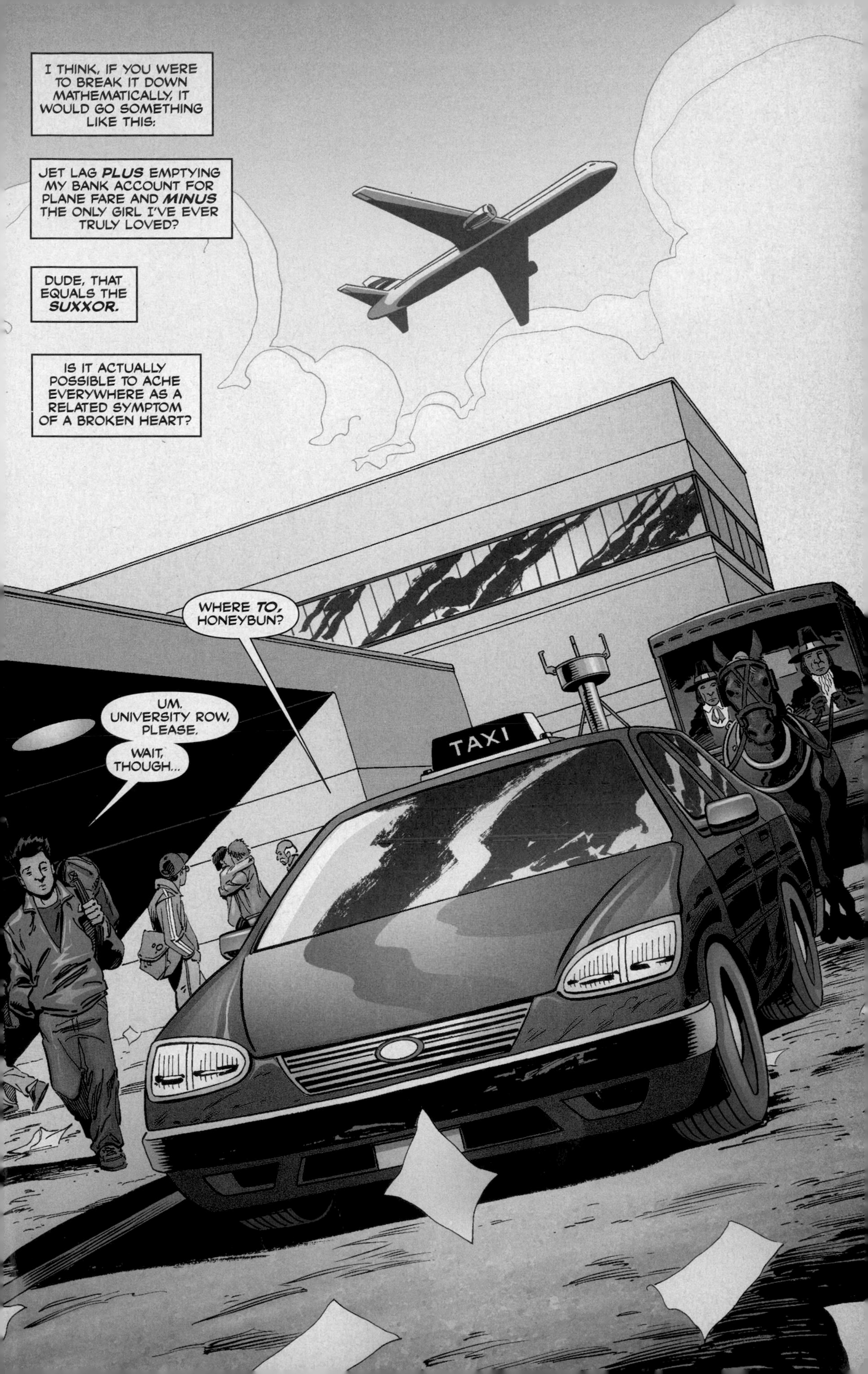
I THINK, IF YOU WERE TO BREAK IT DOWN MATHEMATICALLY, IT WOULD GO SOMETHING LIKE THIS:
JET LAG **PLUS** EMPTYING MY BANK ACCOUNT FOR PLANE FARE AND **MINUS** THE ONLY GIRL I'VE EVER TRULY LOVED?
DUDE, THAT EQUALS THE **SUXXOR.**
IS IT ACTUALLY POSSIBLE TO ACHE EVERYWHERE AS A RELATED SYMPTOM OF A BROKEN HEART?
WHERE **TO,** HONEYBUN?
UM. UNIVERSITY ROW, PLEASE.
WAIT, THOUGH...
TAXI

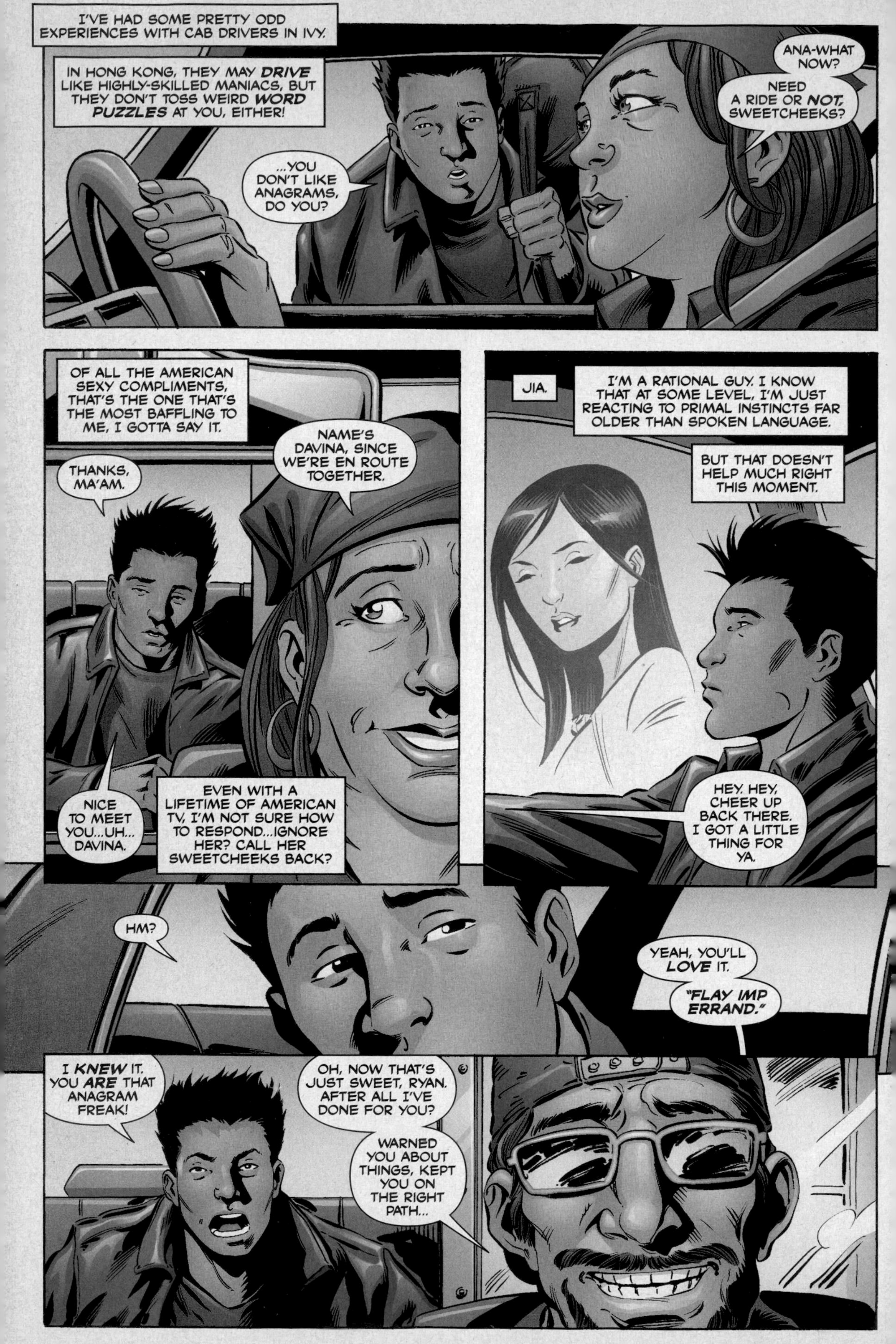
I'VE HAD SOME PRETTY ODD EXPERIENCES WITH CAB DRIVERS IN IVY.
IN HONG KONG, THEY MAY DRIVE LIKE HIGHLY-SKILLED MANIACS, BUT THEY DON'T TOSS WEIRD WORD PUZZLES AT YOU, EITHER!
ANA-WHAT NOW?
NEED A RIDE OR NOT, SWEETCHEEKS?
...YOU DON'T LIKE ANAGRAMS, DO YOU?
OF ALL THE AMERICAN SEXY COMPLIMENTS, THAT'S THE ONE THAT'S THE MOST BAFFLING TO ME, I GOTTA SAY IT.
THANKS, MA'AM.
NAME'S DAVINA, SINCE WE'RE EN ROUTE TOGETHER.
NICE TO MEET YOU...UH... DAVINA.
EVEN WITH A LIFETIME OF AMERICAN TV, I'M NOT SURE HOW TO RESPOND...IGNORE HER? CALL HER SWEETCHEEKS BACK?
JIA.
I'M A RATIONAL GUY. I KNOW THAT AT SOME LEVEL, I'M JUST REACTING TO PRIMAL INSTINCTS FAR OLDER THAN SPOKEN LANGUAGE.
BUT THAT DOESN'T HELP MUCH RIGHT THIS MOMENT.
HEY. HEY, CHEER UP BACK THERE. I GOT A LITTLE THING FOR YA.
HM?
YEAH, YOU'LL LOVE IT.
"FLAY IMP ERRAND."
I KNEW IT. YOU ARE THAT ANAGRAM FREAK!
OH, NOW THAT'S JUST SWEET, RYAN. AFTER ALL I'VE DONE FOR YOU?
WARNED YOU ABOUT THINGS, KEPT YOU ON THE RIGHT PATH...

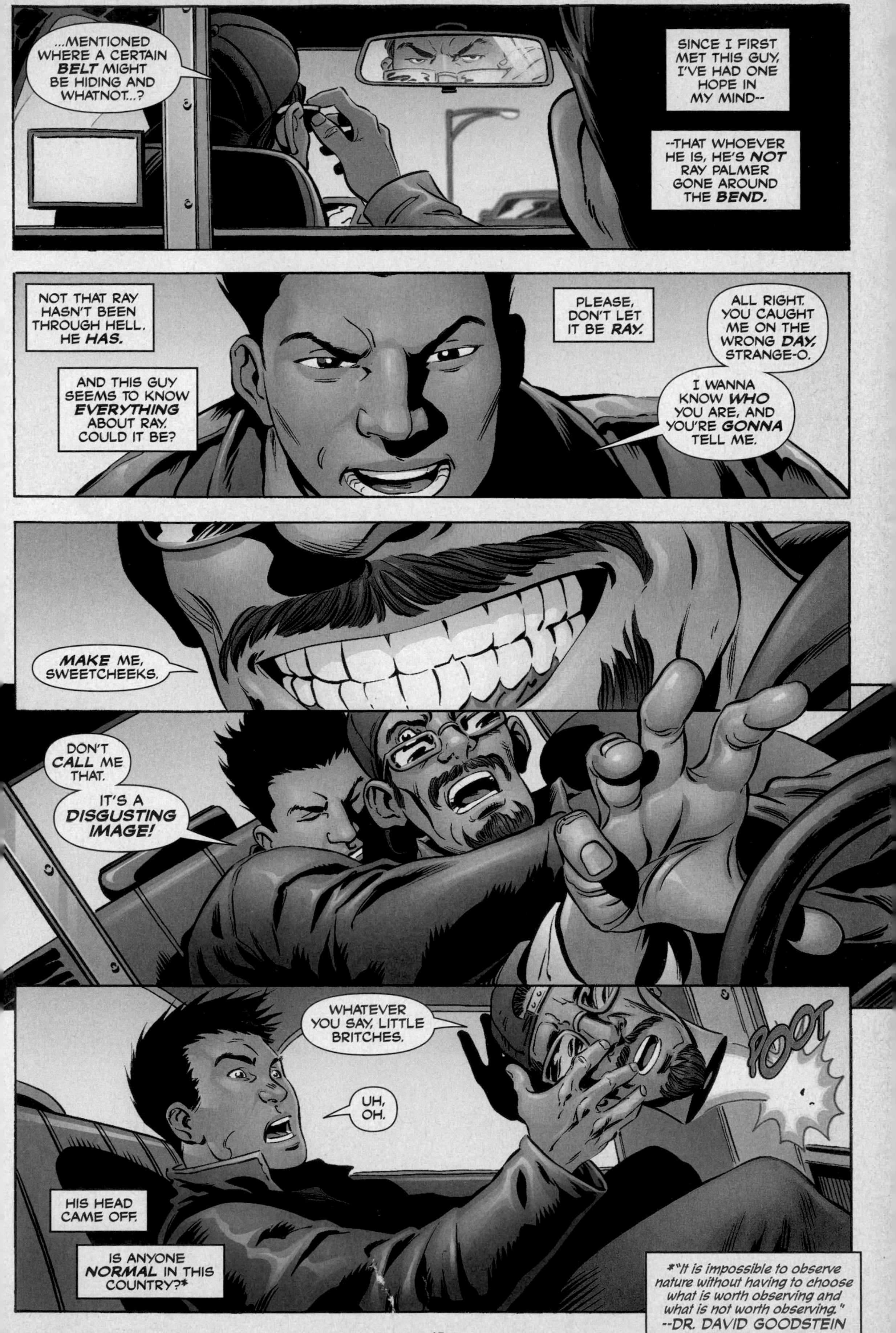
...MENTIONED WHERE A CERTAIN BELT MIGHT BE HIDING AND WHATNOT...?
SINCE I FIRST MET THIS GUY, I'VE HAD ONE HOPE IN MY MIND--
--THAT WHOEVER HE IS, HE'S NOT RAY PALMER GONE AROUND THE BEND.
NOT THAT RAY HASN'T BEEN THROUGH HELL. HE HAS.
AND THIS GUY SEEMS TO KNOW EVERYTHING ABOUT RAY. COULD IT BE?
PLEASE, DON'T LET IT BE RAY.
ALL RIGHT. YOU CAUGHT ME ON THE WRONG DAY, STRANGE-O.
I WANNA KNOW WHO YOU ARE, AND YOU'RE GONNA TELL ME.
MAKE ME, SWEETCHEEKS.
DON'T CALL ME THAT.
IT'S A DISGUSTING IMAGE!
WHATEVER YOU SAY, LITTLE BRITCHES.
POOT
UH, OH.
HIS HEAD CAME OFF.
IS ANYONE NORMAL IN THIS COUNTRY?*
*"It is impossible to observe nature without having to choose what is worth observing and what is not worth observing." --DR. DAVID GOODSTEIN

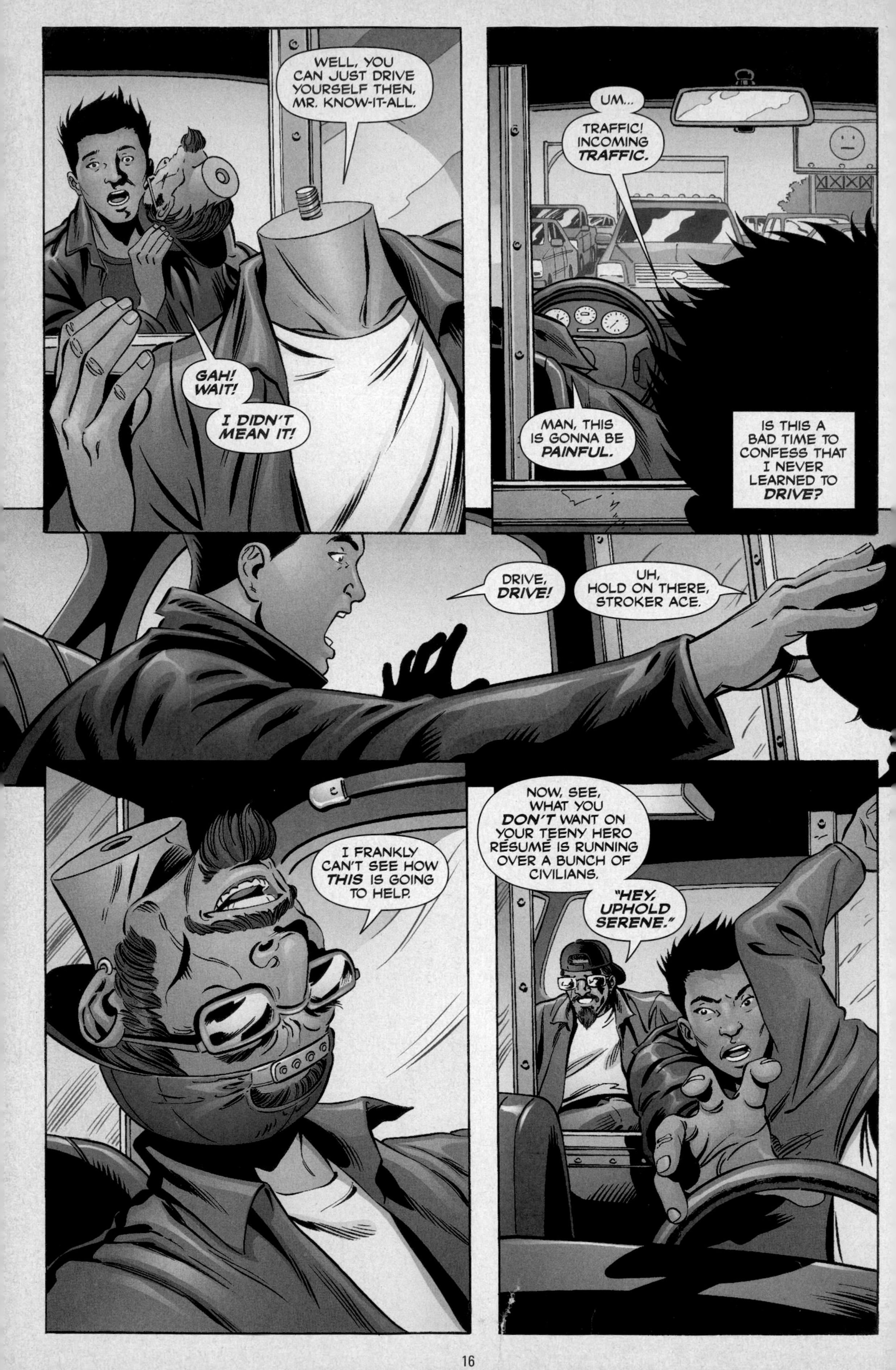
WELL, YOU CAN JUST DRIVE YOURSELF THEN, MR. KNOW-IT-ALL.
GAH! WAIT!
I DIDN'T MEAN IT!
UM...
TRAFFIC! INCOMING TRAFFIC.
MAN, THIS IS GONNA BE PAINFUL.
IS THIS A BAD TIME TO CONFESS THAT I NEVER LEARNED TO DRIVE?
DRIVE, DRIVE!
UH, HOLD ON THERE, STROKER ACE.
I FRANKLY CAN'T SEE HOW THIS IS GOING TO HELP.
NOW, SEE, WHAT YOU DON'T WANT ON YOUR TEENY HERO RÉSUMÉ IS RUNNING OVER A BUNCH OF CIVILIANS.
"HEY, UPHOLD SERENE."

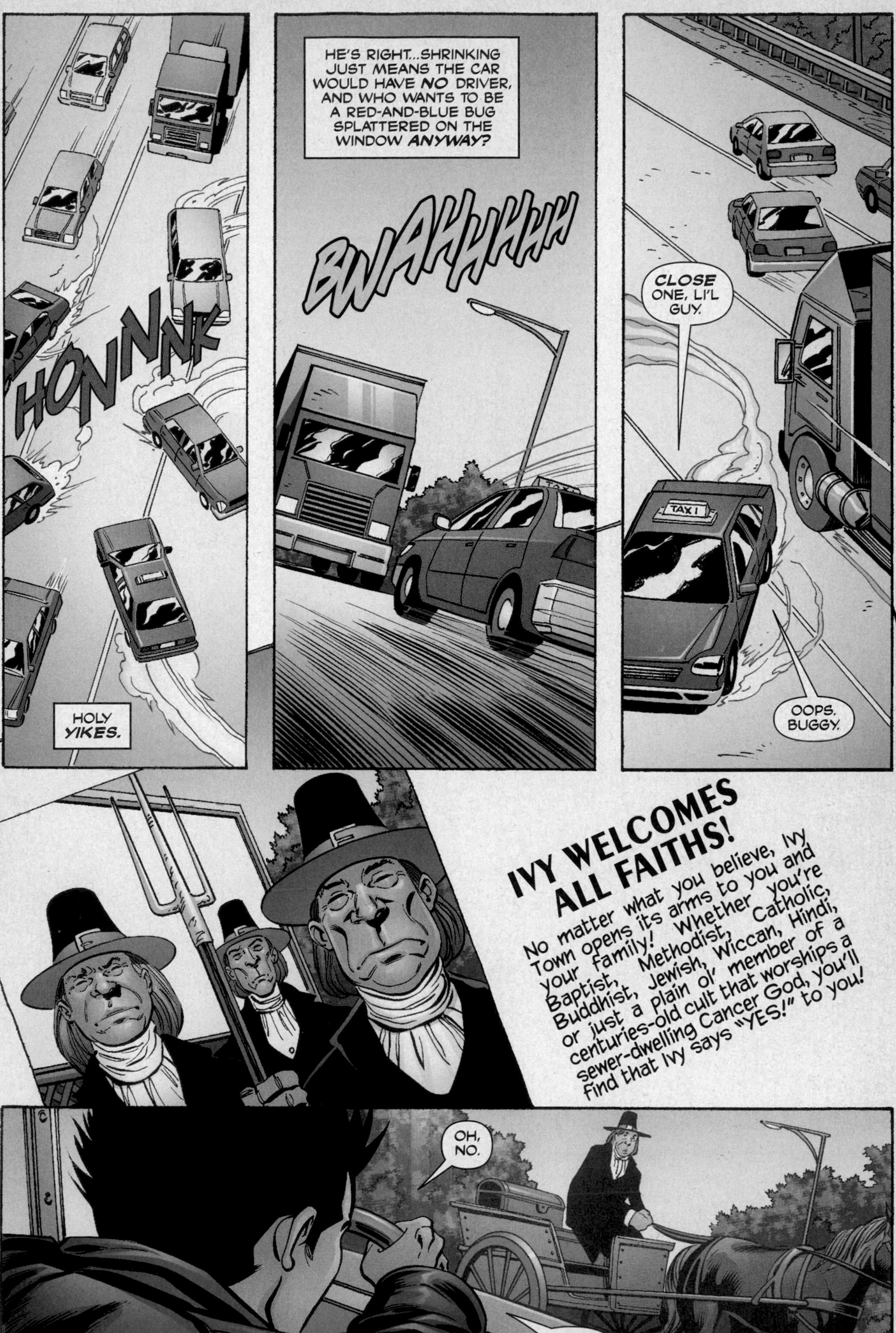
HONNNK
HOLY YIKES.
HE'S RIGHT...SHRINKING JUST MEANS THE CAR WOULD HAVE NO DRIVER, AND WHO WANTS TO BE A RED-AND-BLUE BUG SPLATTERED ON THE WINDOW ANYWAY?
BWAHHHHH
TAXI
CLOSE ONE, LI'L GUY.
TAXI
OOPS. BUGGY.
IVY WELCOMES ALL FAITHS!
No matter what you believe, Ivy Town opens its arms to you and your family! Whether you're Baptist, Methodist, Catholic, Buddhist, Jewish, Wiccan, Hindi, or just a plain ol' member of a centuries-old cult that worships a sewer-dwelling Cancer God, you'll find that Ivy says "YES!" to you!
OH, NO.
COME ON! COME ON!

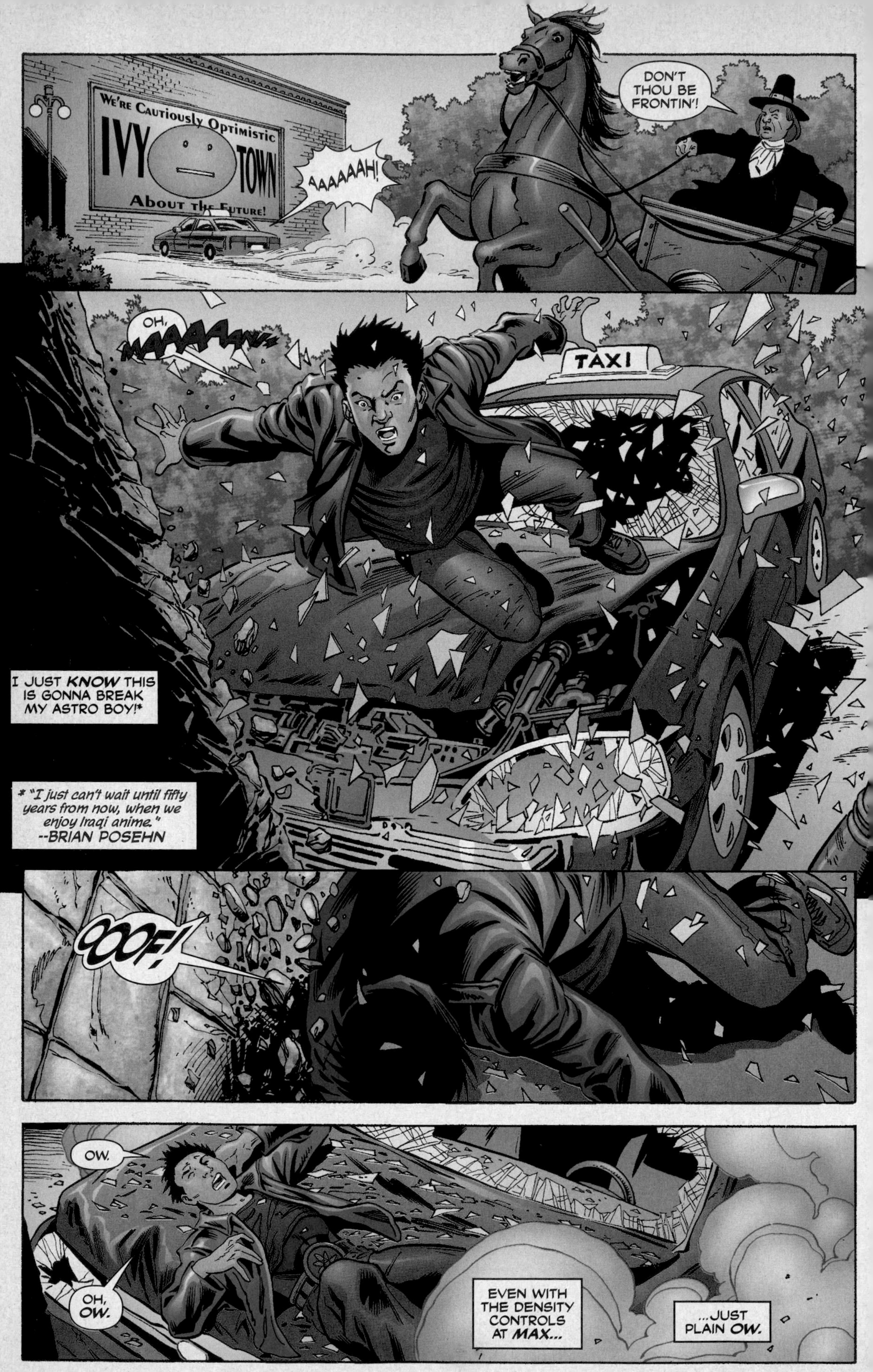

WE'RE CAUTIOUSLY OPTIMISTIC
IVY TOWN
ABOUT THE FUTURE!
AAAAAAH!
DON'T THOU BE FRONTIN'!
TAXI
OH, MAAAAAN--
I JUST KNOW THIS IS GONNA BREAK MY ASTRO BOY!*
* "I just can't wait until fifty years from now, when we enjoy Iraqi anime." --BRIAN POSEHN
OOOF!
OW.
OH, OW.
EVEN WITH THE DENSITY CONTROLS AT MAX...
...JUST PLAIN OW.

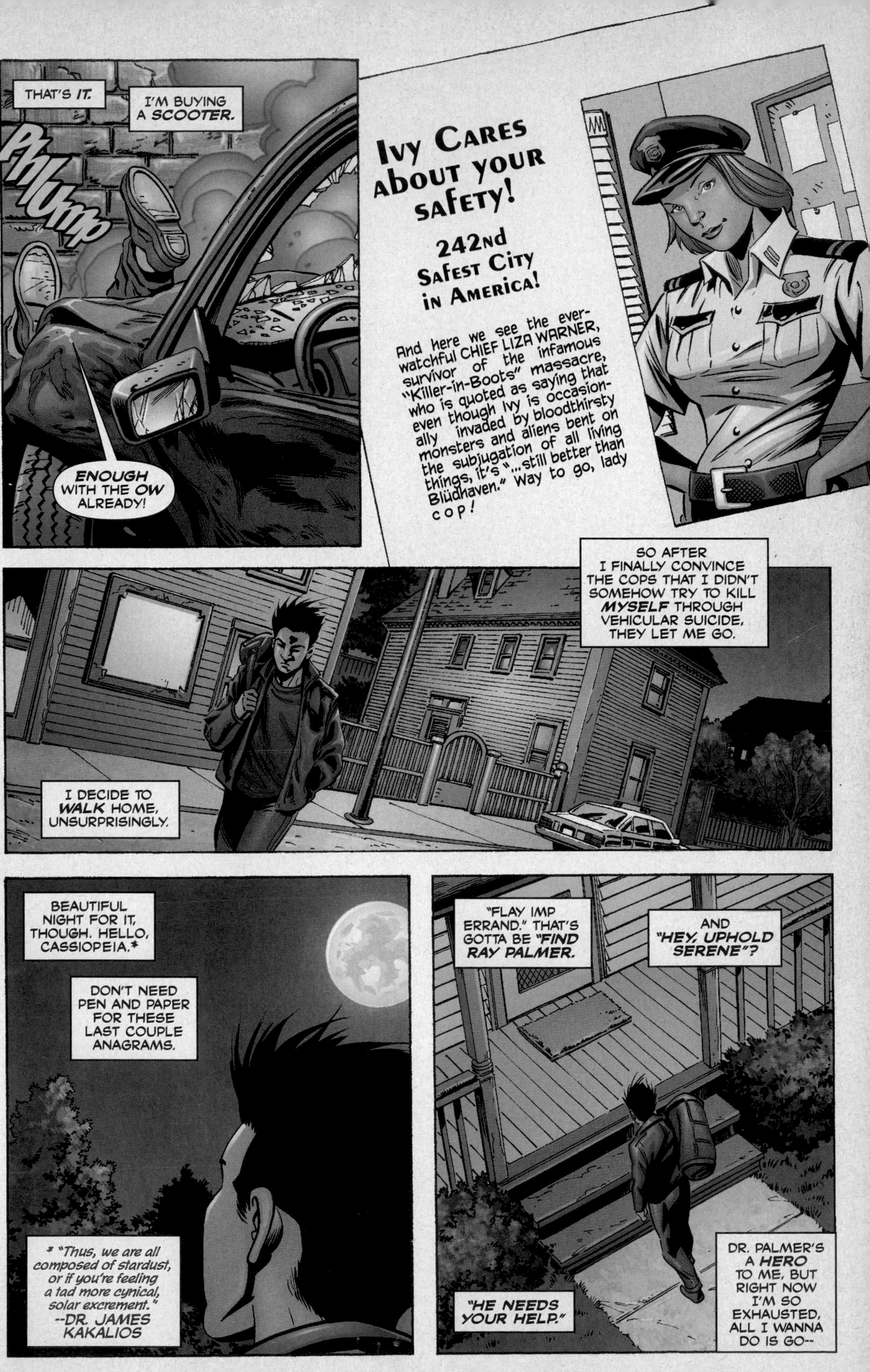
THAT'S IT.
I'M BUYING A SCOOTER.
PHLUMP
ENOUGH WITH THE OW ALREADY!
Ivy Cares about your safety!
242nd Safest City in America!
And here we see the ever-watchful CHIEF LIZA WARNER, survivor of the infamous "Killer-in-Boots" massacre, who is quoted as saying that even though Ivy is occasionally invaded by bloodthirsty monsters and aliens bent on the subjugation of all living things, it's "...still better than Blüdhaven." Way to go, lady cop!
SO AFTER I FINALLY CONVINCE THE COPS THAT I DIDN'T SOMEHOW TRY TO KILL MYSELF THROUGH VEHICULAR SUICIDE, THEY LET ME GO.
I DECIDE TO WALK HOME, UNSURPRISINGLY.
BEAUTIFUL NIGHT FOR IT, THOUGH. HELLO, CASSIOPEIA.*
DON'T NEED PEN AND PAPER FOR THESE LAST COUPLE ANAGRAMS.
* "Thus, we are all composed of stardust, or if you're feeling a tad more cynical, solar excrement." --DR. JAMES KAKALIOS
"FLAY IMP ERRAND." THAT'S GOTTA BE "FIND RAY PALMER.
AND "HEY, UPHOLD SERENE"?
"HE NEEDS YOUR HELP."
DR. PALMER'S A HERO TO ME, BUT RIGHT NOW I'M SO EXHAUSTED, ALL I WANNA DO IS GO--

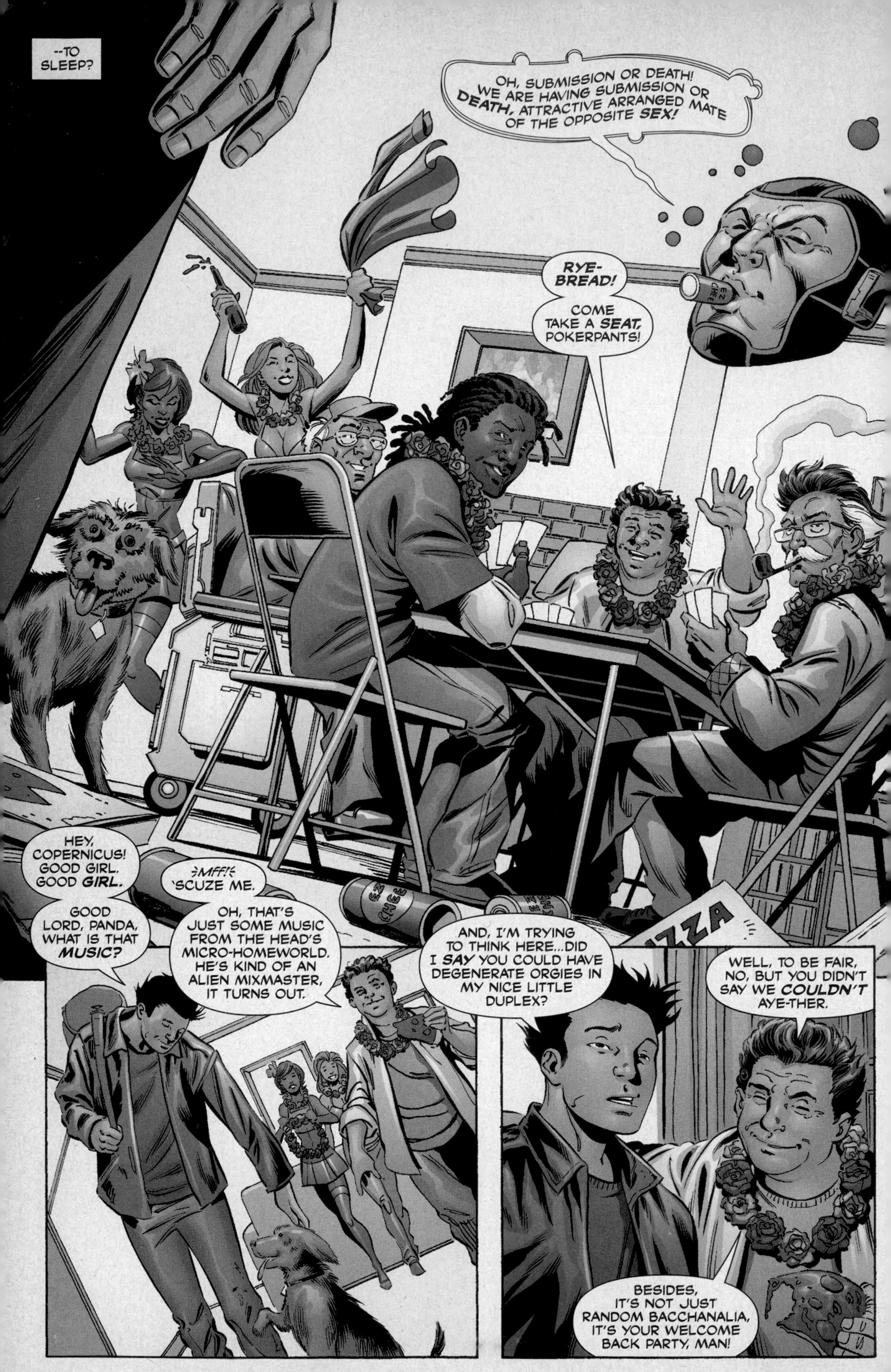
--TO SLEEP?
OH, SUBMISSION OR DEATH! WE ARE HAVING SUBMISSION OR DEATH, ATTRACTIVE ARRANGED MATE OF THE OPPOSITE SEX!
RYE-BREAD!
COME TAKE A SEAT, POKERPANTS!
HEY, COPERNICUS! GOOD GIRL. GOOD GIRL.
MFF! 'SCUZE ME.
GOOD LORD, PANDA, WHAT IS THAT MUSIC?
OH, THAT'S JUST SOME MUSIC FROM THE HEAD'S MICRO-HOMEWORLD. HE'S KIND OF AN ALIEN MIXMASTER, IT TURNS OUT.
AND, I'M TRYING TO THINK HERE...DID I SAY YOU COULD HAVE DEGENERATE ORGIES IN MY NICE LITTLE DUPLEX?
WELL, TO BE FAIR, NO, BUT YOU DIDN'T SAY WE COULDN'T AYE-THER.
BESIDES, IT'S NOT JUST RANDOM BACCHANALIA, IT'S YOUR WELCOME BACK PARTY, MAN!

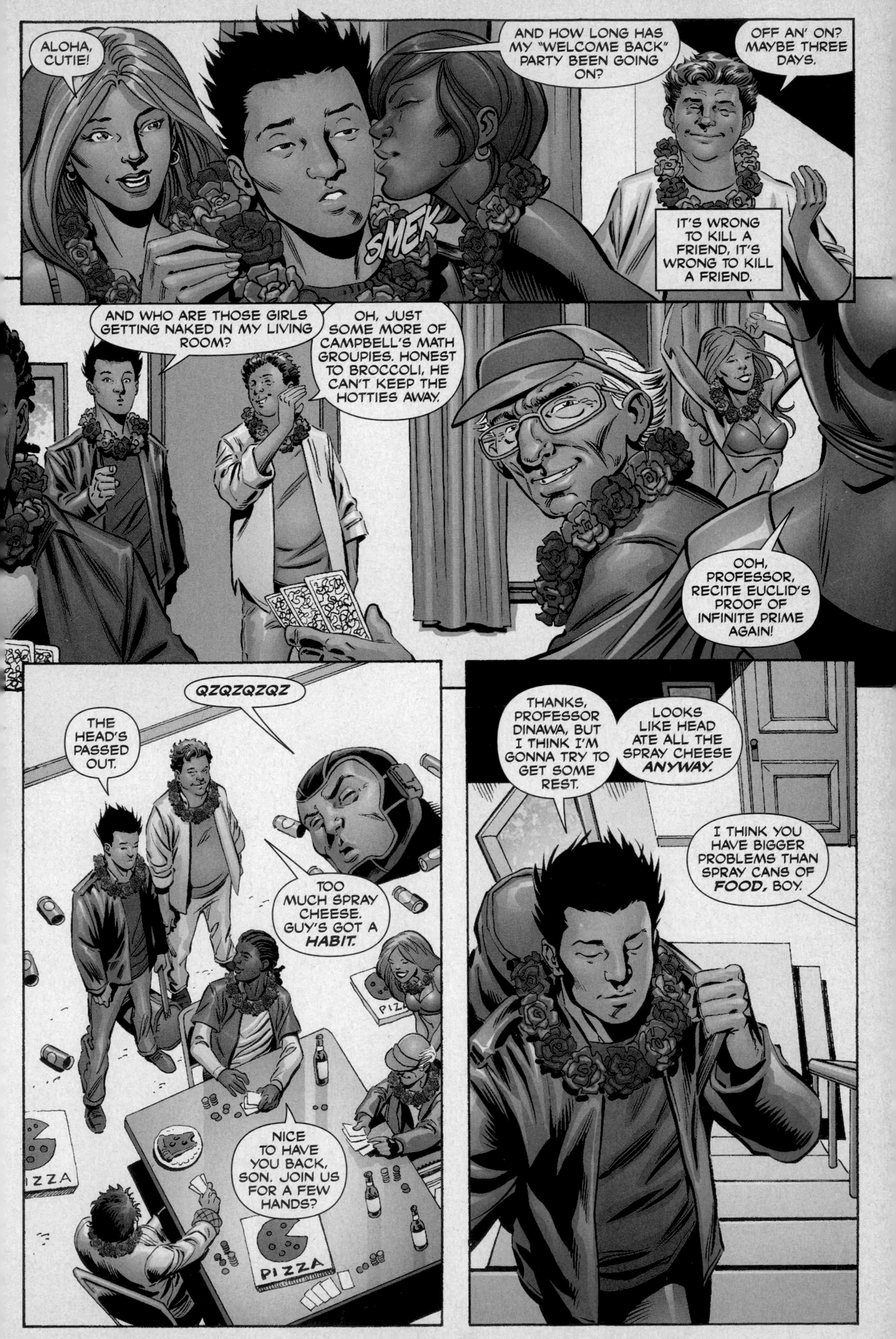
ALOHA, CUTIE!
AND HOW LONG HAS MY "WELCOME BACK" PARTY BEEN GOING ON?
OFF AN' ON? MAYBE THREE DAYS.
SMEK
IT'S WRONG TO KILL A FRIEND, IT'S WRONG TO KILL A FRIEND.
AND WHO ARE THOSE GIRLS GETTING NAKED IN MY LIVING ROOM?
OH, JUST SOME MORE OF CAMPBELL'S MATH GROUPIES. HONEST TO BROCCOLI, HE CAN'T KEEP THE HOTTIES AWAY.
OOH, PROFESSOR, RECITE EUCLID'S PROOF OF INFINITE PRIME AGAIN!
QZQZQZQZ
THE HEAD'S PASSED OUT.
TOO MUCH SPRAY CHEESE. GUY'S GOT A HABIT.
NICE TO HAVE YOU BACK, SON. JOIN US FOR A FEW HANDS?
PIZZA
PIZZA
THANKS, PROFESSOR DINAWA, BUT I THINK I'M GONNA TRY TO GET SOME REST.
LOOKS LIKE HEAD ATE ALL THE SPRAY CHEESE ANYWAY.
I THINK YOU HAVE BIGGER PROBLEMS THAN SPRAY CANS OF FOOD, BOY.

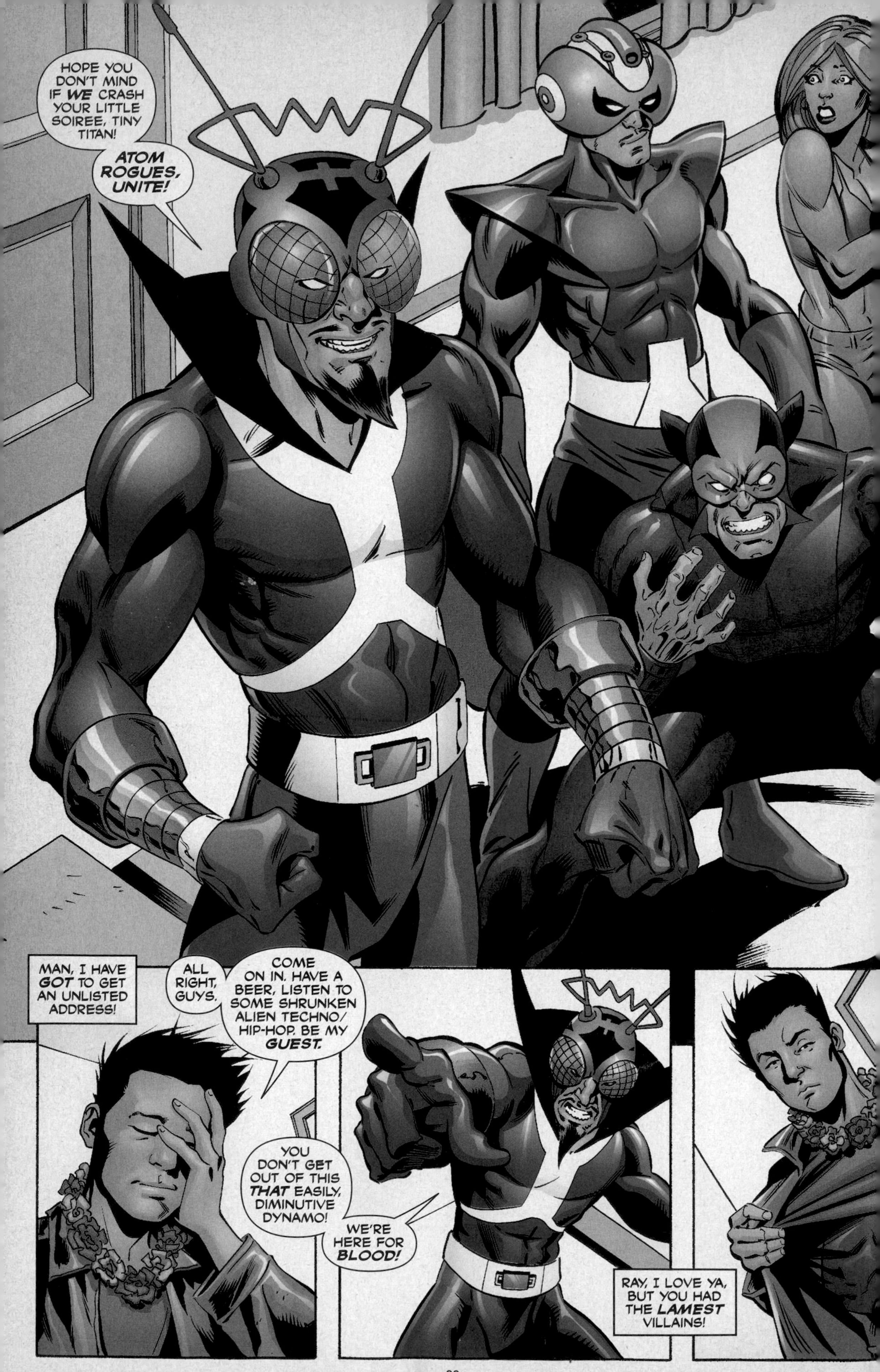

HOPE YOU DON'T MIND IF WE CRASH YOUR LITTLE SOIREE, TINY TITAN!
ATOM ROGUES, UNITE!
MAN, I HAVE GOT TO GET AN UNLISTED ADDRESS!
ALL RIGHT, GUYS.
COME ON IN. HAVE A BEER, LISTEN TO SOME SHRUNKEN ALIEN TECHNO/ HIP-HOP. BE MY GUEST.
YOU DON'T GET OUT OF THIS THAT EASILY, DIMINUTIVE DYNAMO!
WE'RE HERE FOR BLOOD!
RAY, I LOVE YA, BUT YOU HAD THE LAMEST VILLAINS!

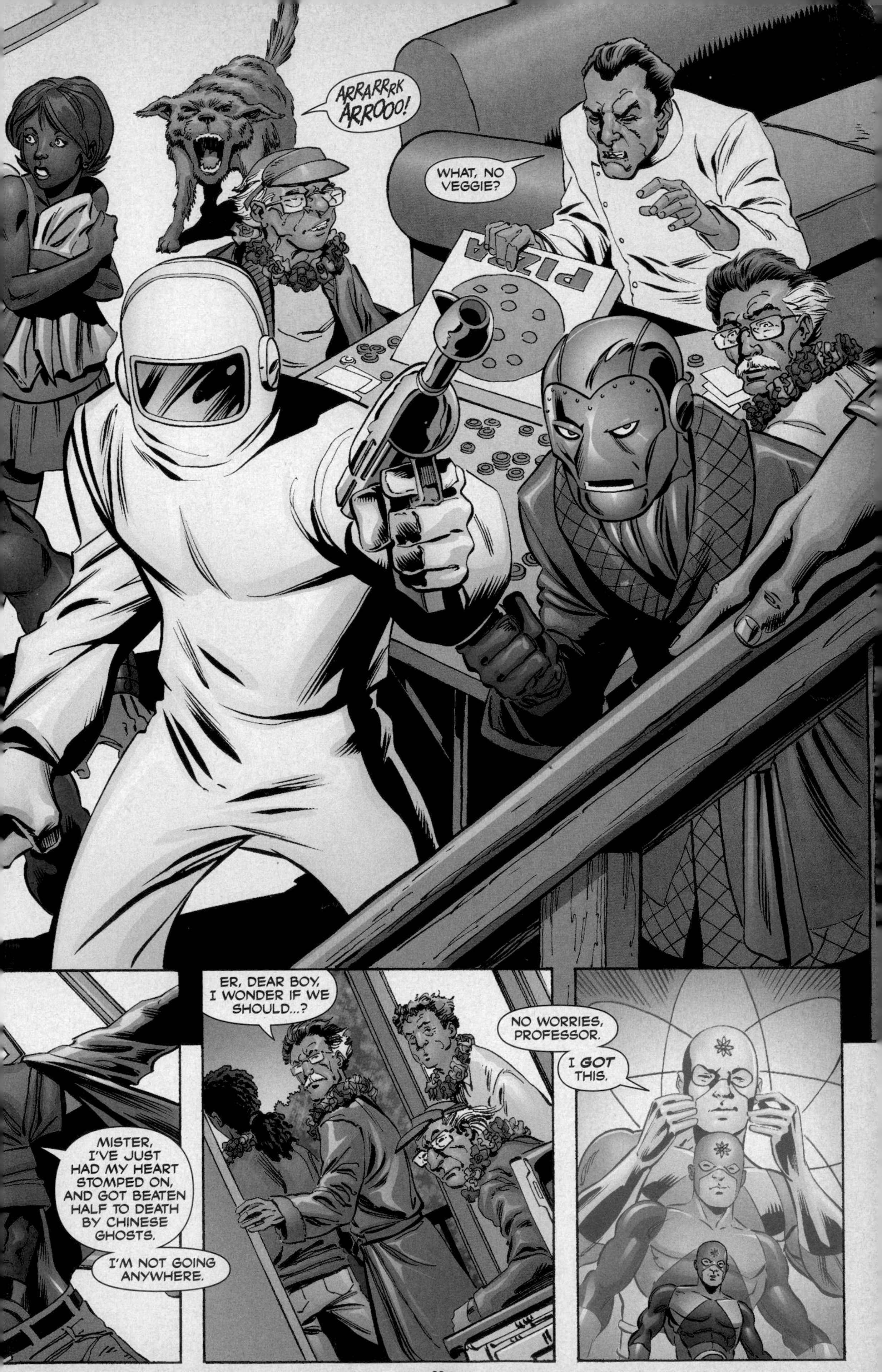
ARRARRRK ARROOO!
WHAT, NO VEGGIE?
PIZZA
ER, DEAR BOY, I WONDER IF WE SHOULD...?
MISTER, I'VE JUST HAD MY HEART STOMPED ON, AND GOT BEATEN HALF TO DEATH BY CHINESE GHOSTS.
I'M NOT GOING ANYWHERE.
NO WORRIES, PROFESSOR.
I GOT THIS.

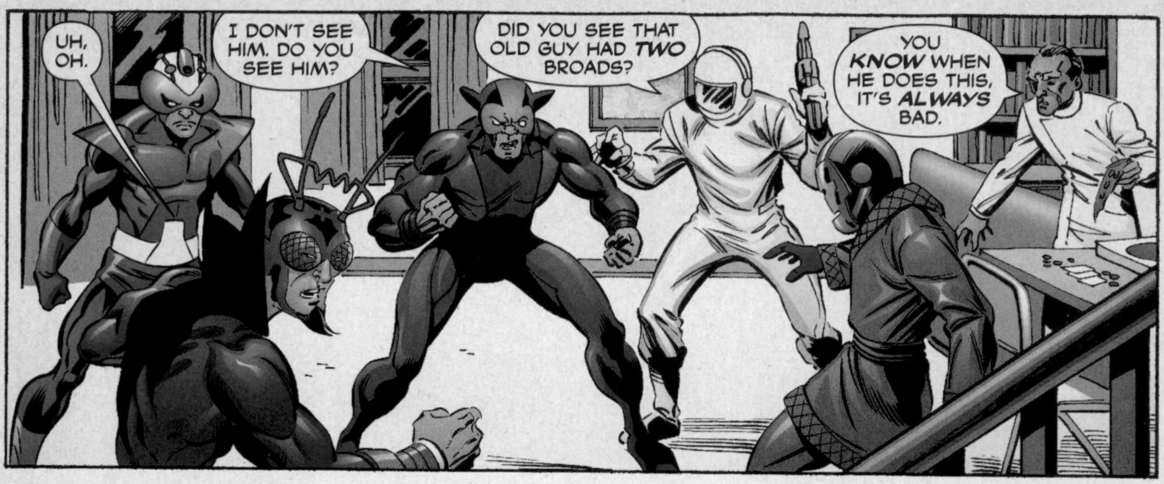
UH, OH.
I DON'T SEE HIM. DO YOU SEE HIM?
DID YOU SEE THAT OLD GUY HAD TWO BROADS?
YOU KNOW WHEN HE DOES THIS, IT'S ALWAYS BAD.

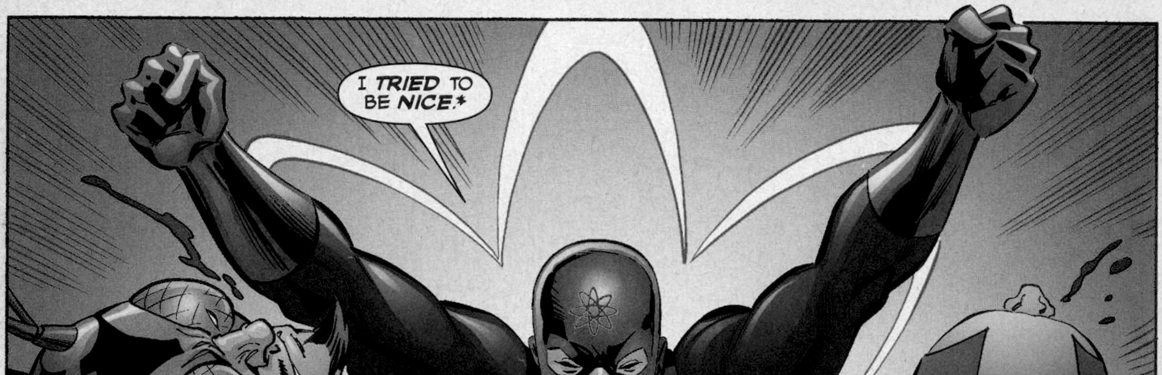
I TRIED TO BE NICE.*
*"Whenever action is born from force, though it be infinitesimal, the cosmic balance is upset and the universal motion results."
--NIKOLA TESLA

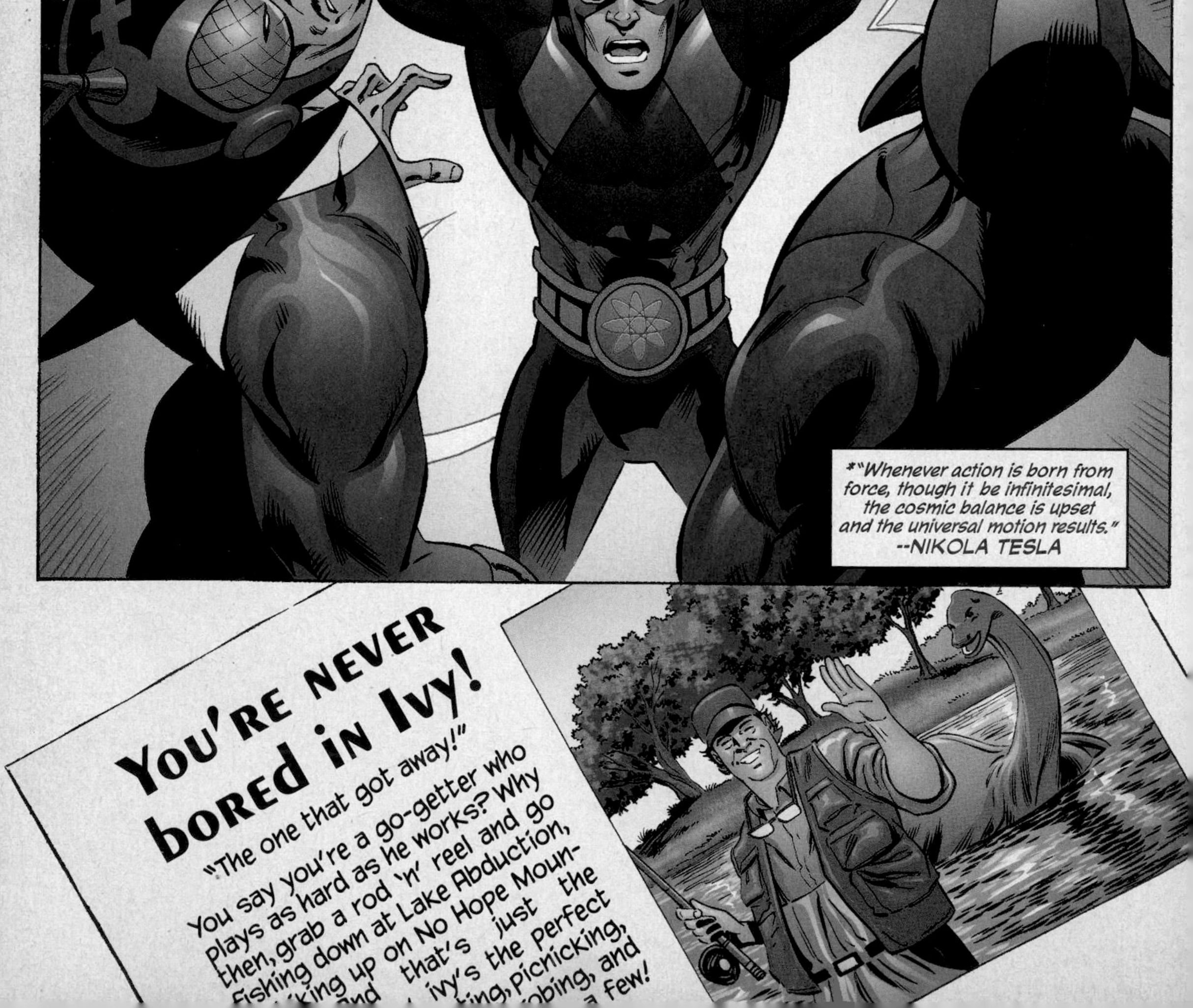
You're NEVER bored in Ivy!
"The one that got away!"
You say you're a go-getter who plays as hard as he works? Why then, grab a rod 'n' reel and go fishing down at Lake Abduction,
No Hope Moun-
that's just the
Ivy's the perfect
picnicking,
and
a few!

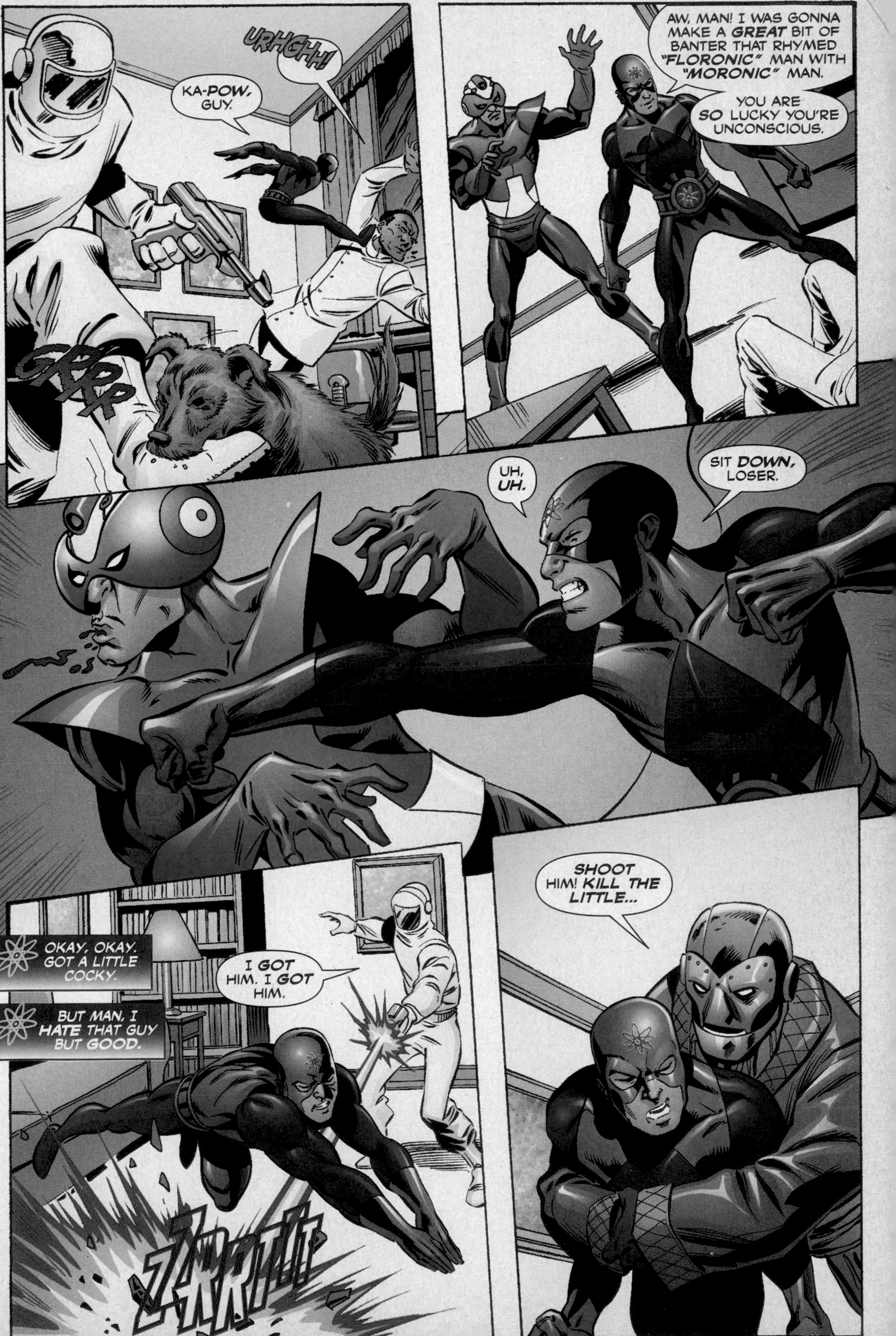
URHGHH!
KA-POW, GUY.
GRRR
AW, MAN! I WAS GONNA MAKE A GREAT BIT OF BANTER THAT RHYMED "FLORONIC" MAN WITH "MORONIC" MAN.
YOU ARE SO LUCKY YOU'RE UNCONSCIOUS.
UH, UH.
SIT DOWN, LOSER.
OKAY, OKAY. GOT A LITTLE COCKY.
BUT MAN, I HATE THAT GUY BUT GOOD.
I GOT HIM. I GOT HIM.
ZZRRTTT
SHOOT HIM! KILL THE LITTLE...

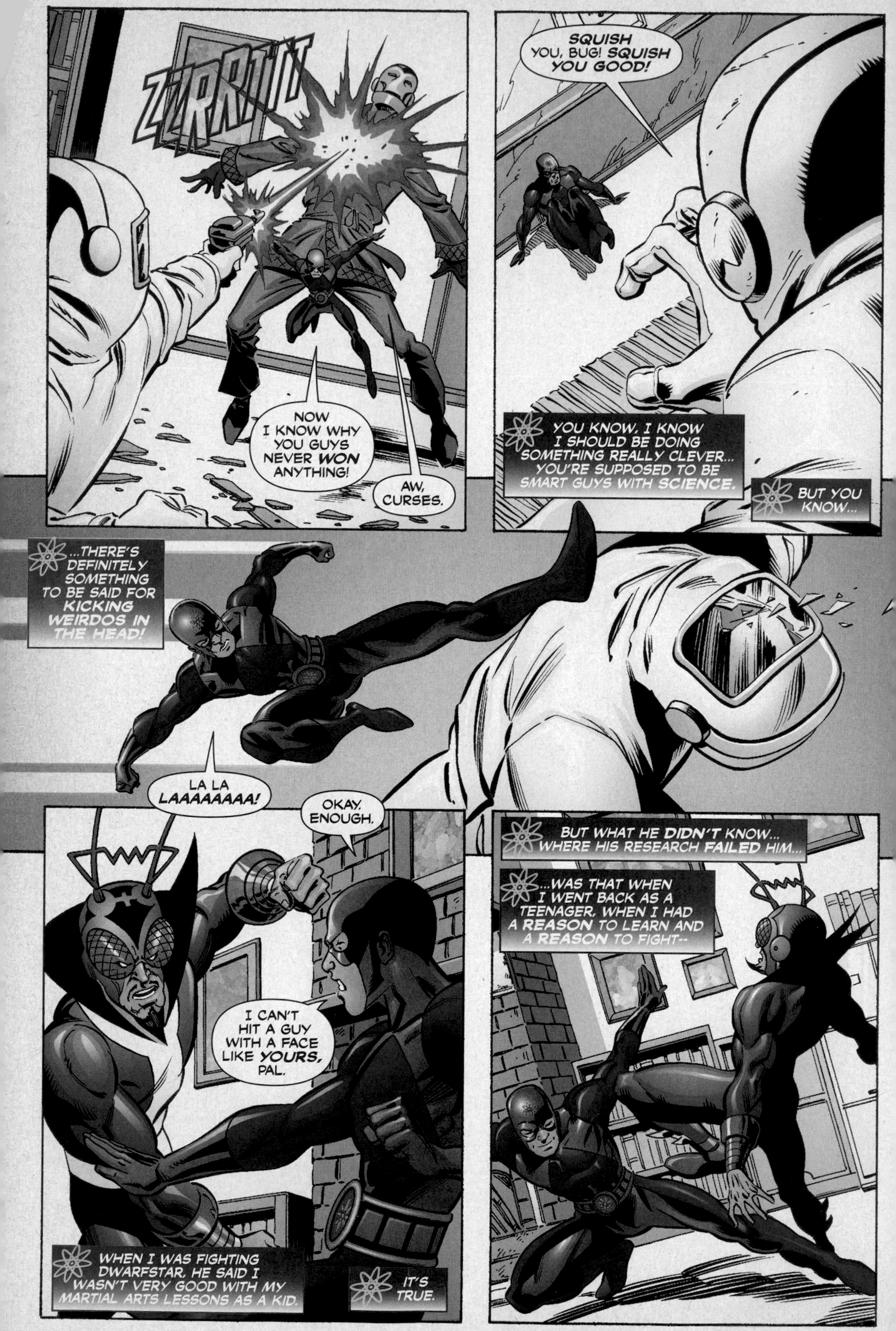
ZZRRTTT
NOW I KNOW WHY YOU GUYS NEVER WON ANYTHING!
AW, CURSES.
SQUISH YOU, BUG! SQUISH YOU GOOD!
YOU KNOW, I KNOW I SHOULD BE DOING SOMETHING REALLY CLEVER... YOU'RE SUPPOSED TO BE SMART GUYS WITH SCIENCE.
BUT YOU KNOW...
...THERE'S DEFINITELY SOMETHING TO BE SAID FOR KICKING WEIRDOS IN THE HEAD!
LA LA LAAAAAAAA!
OKAY. ENOUGH.
I CAN'T HIT A GUY WITH A FACE LIKE YOURS, PAL.
WHEN I WAS FIGHTING DWARFSTAR, HE SAID I WASN'T VERY GOOD WITH MY MARTIAL ARTS LESSONS AS A KID.
IT'S TRUE.
BUT WHAT HE DIDN'T KNOW... WHERE HIS RESEARCH FAILED HIM...
...WAS THAT WHEN I WENT BACK AS A TEENAGER, WHEN I HAD A REASON TO LEARN AND A REASON TO FIGHT--

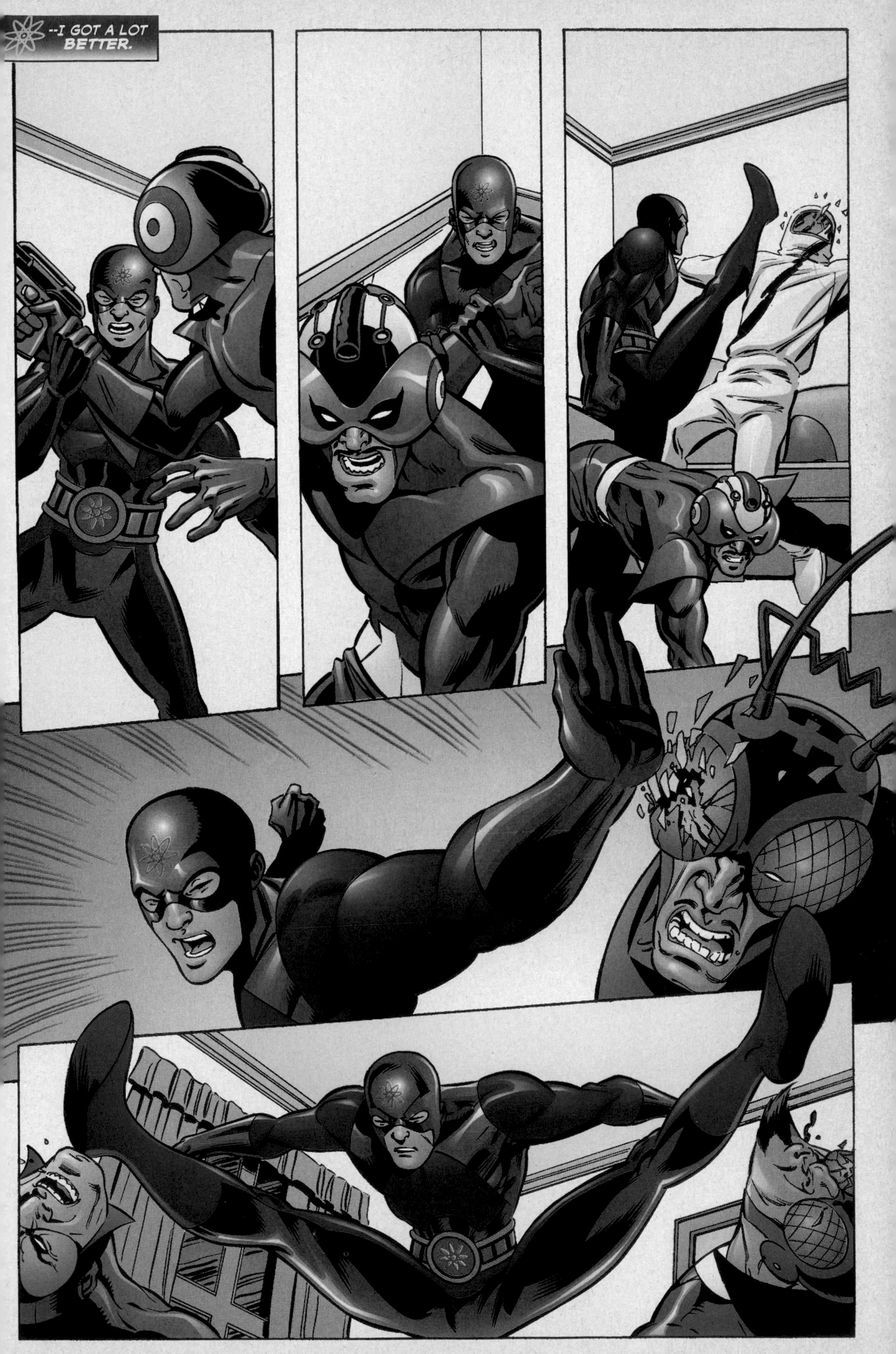
--I GOT A LOT BETTER.

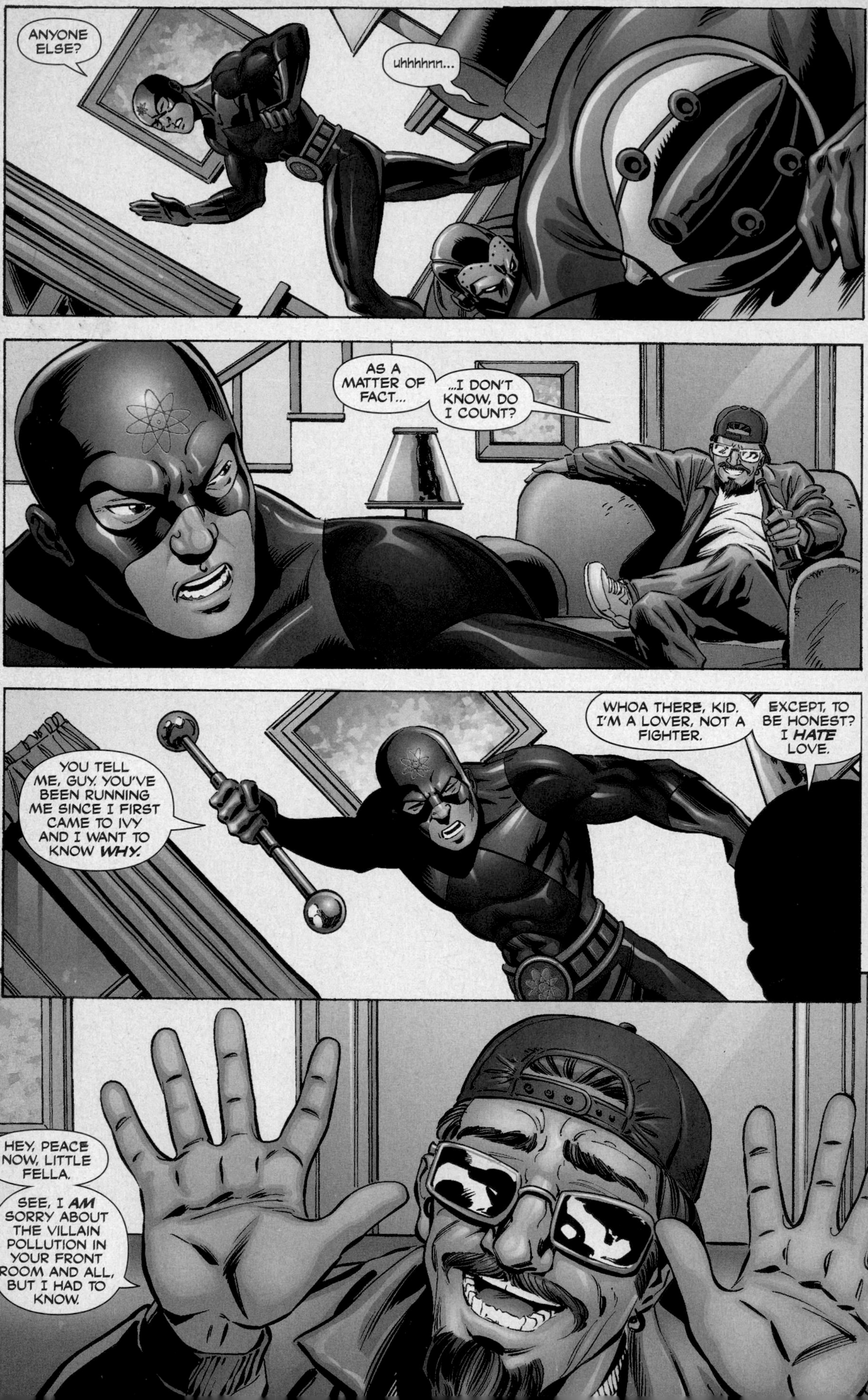
ANYONE ELSE?
uhhhhnn...
AS A MATTER OF FACT...
...I DON'T KNOW, DO I COUNT?
YOU TELL ME, GUY. YOU'VE BEEN RUNNING ME SINCE I FIRST CAME TO IVY AND I WANT TO KNOW WHY.
WHOA THERE, KID. I'M A LOVER, NOT A FIGHTER.
EXCEPT, TO BE HONEST? I HATE LOVE.
HEY, PEACE NOW, LITTLE FELLA.
SEE, I AM SORRY ABOUT THE VILLAIN POLLUTION IN YOUR FRONT ROOM AND ALL, BUT I HAD TO KNOW.

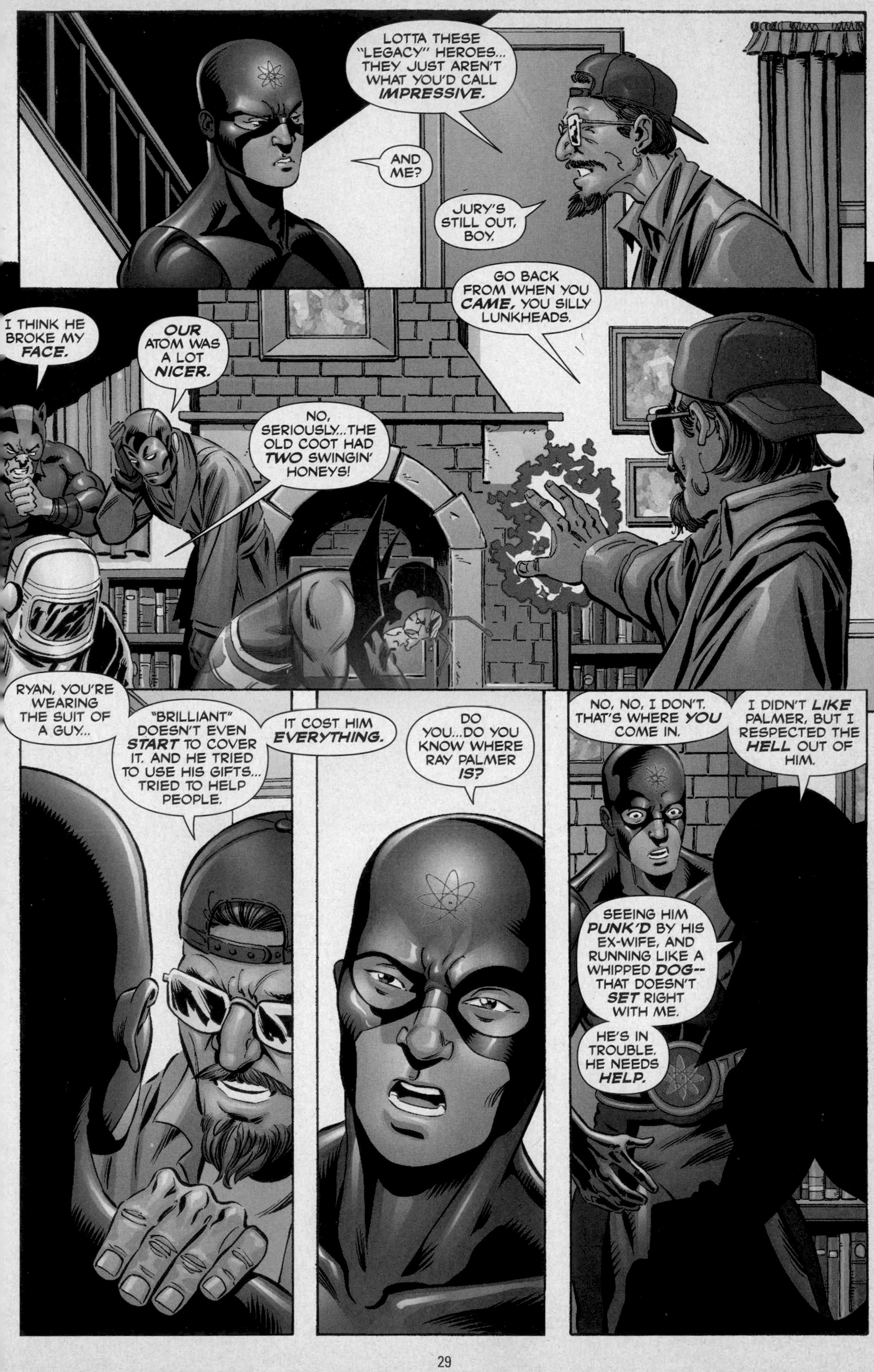
LOTTA THESE "LEGACY" HEROES... THEY JUST AREN'T WHAT YOU'D CALL IMPRESSIVE.
AND ME?
JURY'S STILL OUT, BOY.
GO BACK FROM WHEN YOU CAME, YOU SILLY LUNKHEADS.
I THINK HE BROKE MY FACE.
OUR ATOM WAS A LOT NICER.
NO, SERIOUSLY...THE OLD COOT HAD TWO SWINGIN' HONEYS!
RYAN, YOU'RE WEARING THE SUIT OF A GUY...
"BRILLIANT" DOESN'T EVEN START TO COVER IT. AND HE TRIED TO USE HIS GIFTS... TRIED TO HELP PEOPLE.
IT COST HIM EVERYTHING.
DO YOU...DO YOU KNOW WHERE RAY PALMER IS?
NO, NO, I DON'T. THAT'S WHERE YOU COME IN.
I DIDN'T LIKE PALMER, BUT I RESPECTED THE HELL OUT OF HIM.
SEEING HIM PUNK'D BY HIS EX-WIFE, AND RUNNING LIKE A WHIPPED DOG-- THAT DOESN'T SET RIGHT WITH ME.
HE'S IN TROUBLE. HE NEEDS HELP.

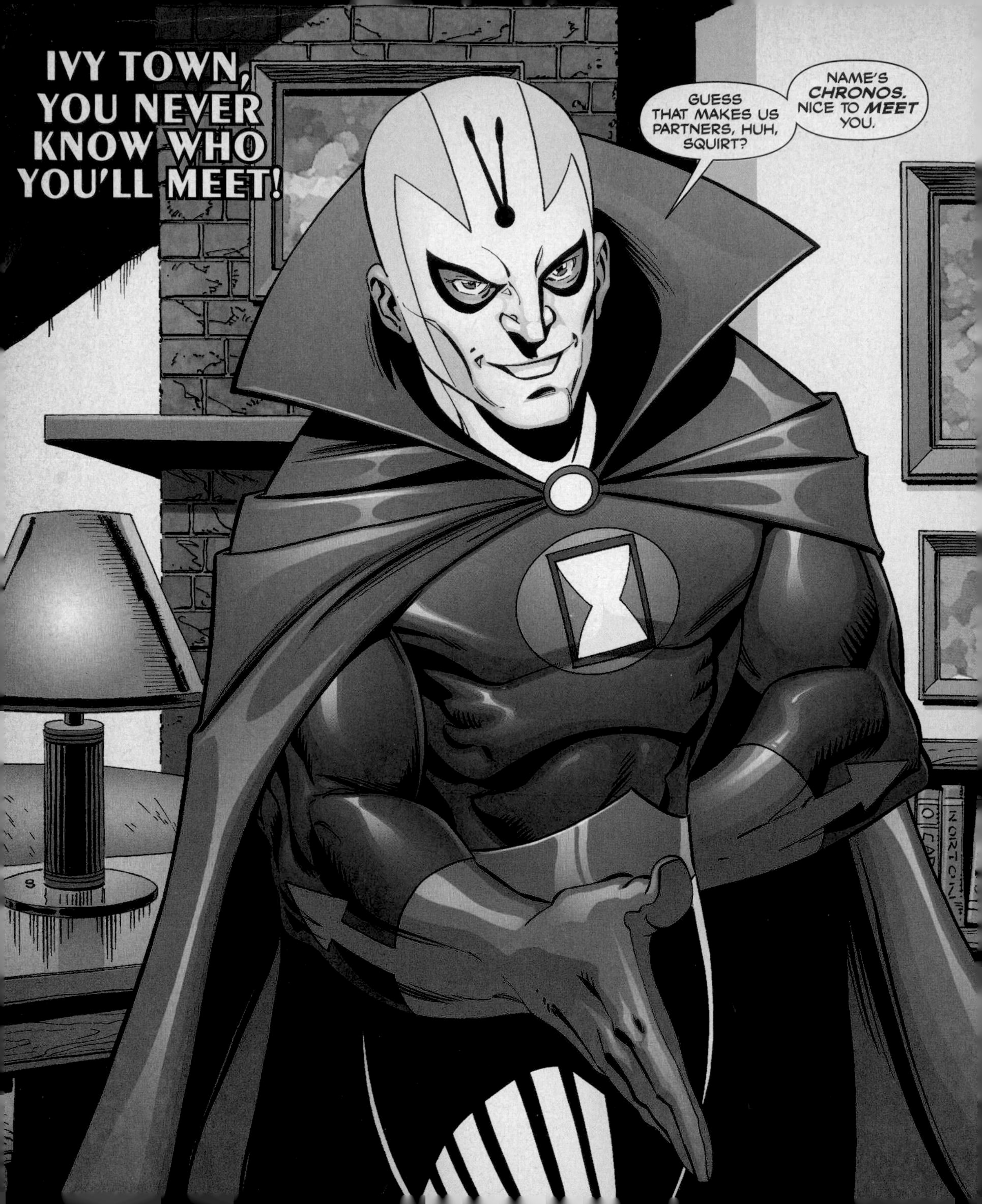
IVY TOWN, YOU NEVER KNOW WHO YOU'LL MEET!
GUESS THAT MAKES US PARTNERS, HUH, SQUIRT?
NAME'S CHRONOS. NICE TO MEET YOU.

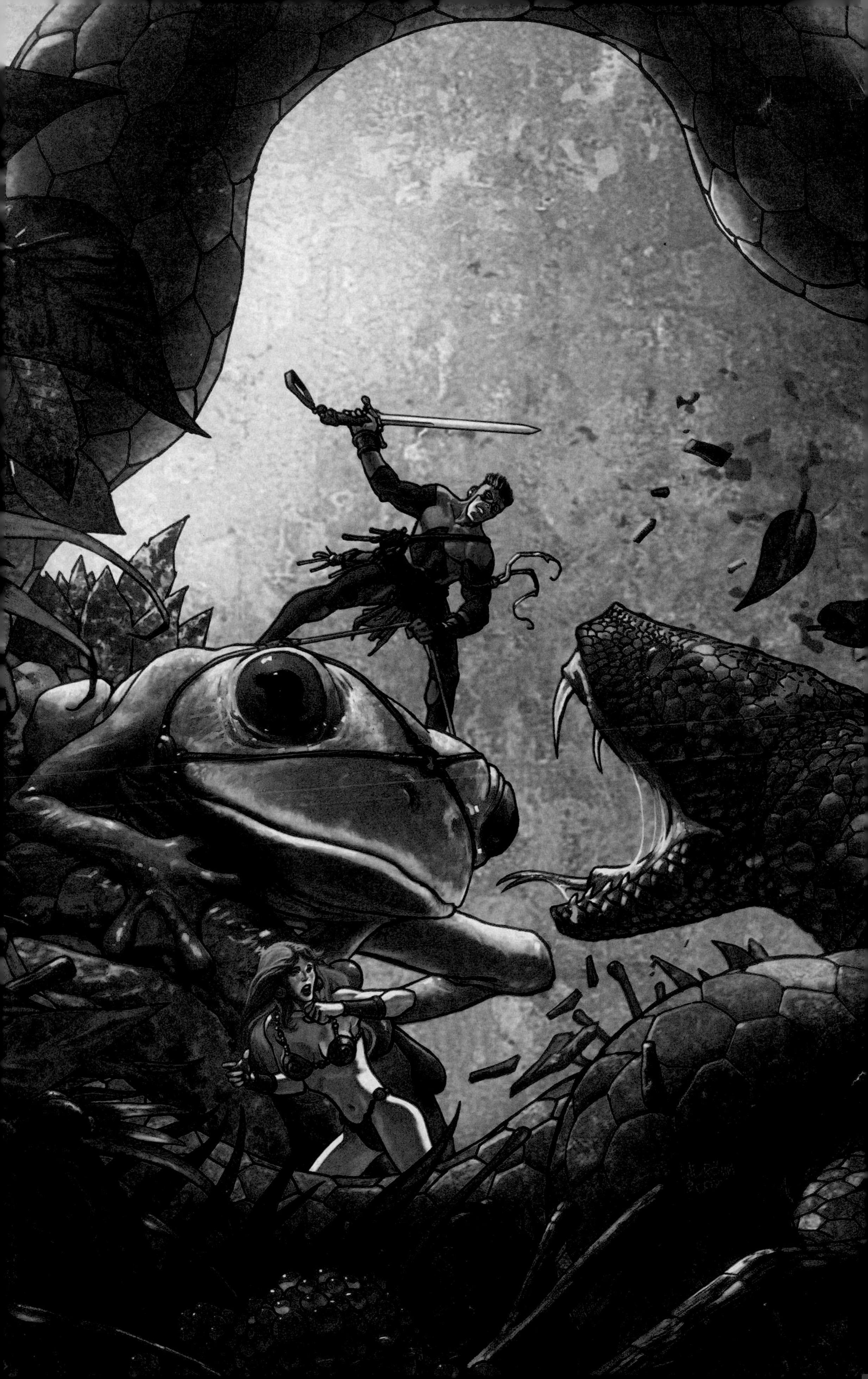

HUNT FOR RAY PALMER: PART TWO
SECOND GENESIS

from **THE ALL NEW ATOM #13**

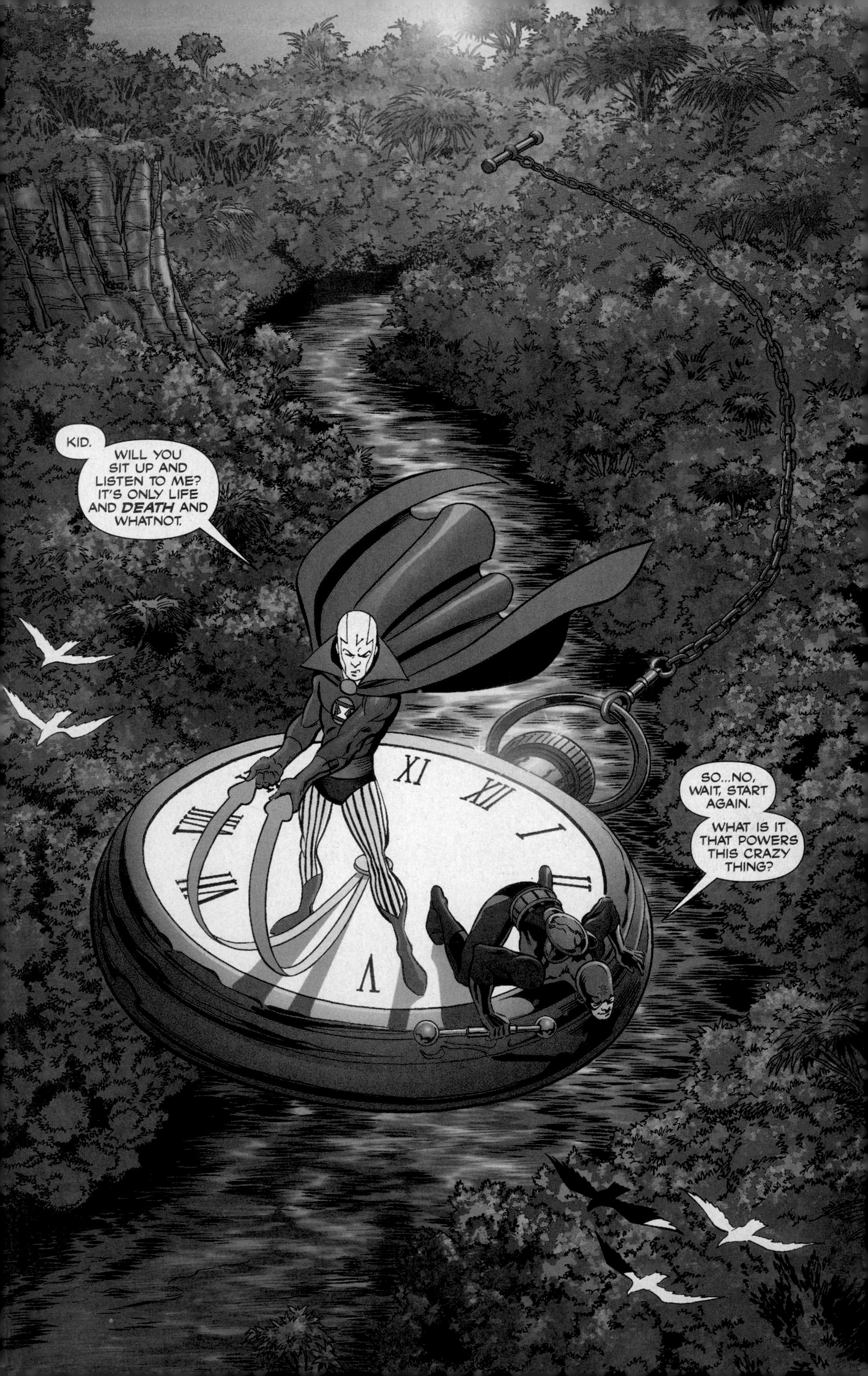
KID.
WILL YOU SIT UP AND LISTEN TO ME? IT'S ONLY LIFE AND *DEATH* AND WHATNOT.
SO...NO, WAIT, START AGAIN.
WHAT IS IT THAT POWERS THIS CRAZY THING?

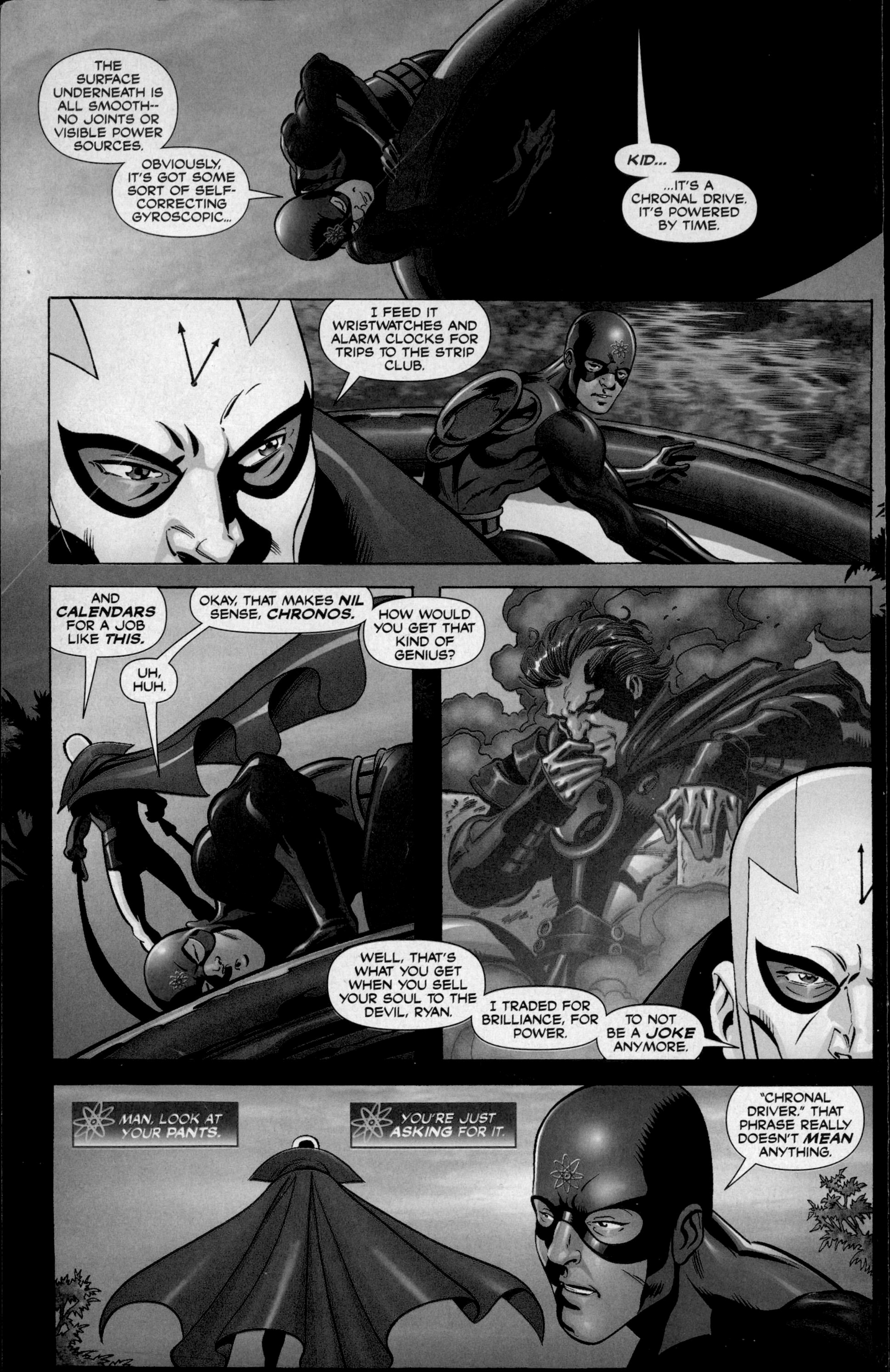
THE SURFACE UNDERNEATH IS ALL SMOOTH-- NO JOINTS OR VISIBLE POWER SOURCES.
OBVIOUSLY, IT'S GOT SOME SORT OF SELF-CORRECTING GYROSCOPIC...
KID...
...IT'S A CHRONAL DRIVE. IT'S POWERED BY TIME.
I FEED IT WRISTWATCHES AND ALARM CLOCKS FOR TRIPS TO THE STRIP CLUB.
AND CALENDARS FOR A JOB LIKE THIS.
UH, HUH.
OKAY, THAT MAKES NIL SENSE, CHRONOS.
HOW WOULD YOU GET THAT KIND OF GENIUS?
WELL, THAT'S WHAT YOU GET WHEN YOU SELL YOUR SOUL TO THE DEVIL, RYAN.
I TRADED FOR BRILLIANCE, FOR POWER.
TO NOT BE A JOKE ANYMORE.
MAN, LOOK AT YOUR PANTS.
YOU'RE JUST ASKING FOR IT.
"CHRONAL DRIVER." THAT PHRASE REALLY DOESN'T MEAN ANYTHING.

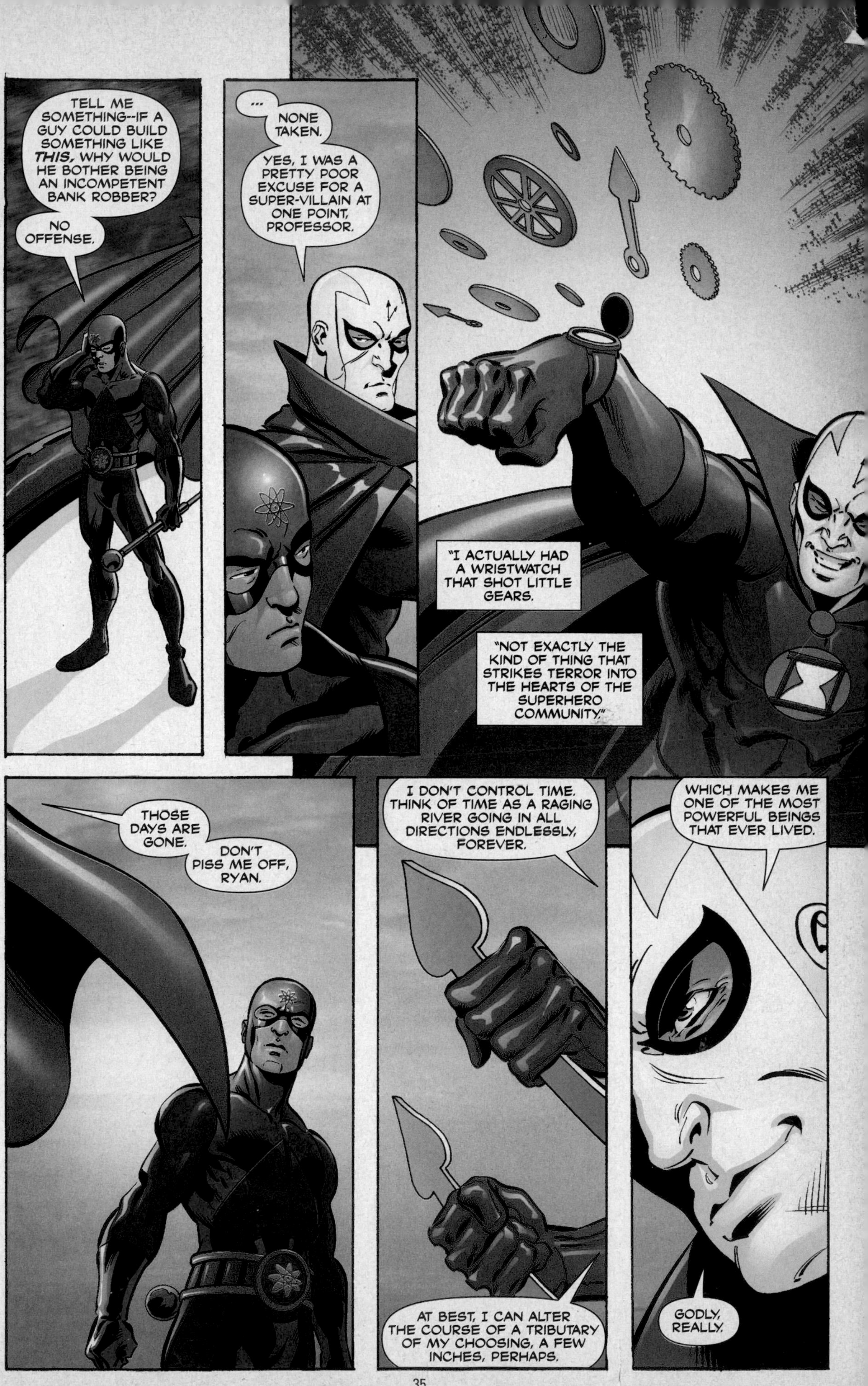
TELL ME SOMETHING--IF A GUY COULD BUILD SOMETHING LIKE THIS, WHY WOULD HE BOTHER BEING AN INCOMPETENT BANK ROBBER?
NO OFFENSE.
...
NONE TAKEN.
YES, I WAS A PRETTY POOR EXCUSE FOR A SUPER-VILLAIN AT ONE POINT, PROFESSOR.
"I ACTUALLY HAD A WRISTWATCH THAT SHOT LITTLE GEARS.
"NOT EXACTLY THE KIND OF THING THAT STRIKES TERROR INTO THE HEARTS OF THE SUPERHERO COMMUNITY."
THOSE DAYS ARE GONE.
DON'T PISS ME OFF, RYAN.
I DON'T CONTROL TIME. THINK OF TIME AS A RAGING RIVER GOING IN ALL DIRECTIONS ENDLESSLY, FOREVER.
AT BEST, I CAN ALTER THE COURSE OF A TRIBUTARY OF MY CHOOSING, A FEW INCHES, PERHAPS.
WHICH MAKES ME ONE OF THE MOST POWERFUL BEINGS THAT EVER LIVED.
GODLY, REALLY.

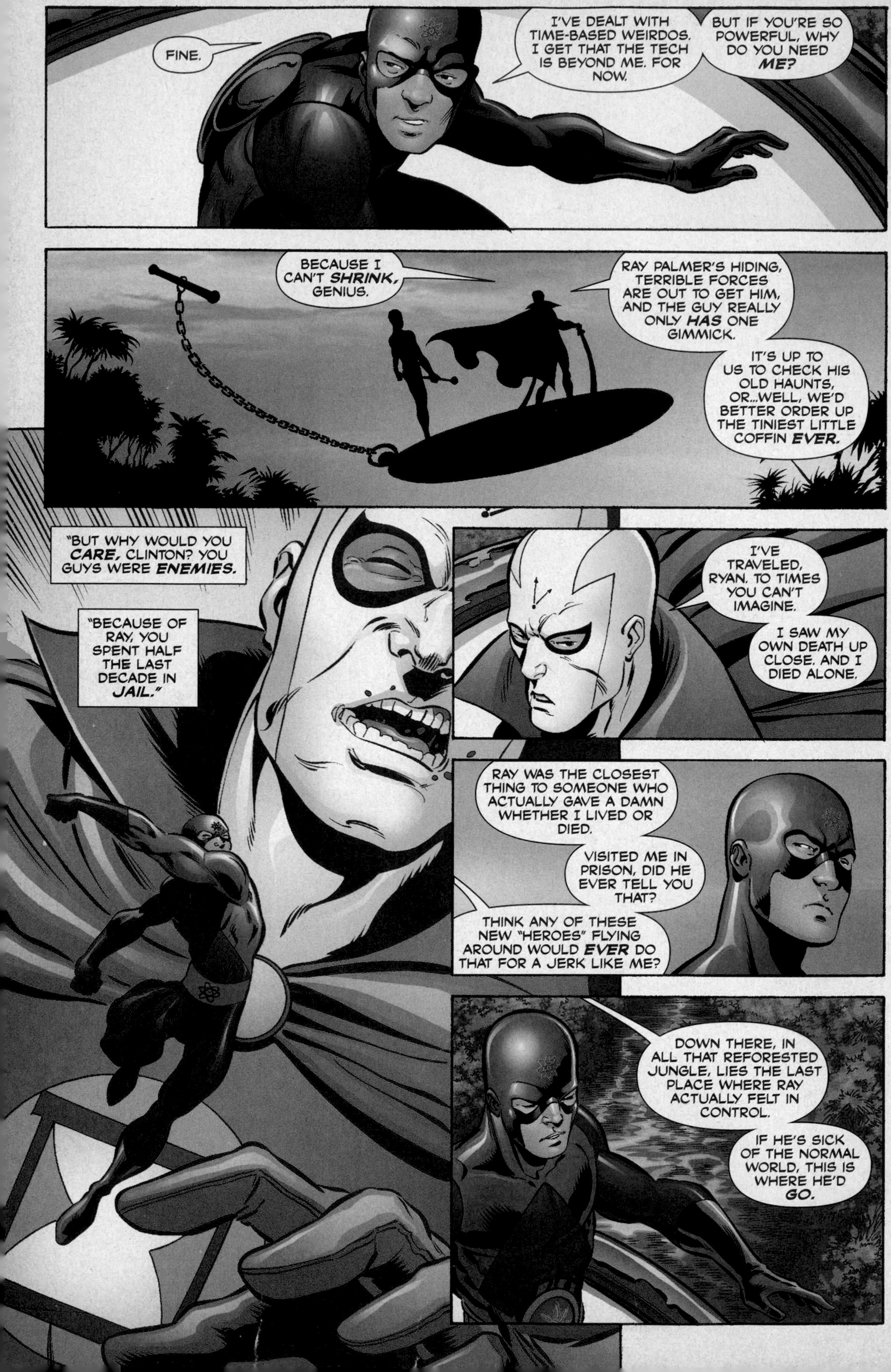
FINE.
I'VE DEALT WITH TIME-BASED WEIRDOS. I GET THAT THE TECH IS BEYOND ME. FOR NOW.
BUT IF YOU'RE SO POWERFUL, WHY DO YOU NEED ME?
BECAUSE I CAN'T SHRINK, GENIUS.
RAY PALMER'S HIDING, TERRIBLE FORCES ARE OUT TO GET HIM, AND THE GUY REALLY ONLY HAS ONE GIMMICK.
IT'S UP TO US TO CHECK HIS OLD HAUNTS, OR...WELL, WE'D BETTER ORDER UP THE TINIEST LITTLE COFFIN EVER.
"BUT WHY WOULD YOU CARE, CLINTON? YOU GUYS WERE ENEMIES.
"BECAUSE OF RAY, YOU SPENT HALF THE LAST DECADE IN JAIL."
I'VE TRAVELED, RYAN, TO TIMES YOU CAN'T IMAGINE.
I SAW MY OWN DEATH UP CLOSE. AND I DIED ALONE.
RAY WAS THE CLOSEST THING TO SOMEONE WHO ACTUALLY GAVE A DAMN WHETHER I LIVED OR DIED.
VISITED ME IN PRISON, DID HE EVER TELL YOU THAT?
THINK ANY OF THESE NEW "HEROES" FLYING AROUND WOULD EVER DO THAT FOR A JERK LIKE ME?
DOWN THERE, IN ALL THAT REFORESTED JUNGLE, LIES THE LAST PLACE WHERE RAY ACTUALLY FELT IN CONTROL.
IF HE'S SICK OF THE NORMAL WORLD, THIS IS WHERE HE'D GO.

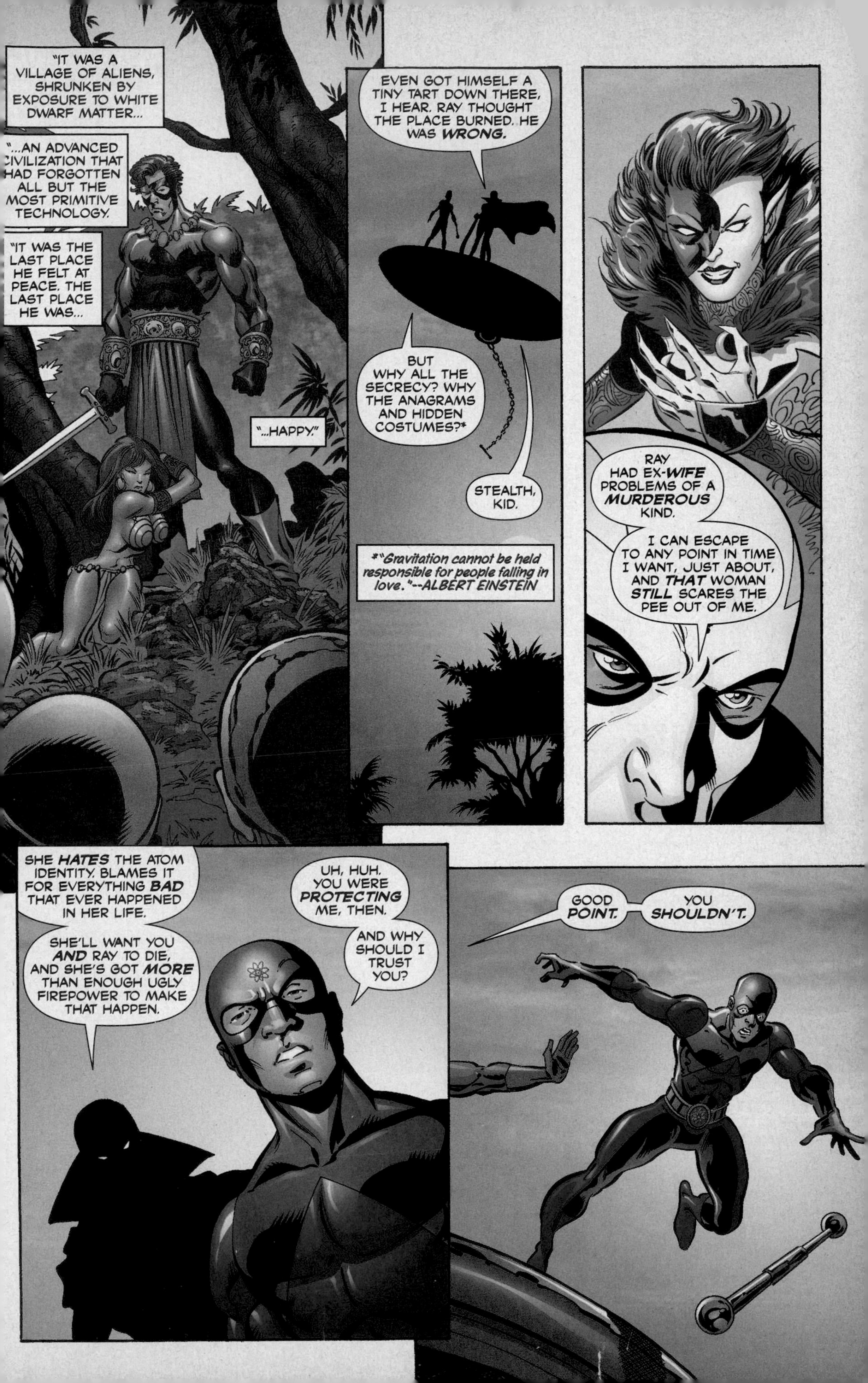
"IT WAS A VILLAGE OF ALIENS, SHRUNKEN BY EXPOSURE TO WHITE DWARF MATTER...
"...AN ADVANCED CIVILIZATION THAT HAD FORGOTTEN ALL BUT THE MOST PRIMITIVE TECHNOLOGY.
"IT WAS THE LAST PLACE HE FELT AT PEACE. THE LAST PLACE HE WAS...
"...HAPPY."
EVEN GOT HIMSELF A TINY TART DOWN THERE, I HEAR. RAY THOUGHT THE PLACE BURNED. HE WAS WRONG.
BUT WHY ALL THE SECRECY? WHY THE ANAGRAMS AND HIDDEN COSTUMES?*
STEALTH, KID.
*"Gravitation cannot be held responsible for people falling in love."--ALBERT EINSTEIN
RAY HAD EX-WIFE PROBLEMS OF A MURDEROUS KIND.
I CAN ESCAPE TO ANY POINT IN TIME I WANT, JUST ABOUT, AND THAT WOMAN STILL SCARES THE PEE OUT OF ME.
SHE HATES THE ATOM IDENTITY. BLAMES IT FOR EVERYTHING BAD THAT EVER HAPPENED IN HER LIFE.
SHE'LL WANT YOU AND RAY TO DIE, AND SHE'S GOT MORE THAN ENOUGH UGLY FIREPOWER TO MAKE THAT HAPPEN.
UH, HUH. YOU WERE PROTECTING ME, THEN.
AND WHY SHOULD I TRUST YOU?
GOOD POINT.
YOU SHOULDN'T.

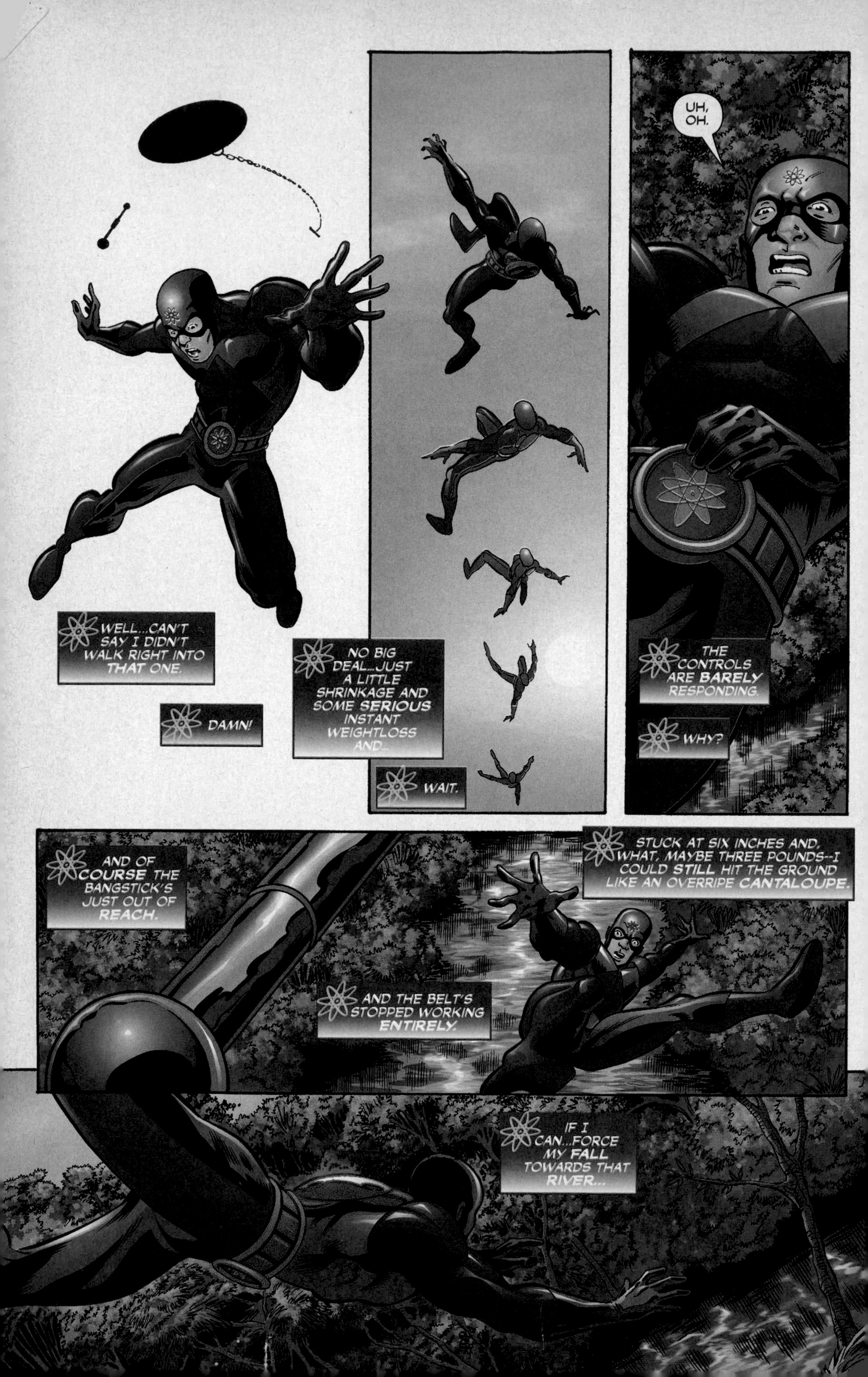
WELL...CAN'T SAY I DIDN'T WALK RIGHT INTO THAT ONE.
DAMN!
NO BIG DEAL...JUST A LITTLE SHRINKAGE AND SOME SERIOUS INSTANT WEIGHTLOSS AND...
WAIT.
UH, OH.
THE CONTROLS ARE BARELY RESPONDING.
WHY?
AND OF COURSE THE BANGSTICK'S JUST OUT OF REACH.
STUCK AT SIX INCHES AND, WHAT, MAYBE THREE POUNDS--I COULD STILL HIT THE GROUND LIKE AN OVERRIPE CANTALOUPE.
AND THE BELT'S STOPPED WORKING ENTIRELY.
IF I CAN...FORCE MY FALL TOWARDS THAT RIVER...

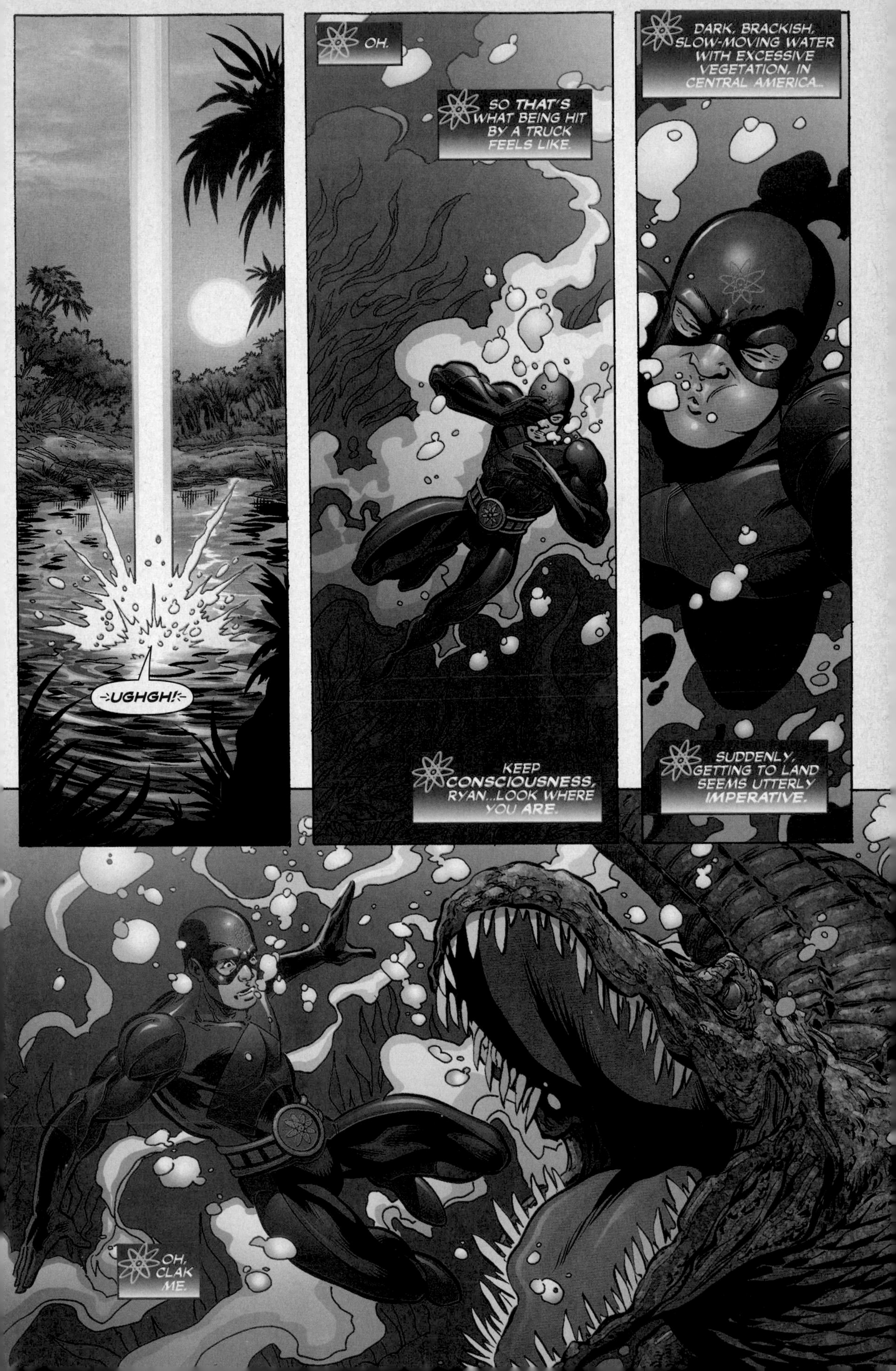
-UGHGH!-
OH.
SO THAT'S WHAT BEING HIT BY A TRUCK FEELS LIKE.
KEEP CONSCIOUSNESS, RYAN...LOOK WHERE YOU ARE.
DARK, BRACKISH, SLOW-MOVING WATER WITH EXCESSIVE VEGETATION, IN CENTRAL AMERICA...
SUDDENLY, GETTING TO LAND SEEMS UTTERLY IMPERATIVE.
OH, CLAK ME.

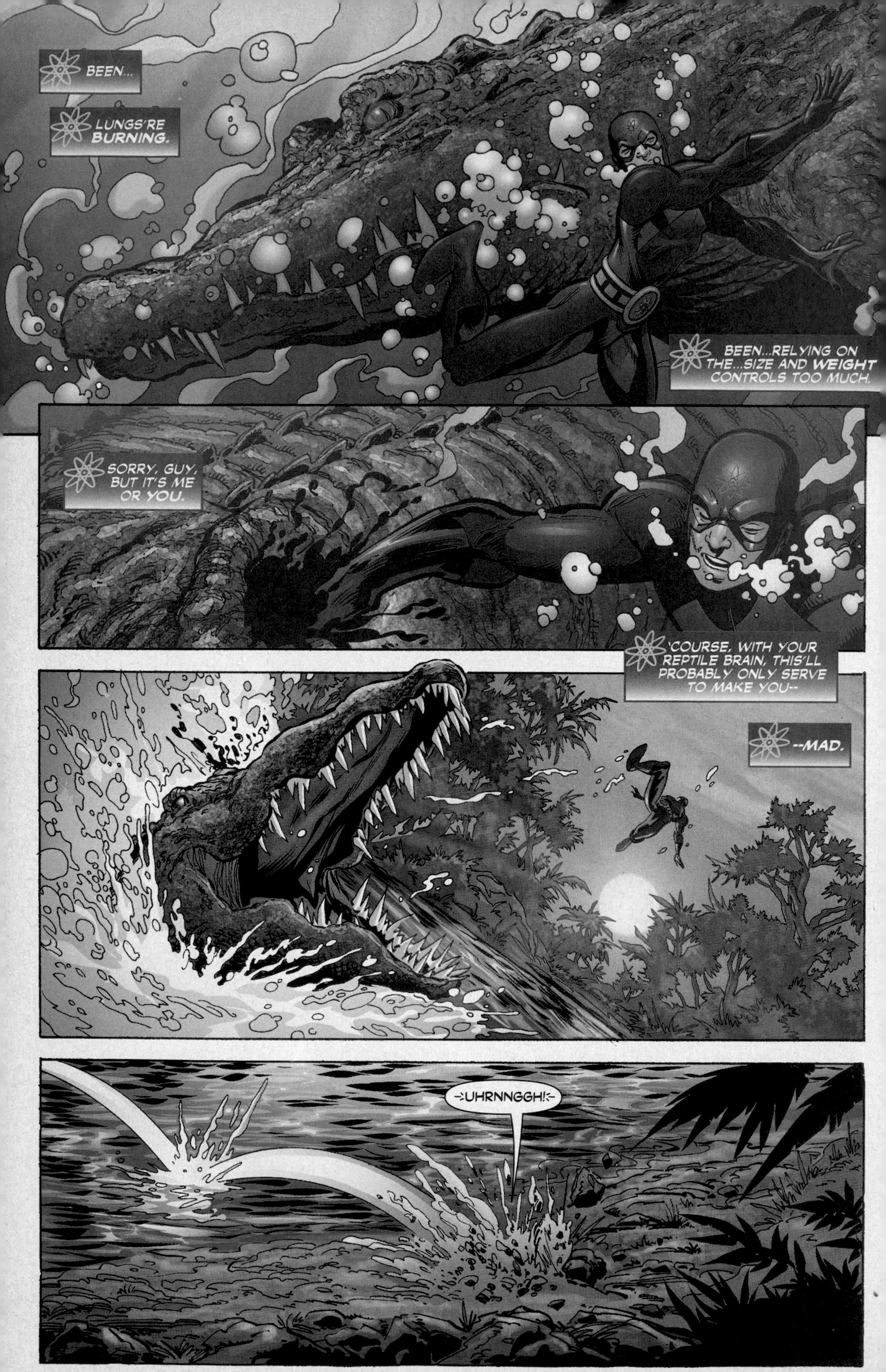
BEEN...
LUNGS'RE BURNING.
BEEN...RELYING ON THE...SIZE AND WEIGHT CONTROLS TOO MUCH.
SORRY, GUY, BUT IT'S ME OR YOU.
'COURSE, WITH YOUR REPTILE BRAIN, THIS'LL PROBABLY ONLY SERVE TO MAKE YOU--
--MAD.
UHRNNGGH!

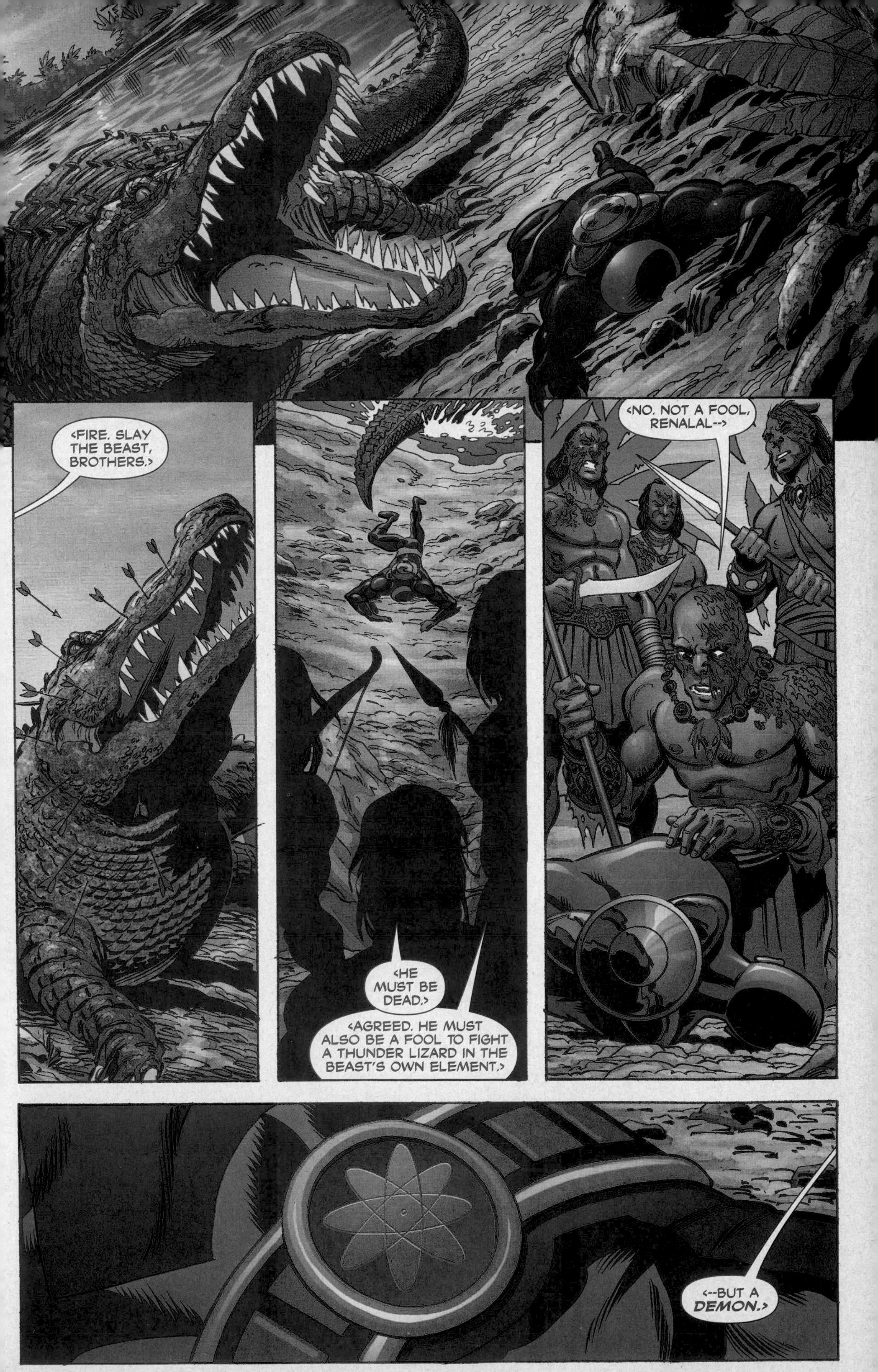

<FIRE. SLAY THE BEAST, BROTHERS.>
<HE MUST BE DEAD.>
<AGREED. HE MUST ALSO BE A FOOL TO FIGHT A THUNDER LIZARD IN THE BEAST'S OWN ELEMENT.>
<NO. NOT A FOOL, RENALAL-->
<--BUT A *DEMON*.>

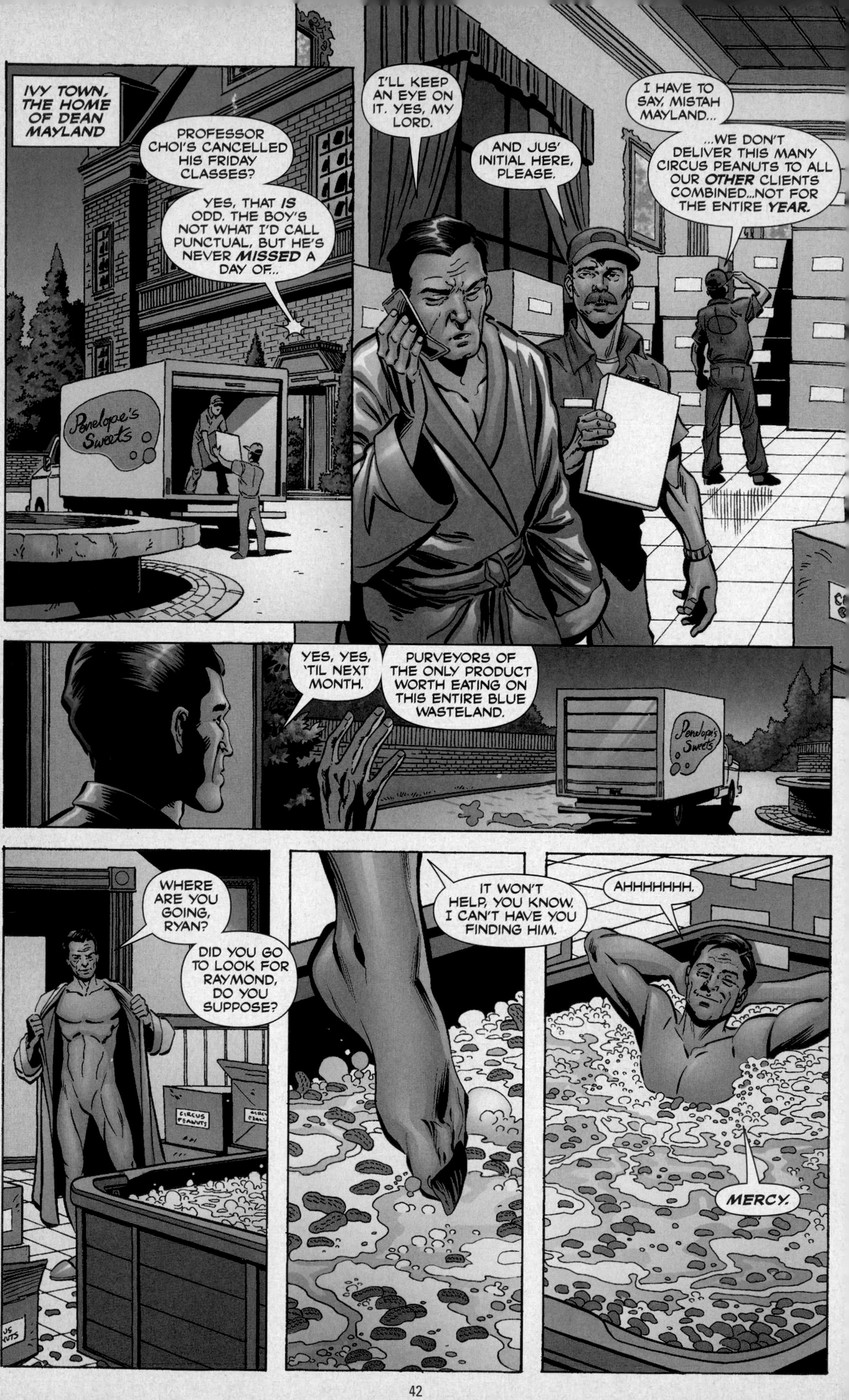
IVY TOWN, THE HOME OF DEAN MAYLAND
PROFESSOR CHOI'S CANCELLED HIS FRIDAY CLASSES?
YES, THAT IS ODD. THE BOY'S NOT WHAT I'D CALL PUNCTUAL, BUT HE'S NEVER MISSED A DAY OF...
Penelope's Sweets
I'LL KEEP AN EYE ON IT. YES, MY LORD.
AND JUS' INITIAL HERE, PLEASE.
I HAVE TO SAY, MISTAH MAYLAND...
...WE DON'T DELIVER THIS MANY CIRCUS PEANUTS TO ALL OUR OTHER CLIENTS COMBINED...NOT FOR THE ENTIRE YEAR.
YES, YES, 'TIL NEXT MONTH.
PURVEYORS OF THE ONLY PRODUCT WORTH EATING ON THIS ENTIRE BLUE WASTELAND.
Penelope's Sweets
WHERE ARE YOU GOING, RYAN?
DID YOU GO TO LOOK FOR RAYMOND, DO YOU SUPPOSE?
CIRCUS PEANUTS
IT WON'T HELP, YOU KNOW. I CAN'T HAVE YOU FINDING HIM.
AHHHHHHH.
MERCY.

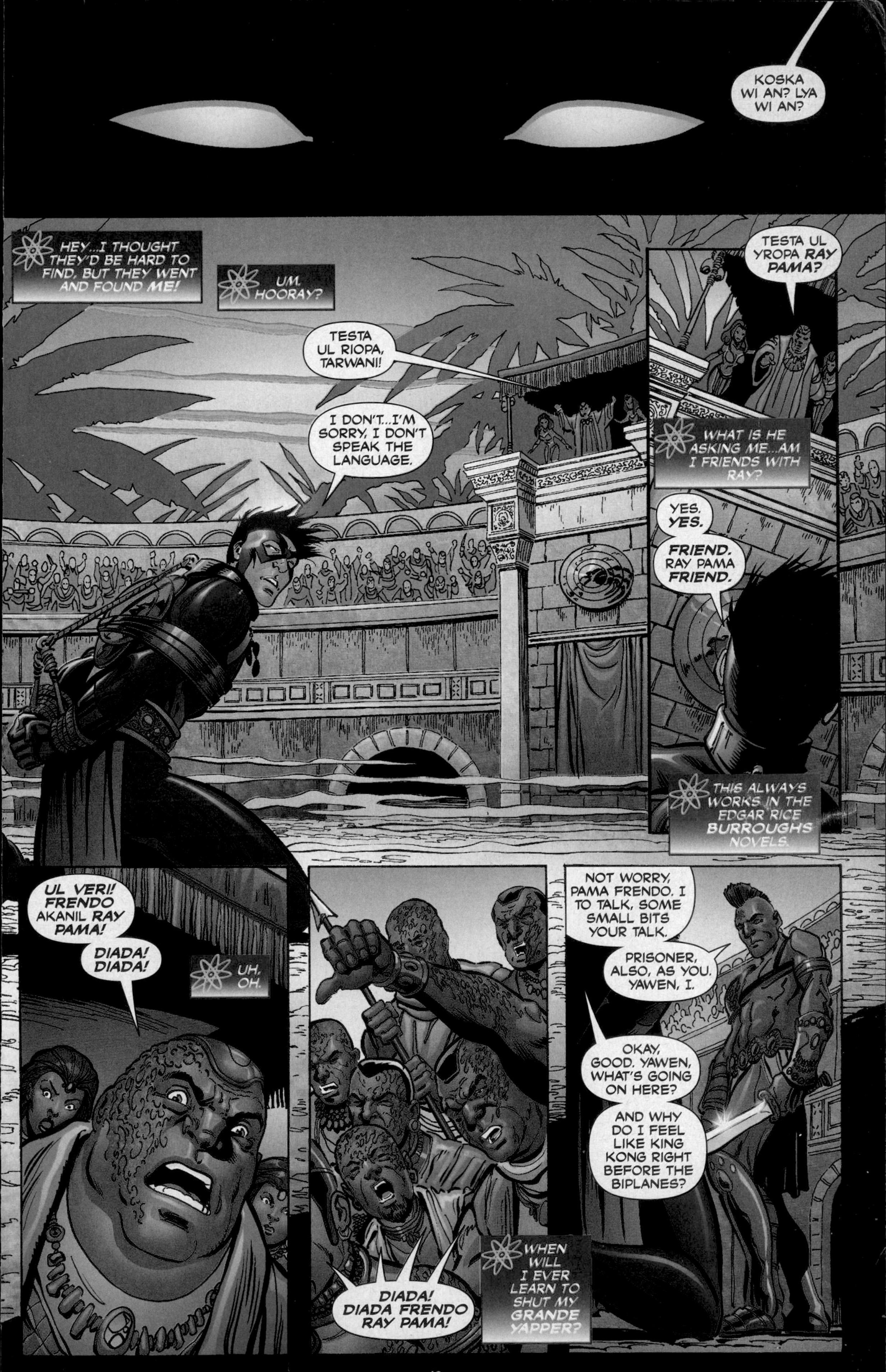
KOSKA WI AN? LYA WI AN?
HEY...I THOUGHT THEY'D BE HARD TO FIND, BUT THEY WENT AND FOUND ME!
UM. HOORAY?
TESTA UL RIOPA, TARWANI!
I DON'T...I'M SORRY, I DON'T SPEAK THE LANGUAGE.
TESTA UL YROPA RAY PAMA?
WHAT IS HE ASKING ME...AM I FRIENDS WITH RAY?
YES. YES.
FRIEND. RAY PAMA FRIEND.
THIS ALWAYS WORKS IN THE EDGAR RICE BURROUGHS NOVELS.
UL VERI! FRENDO AKANIL RAY PAMA!
DIADA! DIADA!
UH, OH.
DIADA! DIADA FRENDO RAY PAMA!
WHEN WILL I EVER LEARN TO SHUT MY GRANDE YAPPER?
NOT WORRY, PAMA FRENDO. I TO TALK, SOME SMALL BITS YOUR TALK.
PRISONER, ALSO, AS YOU. YAWEN, I.
OKAY, GOOD. YAWEN, WHAT'S GOING ON HERE?
AND WHY DO I FEEL LIKE KING KONG RIGHT BEFORE THE BIPLANES?

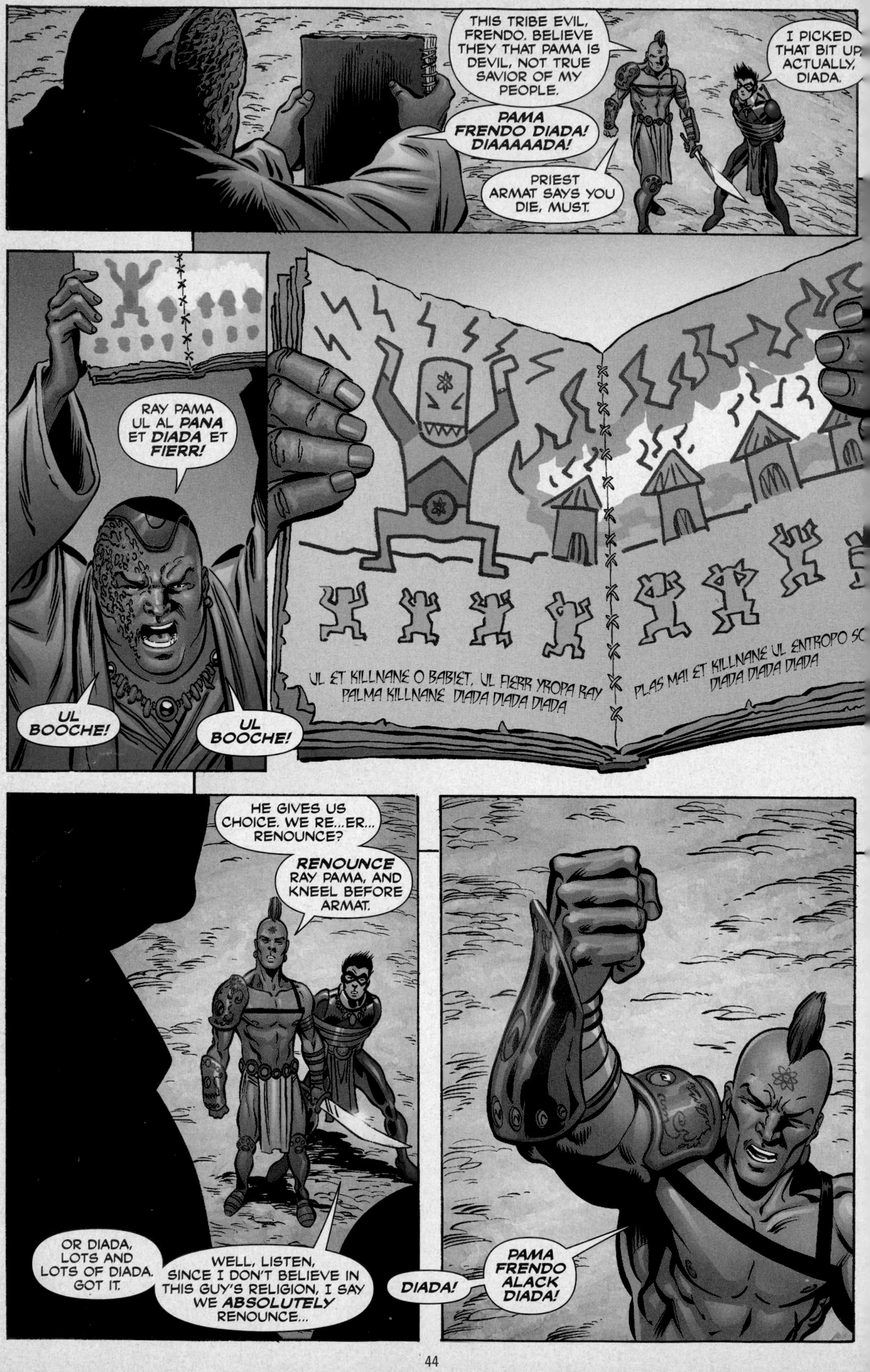
THIS TRIBE EVIL, FRENDO. BELIEVE THEY THAT PAMA IS DEVIL, NOT TRUE SAVIOR OF MY PEOPLE.
I PICKED THAT BIT UP, ACTUALLY, DIADA.
PAMA FRENDO DIADA! DIAAAAADA!
PRIEST ARMAT SAYS YOU DIE, MUST.
RAY PAMA UL AL PANA ET DIADA ET FIERR!
UL ET KILLNANE O BABIET, UL FIERR YROPA RAY PALMA KILLNANE DIADA DIADA DIADA
PLAS MAI ET KILLNANE UL ENTROPO SC DIADA DIADA DIADA
UL BOOCHE!
UL BOOCHE!
HE GIVES US CHOICE. WE RE...ER... RENOUNCE?
RENOUNCE RAY PAMA, AND KNEEL BEFORE ARMAT.
OR DIADA, LOTS AND LOTS OF DIADA. GOT IT.
WELL, LISTEN, SINCE I DON'T BELIEVE IN THIS GUY'S RELIGION, I SAY WE ABSOLUTELY RENOUNCE...
DIADA!
PAMA FRENDO ALACK DIADA!

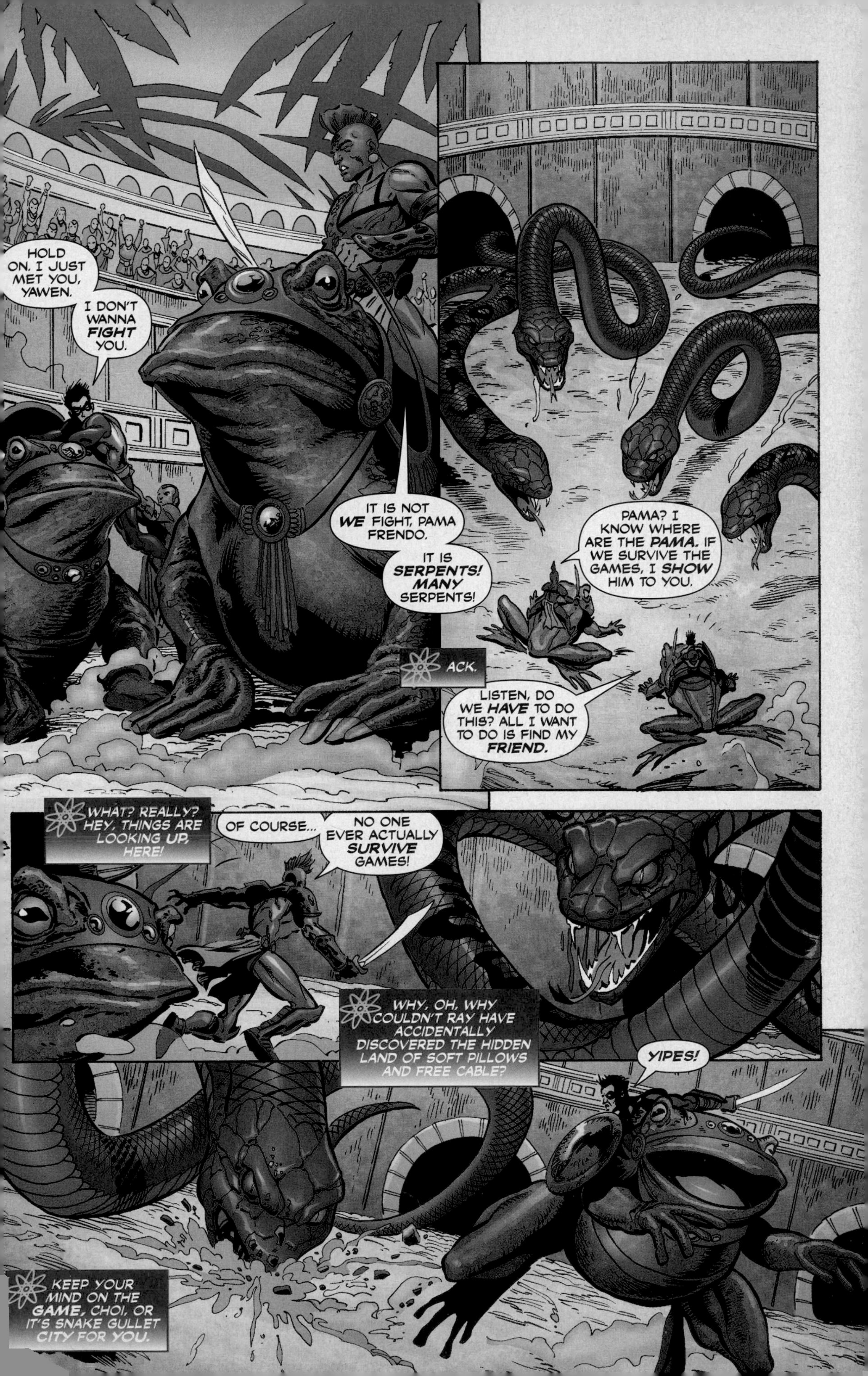
HOLD ON. I JUST MET YOU, YAWEN.
I DON'T WANNA **FIGHT** YOU.
IT IS NOT **WE** FIGHT, PAMA FRENDO.
IT IS **SERPENTS! MANY** SERPENTS!
ACK.
LISTEN, DO WE **HAVE** TO DO THIS? ALL I WANT TO DO IS FIND MY **FRIEND.**
PAMA? I KNOW WHERE ARE THE **PAMA.** IF WE SURVIVE THE GAMES, I **SHOW** HIM TO YOU.
WHAT? REALLY? HEY, THINGS ARE LOOKING **UP,** HERE!
OF COURSE...
NO ONE EVER ACTUALLY **SURVIVE** GAMES!
WHY, OH, WHY COULDN'T RAY HAVE ACCIDENTALLY DISCOVERED THE HIDDEN LAND OF SOFT PILLOWS AND FREE CABLE?
YIPES!
KEEP YOUR MIND ON THE **GAME,** CHOI, OR IT'S SNAKE GULLET CITY FOR **YOU.**

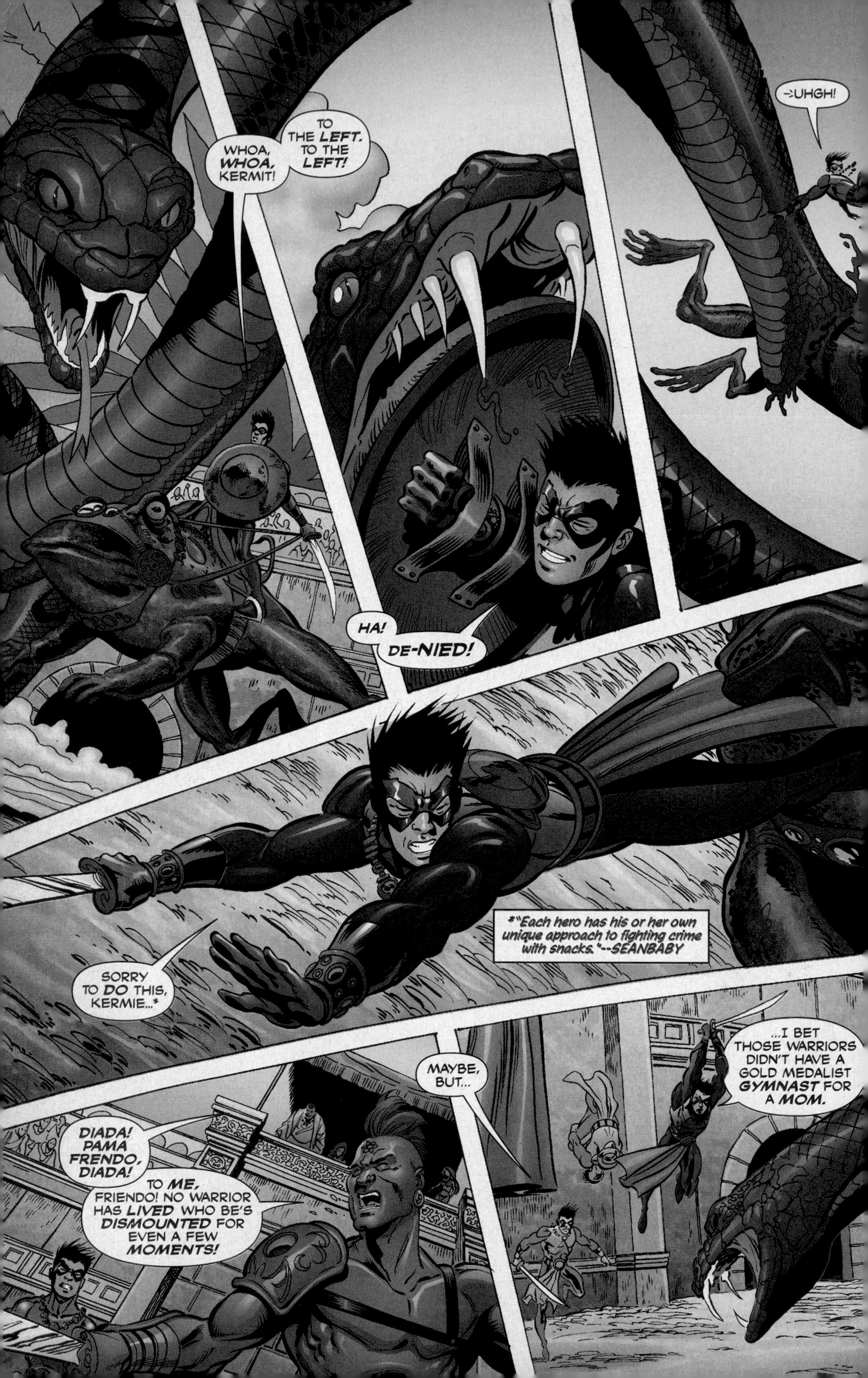
WHOA, WHOA, KERMIT!
TO THE LEFT. TO THE LEFT!
–UHGH!
HA! DE-NIED!
SORRY TO DO THIS, KERMIE...*
*"Each hero has his or her own unique approach to fighting crime with snacks."--SEANBABY
DIADA! PAMA FRENDO, DIADA!
TO ME, FRIENDO! NO WARRIOR HAS LIVED WHO BE'S DISMOUNTED FOR EVEN A FEW MOMENTS!
MAYBE, BUT...
...I BET THOSE WARRIORS DIDN'T HAVE A GOLD MEDALIST GYMNAST FOR A MOM.

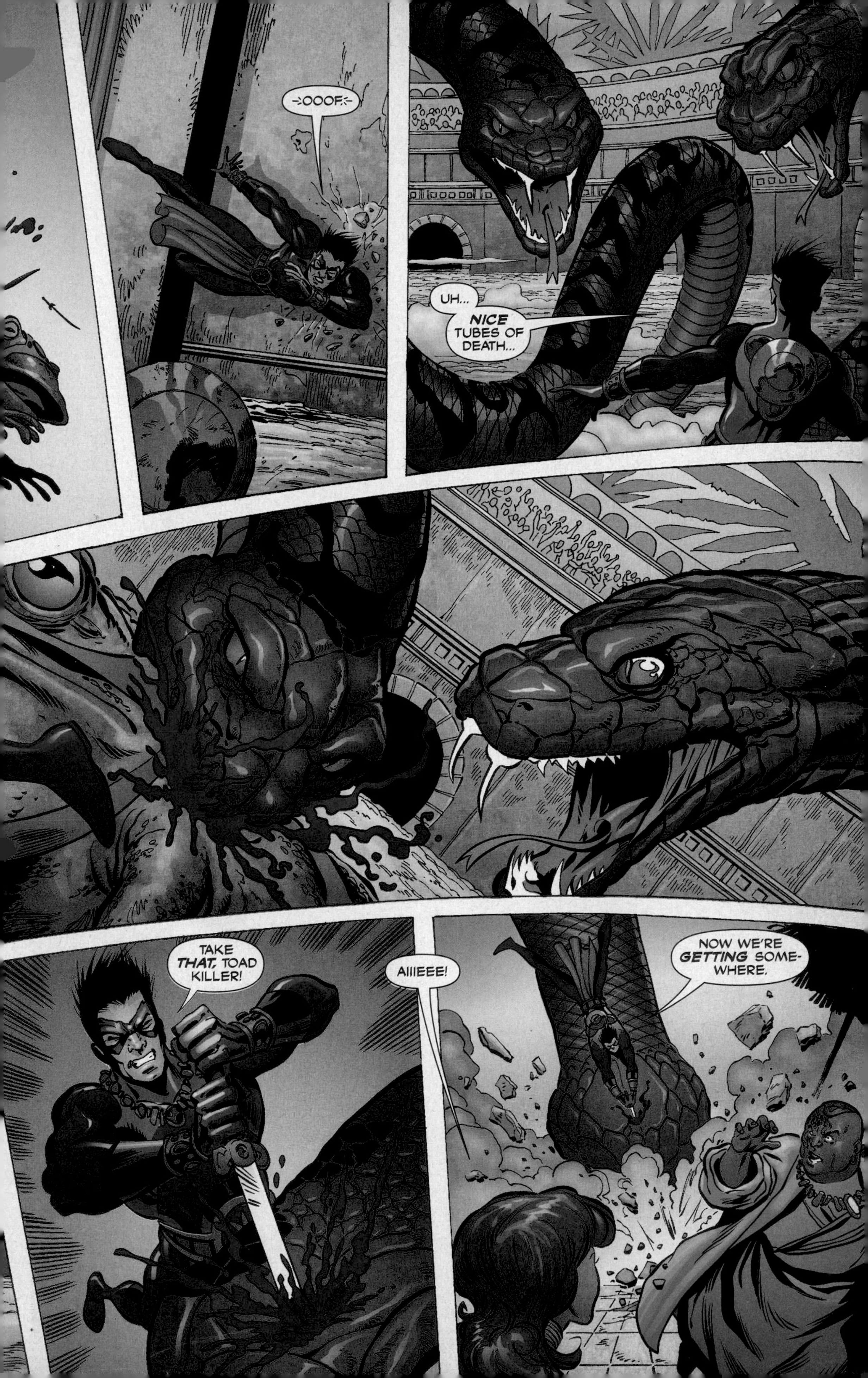
-OOOF-
UH... NICE TUBES OF DEATH...
TAKE THAT, TOAD KILLER!
AIIIEEE!
NOW WE'RE GETTING SOME-WHERE.

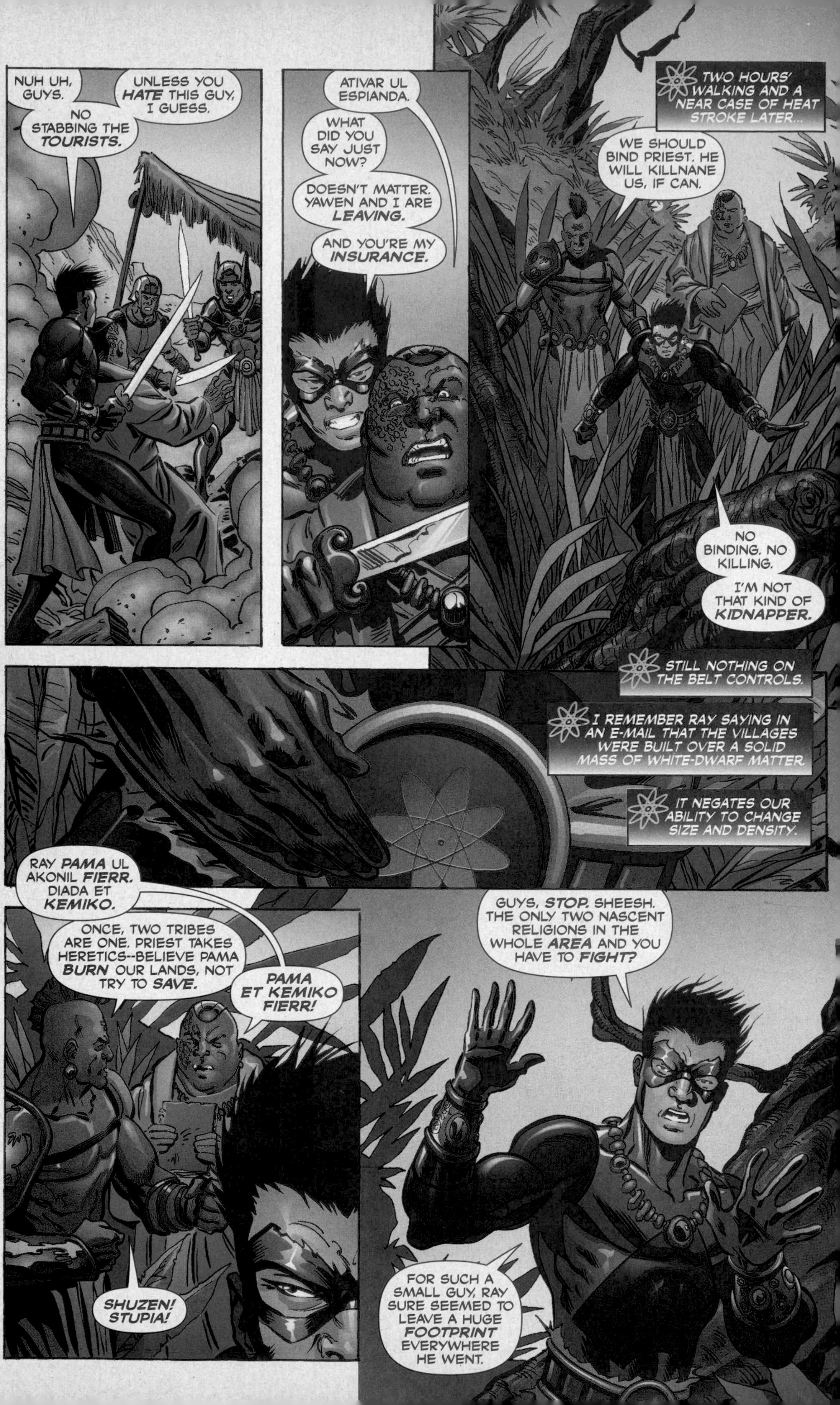
NUH UH, GUYS.
NO STABBING THE TOURISTS.
UNLESS YOU HATE THIS GUY, I GUESS.
ATIVAR UL ESPIANDA.
WHAT DID YOU SAY JUST NOW?
DOESN'T MATTER. YAWEN AND I ARE LEAVING.
AND YOU'RE MY INSURANCE.
TWO HOURS' WALKING AND A NEAR CASE OF HEAT STROKE LATER...
WE SHOULD BIND PRIEST. HE WILL KILLNANE US, IF CAN.
NO BINDING. NO KILLING.
I'M NOT THAT KIND OF KIDNAPPER.
STILL NOTHING ON THE BELT CONTROLS.
I REMEMBER RAY SAYING IN AN E-MAIL THAT THE VILLAGES WERE BUILT OVER A SOLID MASS OF WHITE-DWARF MATTER.
IT NEGATES OUR ABILITY TO CHANGE SIZE AND DENSITY.
RAY PAMA UL AKONIL FIERR. DIADA ET KEMIKO.
ONCE, TWO TRIBES ARE ONE. PRIEST TAKES HERETICS--BELIEVE PAMA BURN OUR LANDS, NOT TRY TO SAVE.
PAMA ET KEMIKO FIERR!
SHUZEN! STUPIA!
GUYS, STOP. SHEESH. THE ONLY TWO NASCENT RELIGIONS IN THE WHOLE AREA AND YOU HAVE TO FIGHT?
FOR SUCH A SMALL GUY, RAY SURE SEEMED TO LEAVE A HUGE FOOTPRINT EVERYWHERE HE WENT.

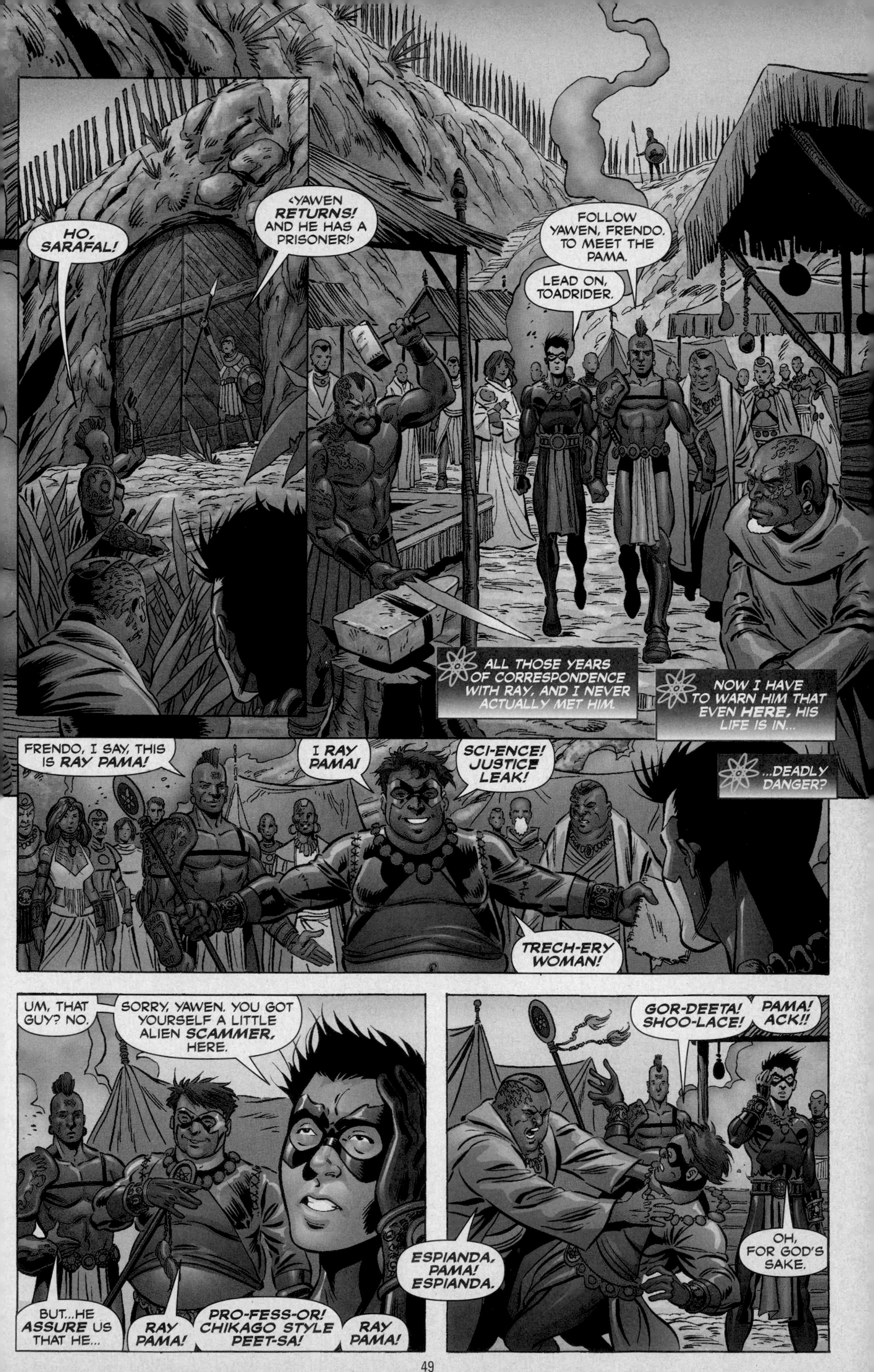
HO, SARAFAL!
<YAWEN RETURNS! AND HE HAS A PRISONER!>
FOLLOW YAWEN, FRENDO, TO MEET THE PAMA.
LEAD ON, TOADRIDER.
ALL THOSE YEARS OF CORRESPONDENCE WITH RAY, AND I NEVER ACTUALLY MET HIM.
NOW I HAVE TO WARN HIM THAT EVEN HERE, HIS LIFE IS IN...
FRENDO, I SAY, THIS IS RAY PAMA!
I RAY PAMA!
SCI-ENCE! JUSTICE LEAK!
...DEADLY DANGER?
TRECH-ERY WOMAN!
UM, THAT GUY? NO.
SORRY, YAWEN. YOU GOT YOURSELF A LITTLE ALIEN SCAMMER, HERE.
BUT...HE ASSURE US THAT HE...
RAY PAMA!
PRO-FESS-OR! CHIKAGO STYLE PEET-SA!
RAY PAMA!
ESPIANDA, PAMA! ESPIANDA.
GOR-DEETA! SHOO-LACE!
PAMA! ACK!!
OH, FOR GOD'S SAKE.

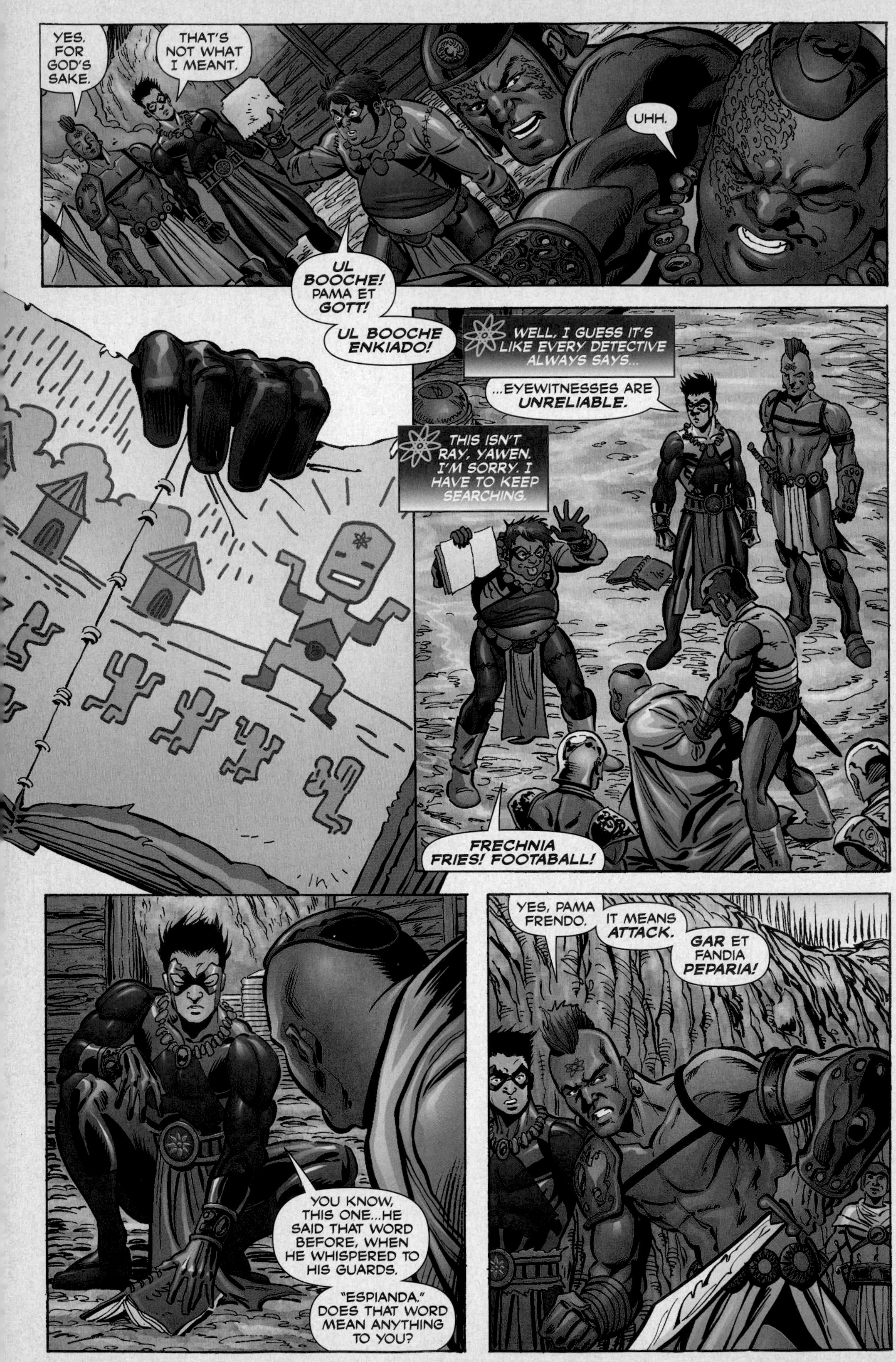
YES. FOR GOD'S SAKE.
THAT'S NOT WHAT I MEANT.
UHH.
UL BOOCHE! PAMA ET GOTT!
UL BOOCHE ENKIADO!
WELL, I GUESS IT'S LIKE EVERY DETECTIVE ALWAYS SAYS...
...EYEWITNESSES ARE UNRELIABLE.
THIS ISN'T RAY, YAWEN. I'M SORRY. I HAVE TO KEEP SEARCHING.
FRECHNIA FRIES! FOOTABALL!
YOU KNOW, THIS ONE...HE SAID THAT WORD BEFORE, WHEN HE WHISPERED TO HIS GUARDS.
"ESPIANDA." DOES THAT WORD MEAN ANYTHING TO YOU?
YES, PAMA FRENDO.
IT MEANS ATTACK.
GAR ET FANDIA PEPARIA!

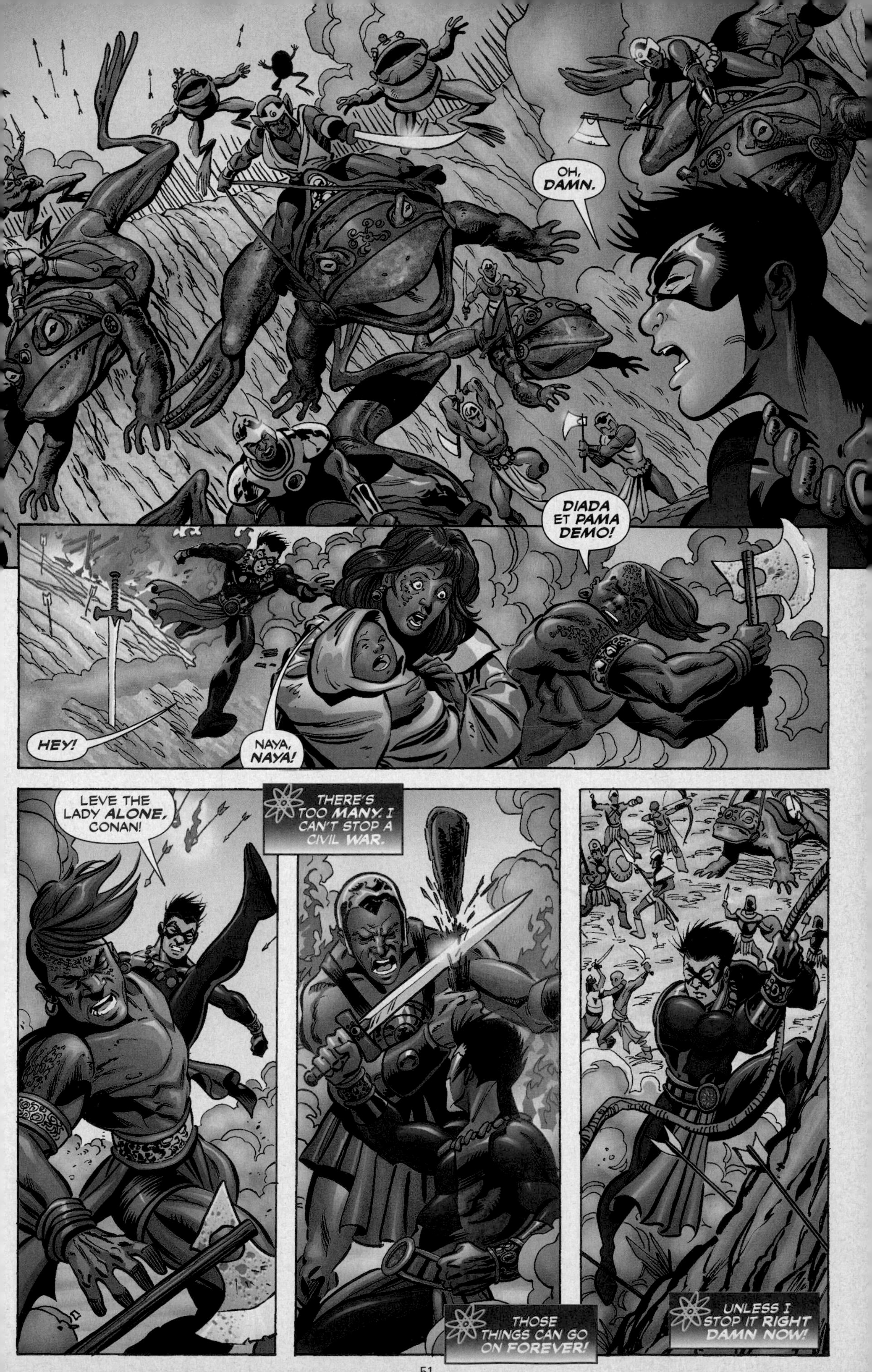
OH, DAMN.
DIADA ET PAMA DEMO!
HEY!
NAYA, NAYA!
LEVE THE LADY ALONE, CONAN!
THERE'S TOO MANY. I CAN'T STOP A CIVIL WAR.
THOSE THINGS CAN GO ON FOREVER!
UNLESS I STOP IT RIGHT DAMN NOW!

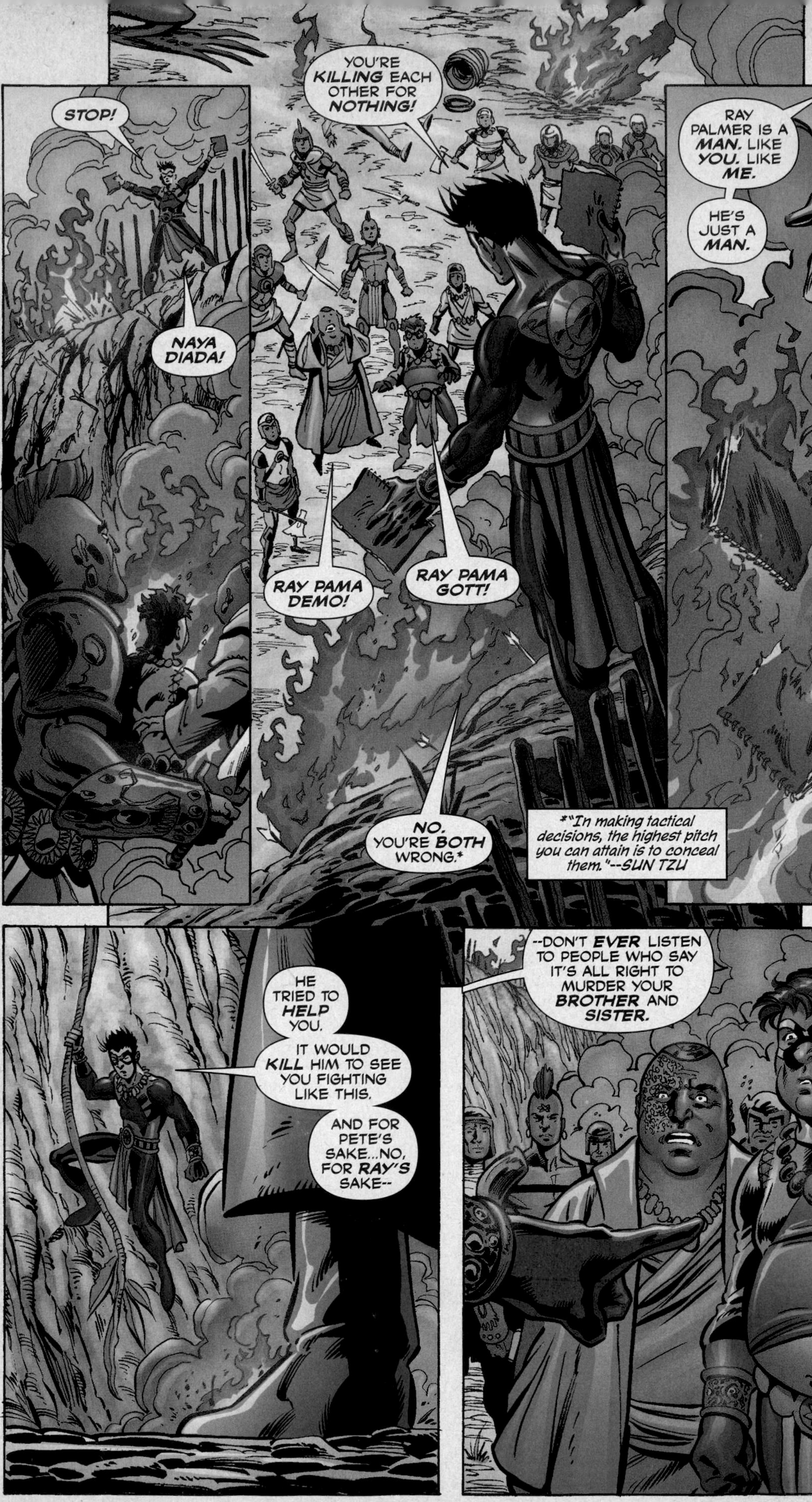
STOP!
YOU'RE KILLING EACH OTHER FOR NOTHING!
RAY PALMER IS A MAN. LIKE YOU. LIKE ME.
HE'S JUST A MAN.
NAYA DIADA!
RAY PAMA DEMO!
RAY PAMA GOTT!
NO. YOU'RE BOTH WRONG.*
*"In making tactical decisions, the highest pitch you can attain is to conceal them."--SUN TZU
HE TRIED TO HELP YOU.
IT WOULD KILL HIM TO SEE YOU FIGHTING LIKE THIS.
AND FOR PETE'S SAKE...NO, FOR RAY'S SAKE--
--DON'T EVER LISTEN TO PEOPLE WHO SAY IT'S ALL RIGHT TO MURDER YOUR BROTHER AND SISTER.

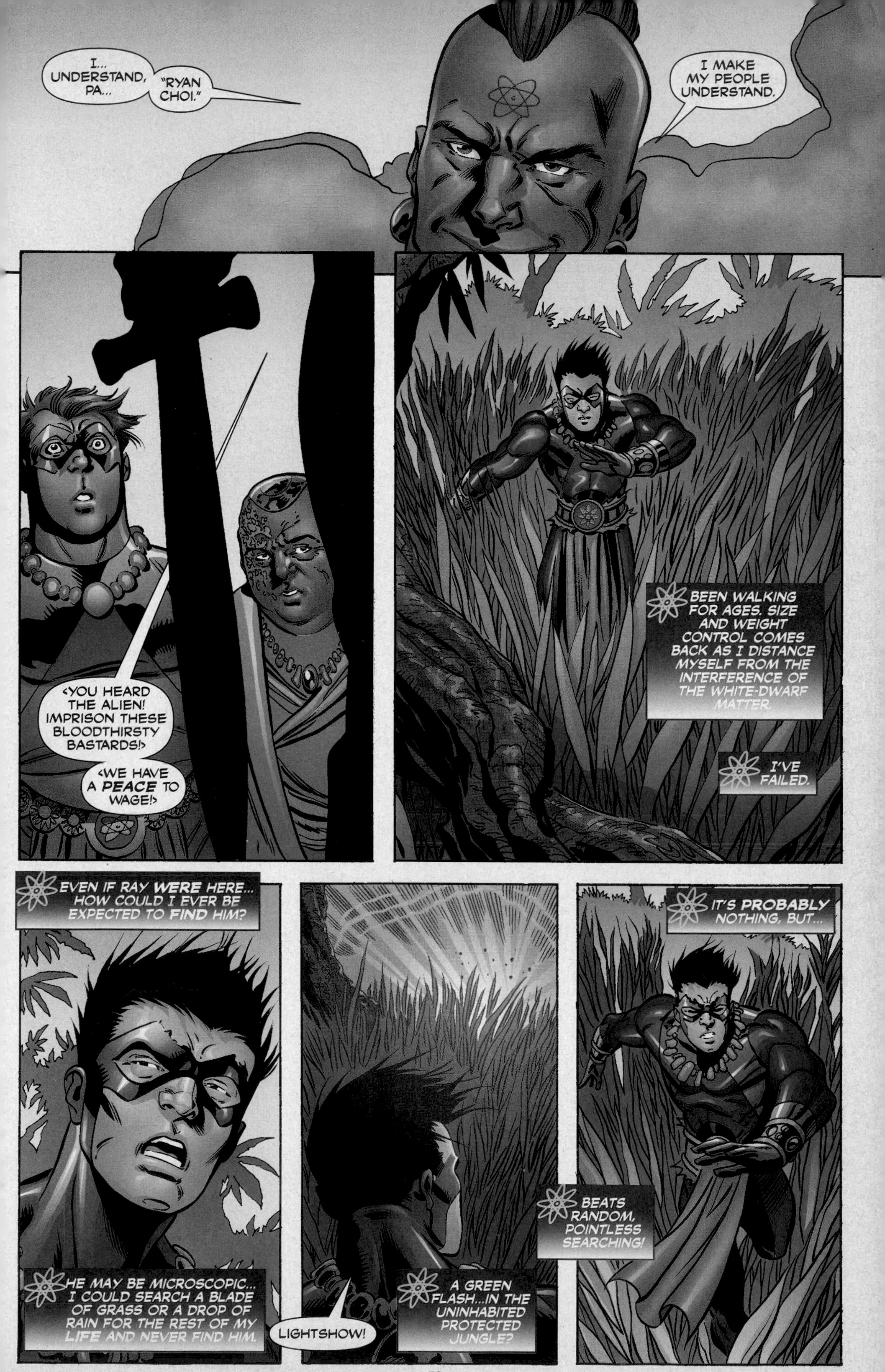
I... UNDERSTAND, PA...
"RYAN CHOI."
I MAKE MY PEOPLE UNDERSTAND.
‹YOU HEARD THE ALIEN! IMPRISON THESE BLOODTHIRSTY BASTARDS!›
‹WE HAVE A PEACE TO WAGE!›
BEEN WALKING FOR AGES. SIZE AND WEIGHT CONTROL COMES BACK AS I DISTANCE MYSELF FROM THE INTERFERENCE OF THE WHITE-DWARF MATTER.
I'VE FAILED.
EVEN IF RAY WERE HERE... HOW COULD I EVER BE EXPECTED TO FIND HIM?
HE MAY BE MICROSCOPIC... I COULD SEARCH A BLADE OF GRASS OR A DROP OF RAIN FOR THE REST OF MY LIFE AND NEVER FIND HIM.
LIGHTSHOW!
A GREEN FLASH...IN THE UNINHABITED PROTECTED JUNGLE?
BEATS RANDOM, POINTLESS SEARCHING!
IT'S PROBABLY NOTHING, BUT...

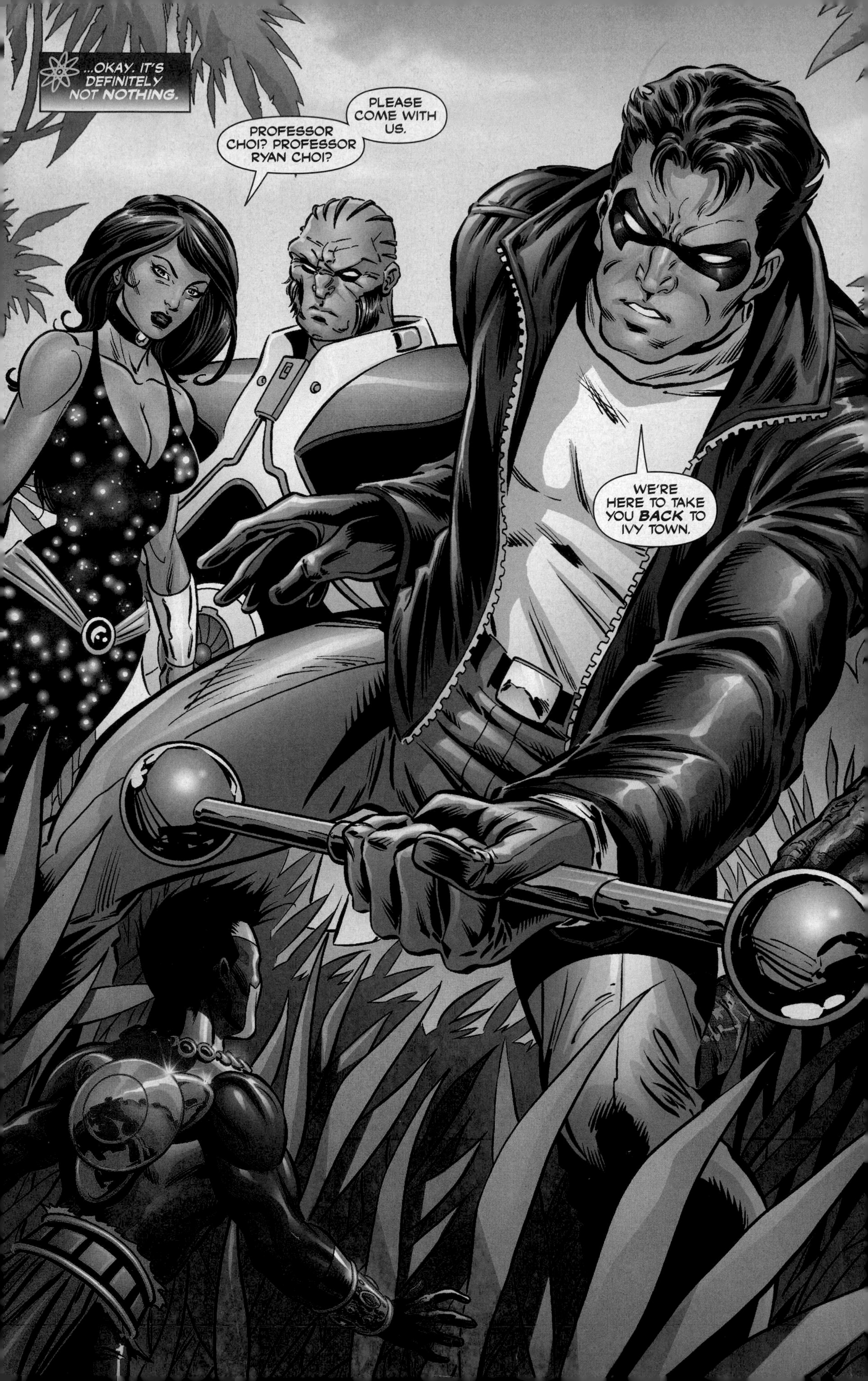
...OKAY. IT'S DEFINITELY NOT NOTHING.
PROFESSOR CHOI? PROFESSOR RYAN CHOI?
PLEASE COME WITH US.
WE'RE HERE TO TAKE YOU BACK TO IVY TOWN.

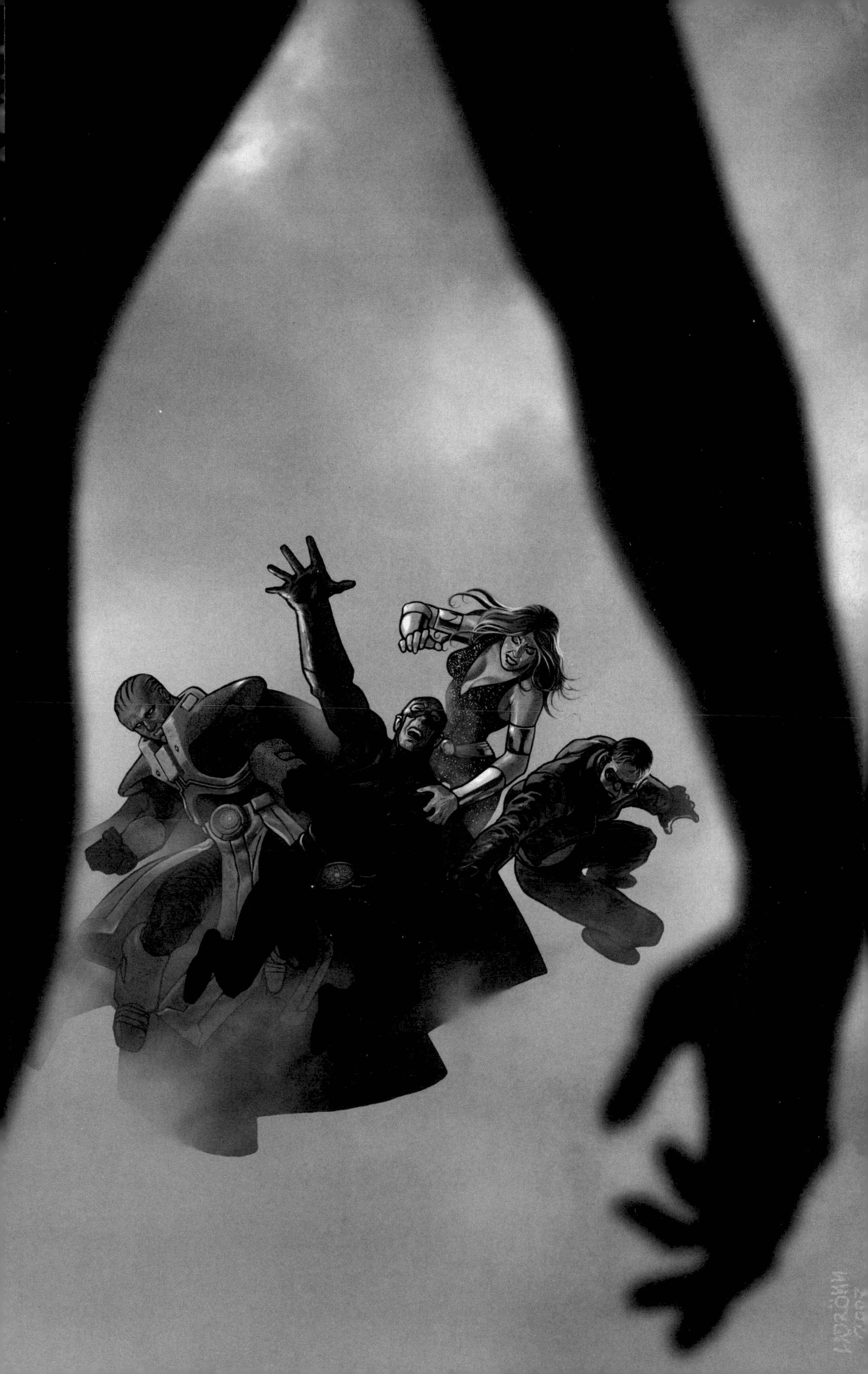

HUNT FOR RAY PALMER: PART THREE
HEAVENS TO BITSY

from **THE ALL NEW ATOM #14**

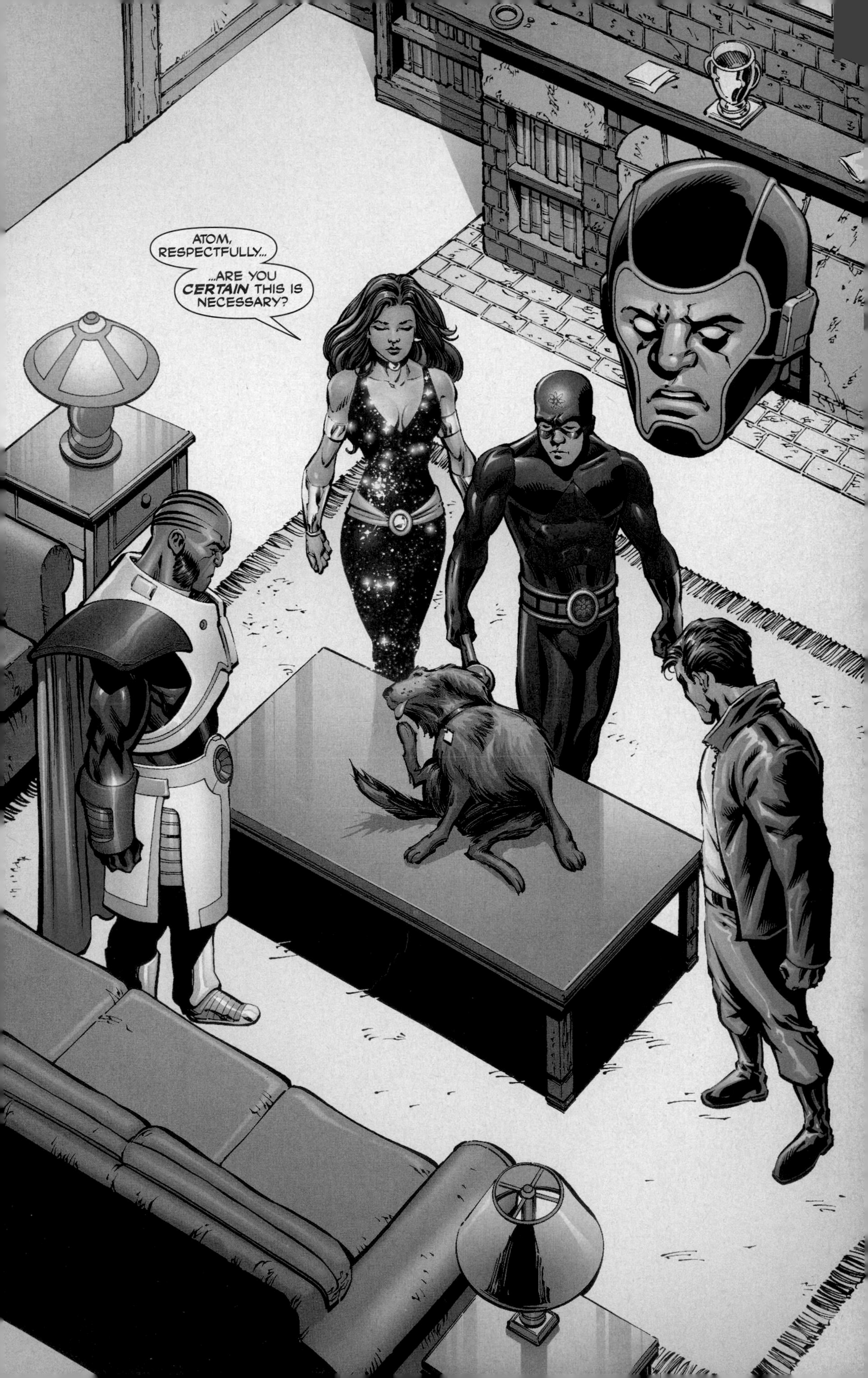
ATOM, RESPECTFULLY...
...ARE YOU CERTAIN THIS IS NECESSARY?

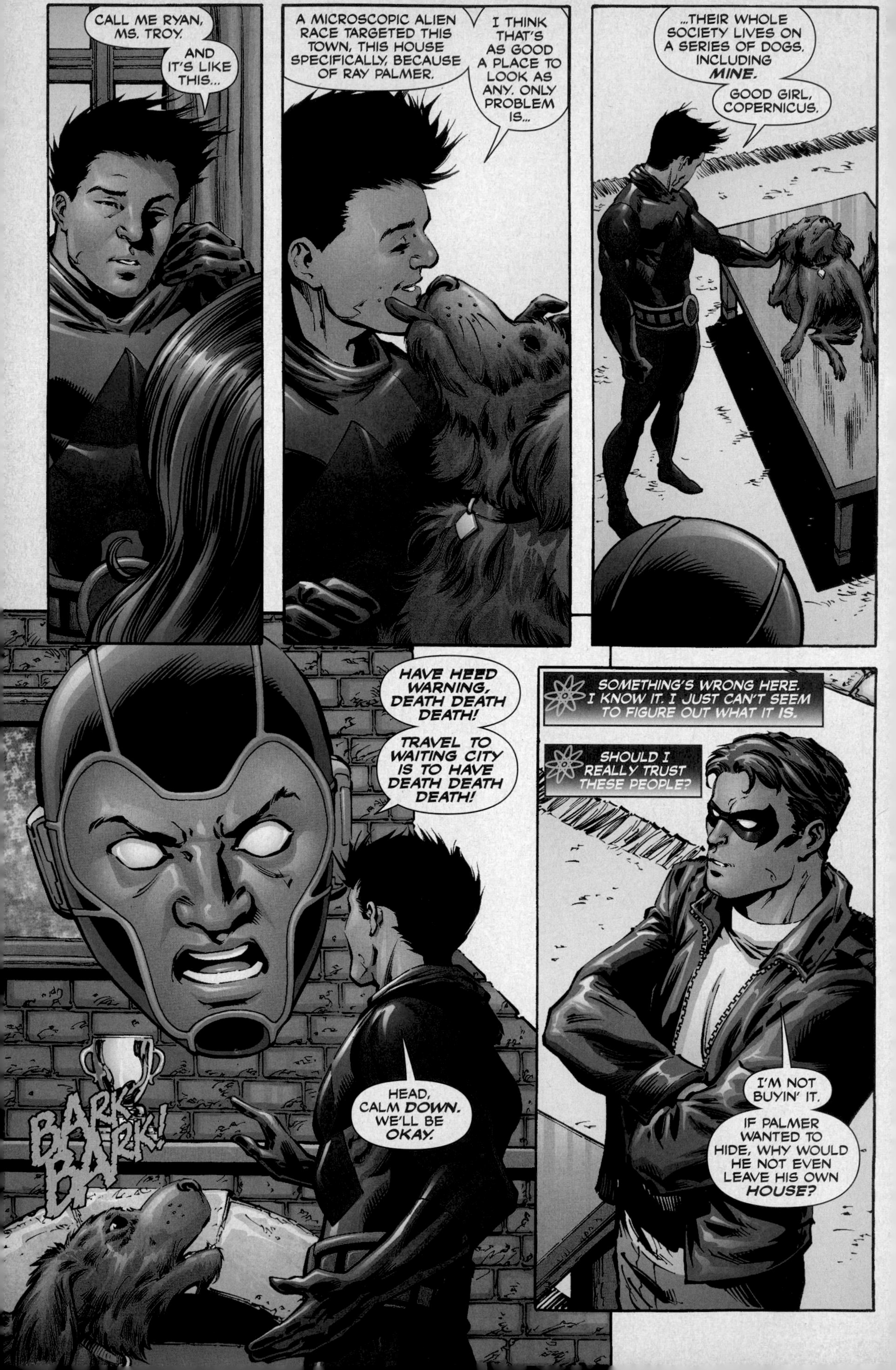

CALL ME RYAN, MS. TROY.
AND IT'S LIKE THIS...
A MICROSCOPIC ALIEN RACE TARGETED THIS TOWN, THIS HOUSE SPECIFICALLY, BECAUSE OF RAY PALMER.
I THINK THAT'S AS GOOD A PLACE TO LOOK AS ANY. ONLY PROBLEM IS...
...THEIR WHOLE SOCIETY LIVES ON A SERIES OF DOGS. INCLUDING MINE.
GOOD GIRL, COPERNICUS.
HAVE HEED WARNING, DEATH DEATH DEATH!
TRAVEL TO WAITING CITY IS TO HAVE DEATH DEATH DEATH!
BARK! BARK!
HEAD, CALM DOWN. WE'LL BE OKAY.
SOMETHING'S WRONG HERE. I KNOW IT. I JUST CAN'T SEEM TO FIGURE OUT WHAT IT IS.
SHOULD I REALLY TRUST THESE PEOPLE?
I'M NOT BUYIN' IT.
IF PALMER WANTED TO HIDE, WHY WOULD HE NOT EVEN LEAVE HIS OWN HOUSE?

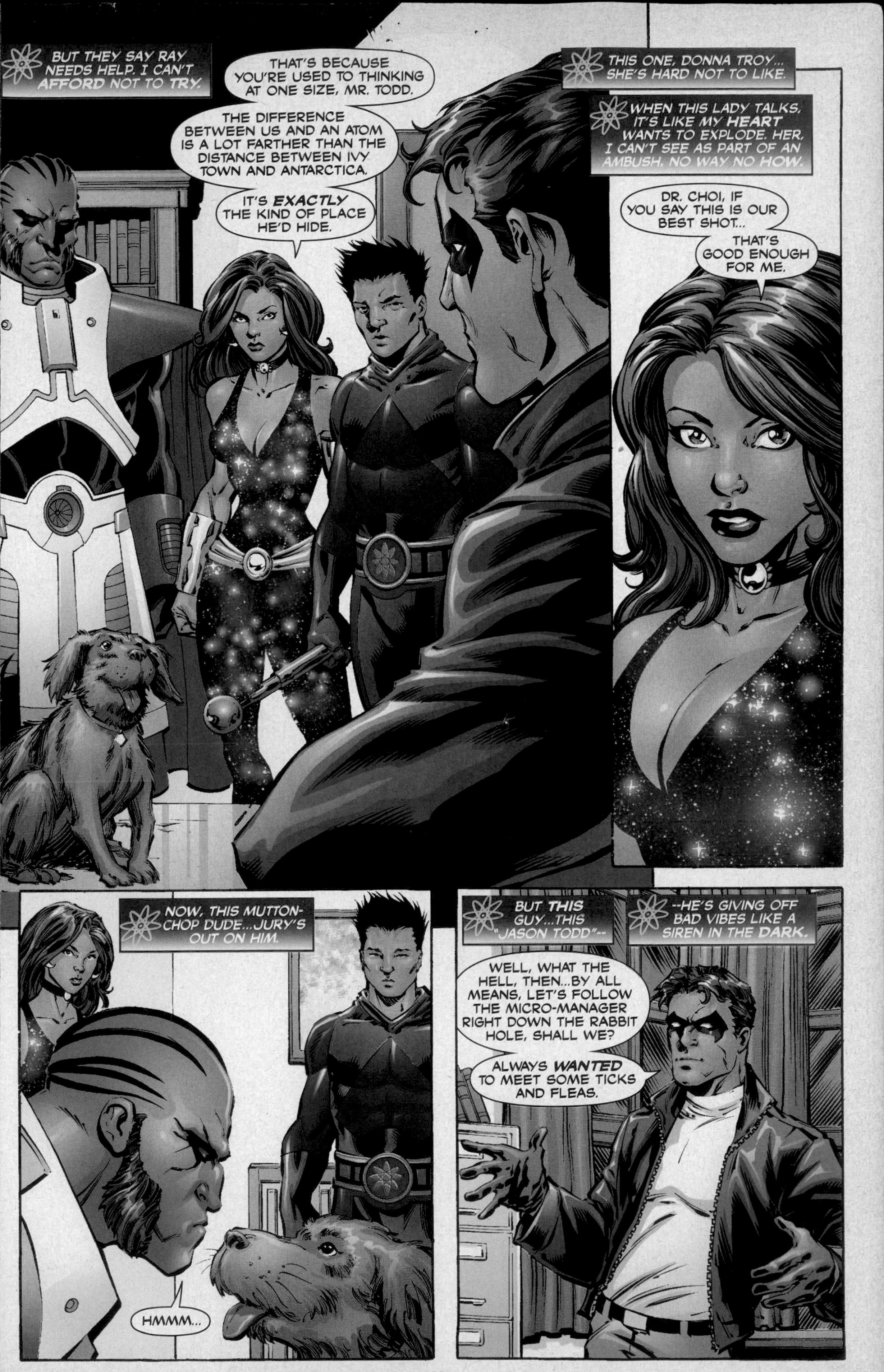

BUT THEY SAY RAY NEEDS HELP. I CAN'T AFFORD NOT TO TRY.
THAT'S BECAUSE YOU'RE USED TO THINKING AT ONE SIZE, MR. TODD.
THE DIFFERENCE BETWEEN US AND AN ATOM IS A LOT FARTHER THAN THE DISTANCE BETWEEN IVY TOWN AND ANTARCTICA.
IT'S EXACTLY THE KIND OF PLACE HE'D HIDE.
THIS ONE, DONNA TROY... SHE'S HARD NOT TO LIKE.
WHEN THIS LADY TALKS, IT'S LIKE MY HEART WANTS TO EXPLODE. HER, I CAN'T SEE AS PART OF AN AMBUSH, NO WAY NO HOW.
DR. CHOI, IF YOU SAY THIS IS OUR BEST SHOT...
THAT'S GOOD ENOUGH FOR ME.
NOW, THIS MUTTON-CHOP DUDE...JURY'S OUT ON HIM.
HMMM...
BUT THIS GUY...THIS "JASON TODD"--
--HE'S GIVING OFF BAD VIBES LIKE A SIREN IN THE DARK.
WELL, WHAT THE HELL, THEN...BY ALL MEANS, LET'S FOLLOW THE MICRO-MANAGER RIGHT DOWN THE RABBIT HOLE, SHALL WE?
ALWAYS WANTED TO MEET SOME TICKS AND FLEAS.

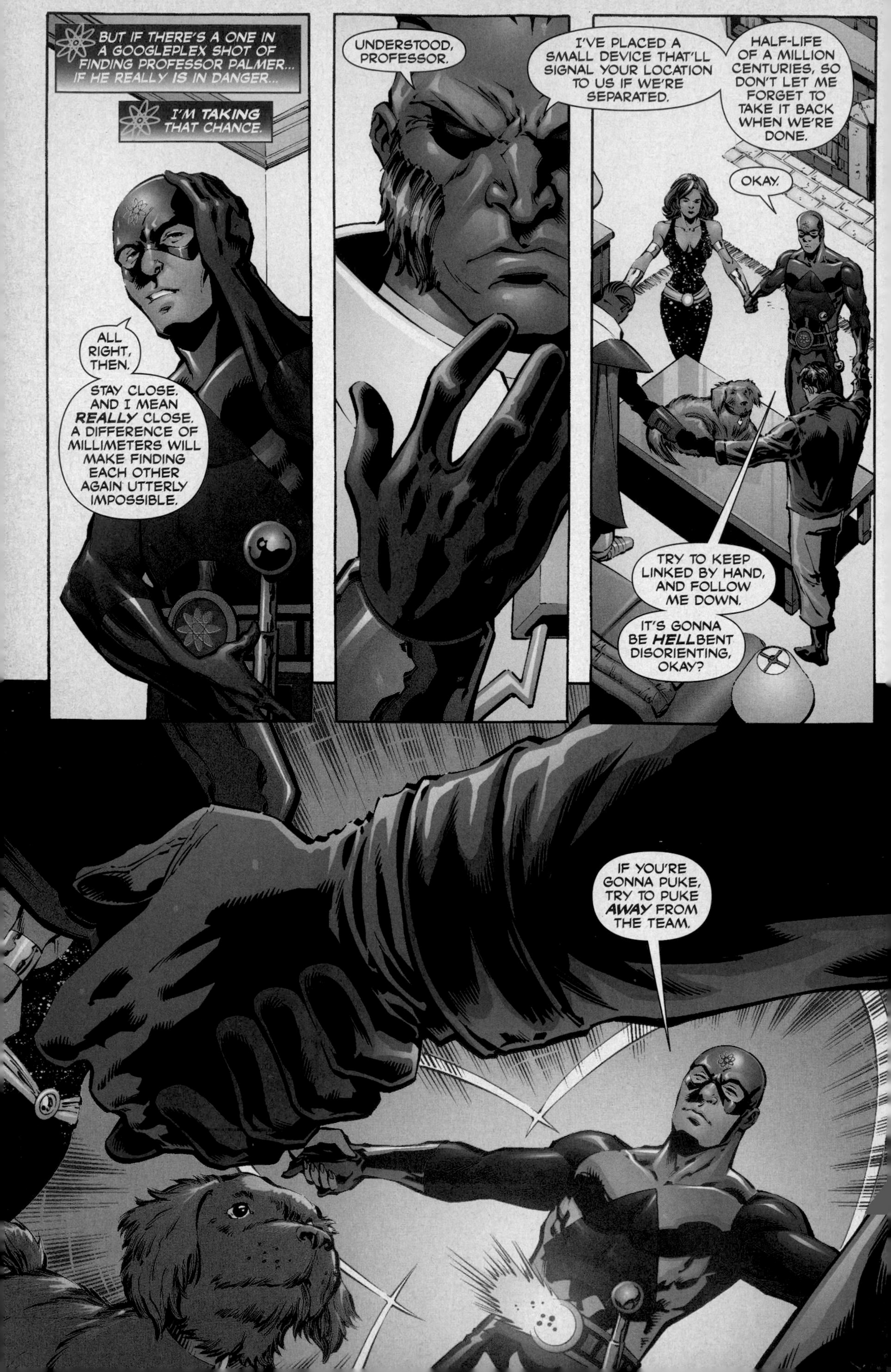
BUT IF THERE'S A ONE IN A GOOGLEPLEX SHOT OF FINDING PROFESSOR PALMER... IF HE REALLY IS IN DANGER...
I'M TAKING THAT CHANCE.
ALL RIGHT, THEN.
STAY CLOSE. AND I MEAN REALLY CLOSE. A DIFFERENCE OF MILLIMETERS WILL MAKE FINDING EACH OTHER AGAIN UTTERLY IMPOSSIBLE.
UNDERSTOOD, PROFESSOR.
I'VE PLACED A SMALL DEVICE THAT'LL SIGNAL YOUR LOCATION TO US IF WE'RE SEPARATED.
HALF-LIFE OF A MILLION CENTURIES, SO DON'T LET ME FORGET TO TAKE IT BACK WHEN WE'RE DONE.
OKAY.
TRY TO KEEP LINKED BY HAND, AND FOLLOW ME DOWN.
IT'S GONNA BE HELLBENT DISORIENTING, OKAY?
IF YOU'RE GONNA PUKE, TRY TO PUKE AWAY FROM THE TEAM.

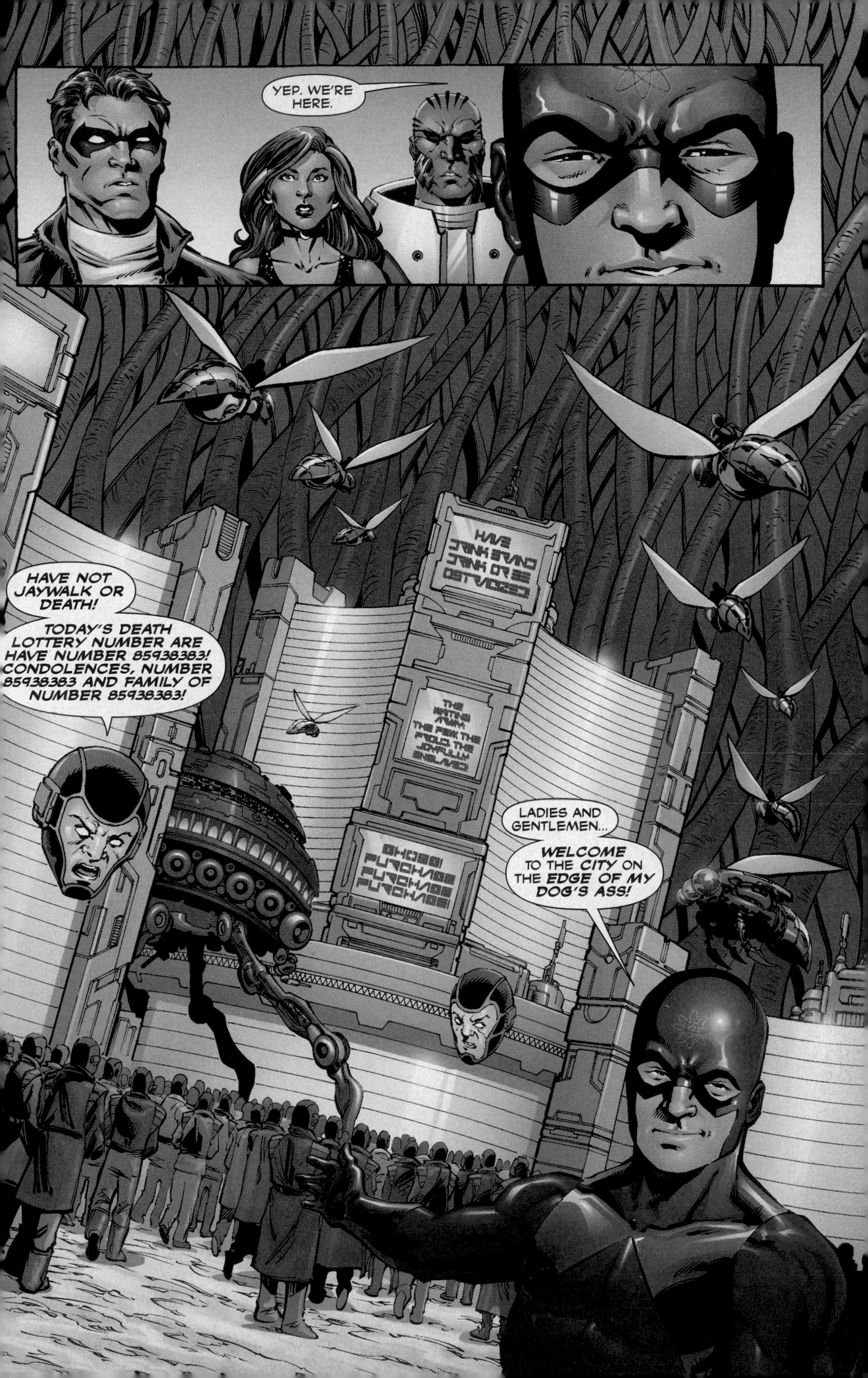
YEP. WE'RE HERE.
HAVE NOT JAYWALK OR DEATH!
TODAY'S DEATH LOTTERY NUMBER ARE HAVE NUMBER 85938383! CONDOLENCES, NUMBER 85938383 AND FAMILY OF NUMBER 85938383!
LADIES AND GENTLEMEN...
WELCOME TO THE CITY ON THE EDGE OF MY DOG'S ASS!

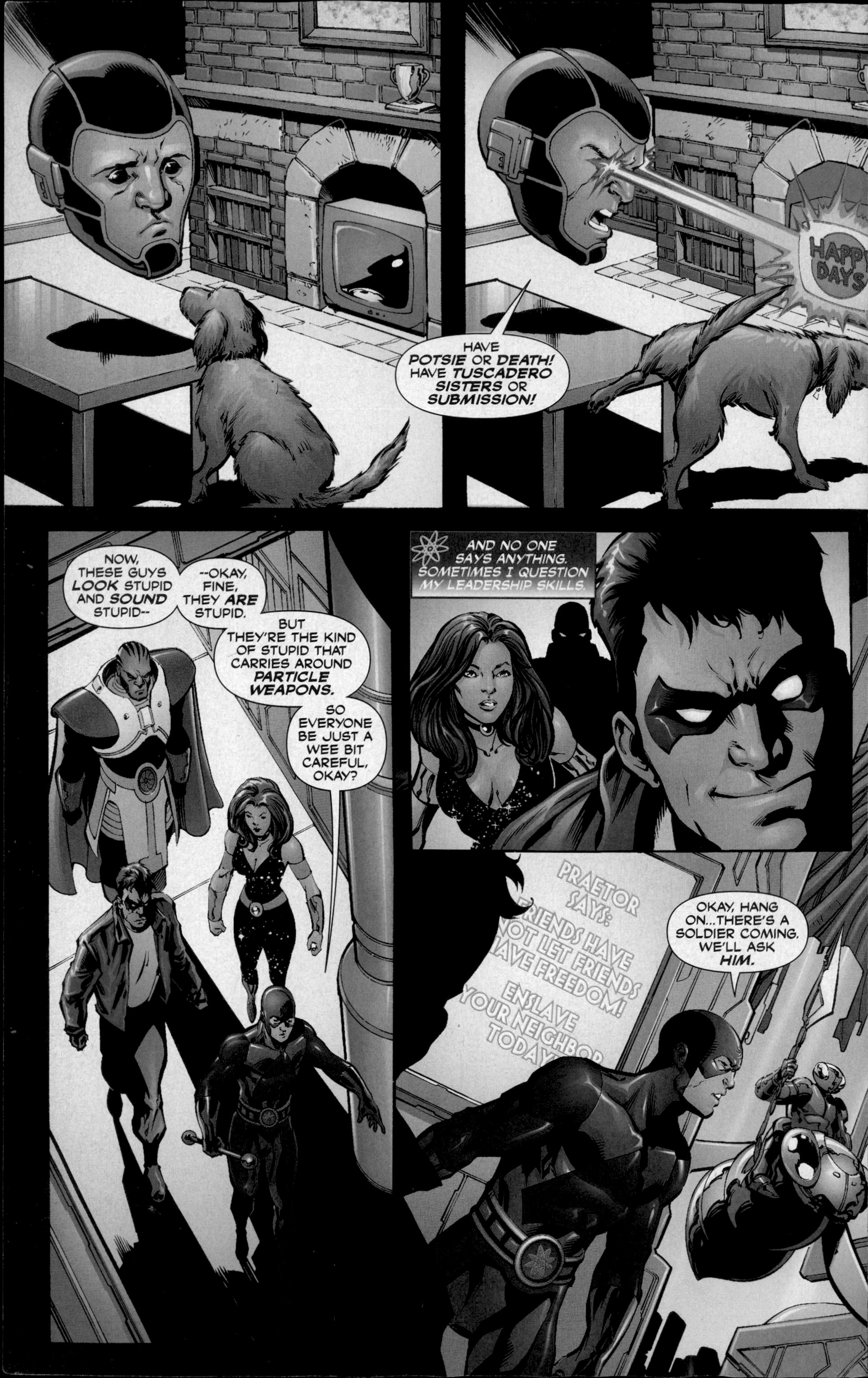
HAPPY DAYS
HAVE POTSIE OR DEATH! HAVE TUSCADERO SISTERS OR SUBMISSION!
NOW, THESE GUYS LOOK STUPID AND SOUND STUPID--
--OKAY, FINE, THEY ARE STUPID.
BUT THEY'RE THE KIND OF STUPID THAT CARRIES AROUND PARTICLE WEAPONS.
SO EVERYONE BE JUST A WEE BIT CAREFUL, OKAY?
AND NO ONE SAYS ANYTHING. SOMETIMES I QUESTION MY LEADERSHIP SKILLS.
PRAETOR SAYS:
FRIENDS HAVE NOT LET FRIENDS HAVE FREEDOM!
ENSLAVE YOUR NEIGHBOR TODAY
OKAY, HANG ON...THERE'S A SOLDIER COMING. WE'LL ASK HIM.

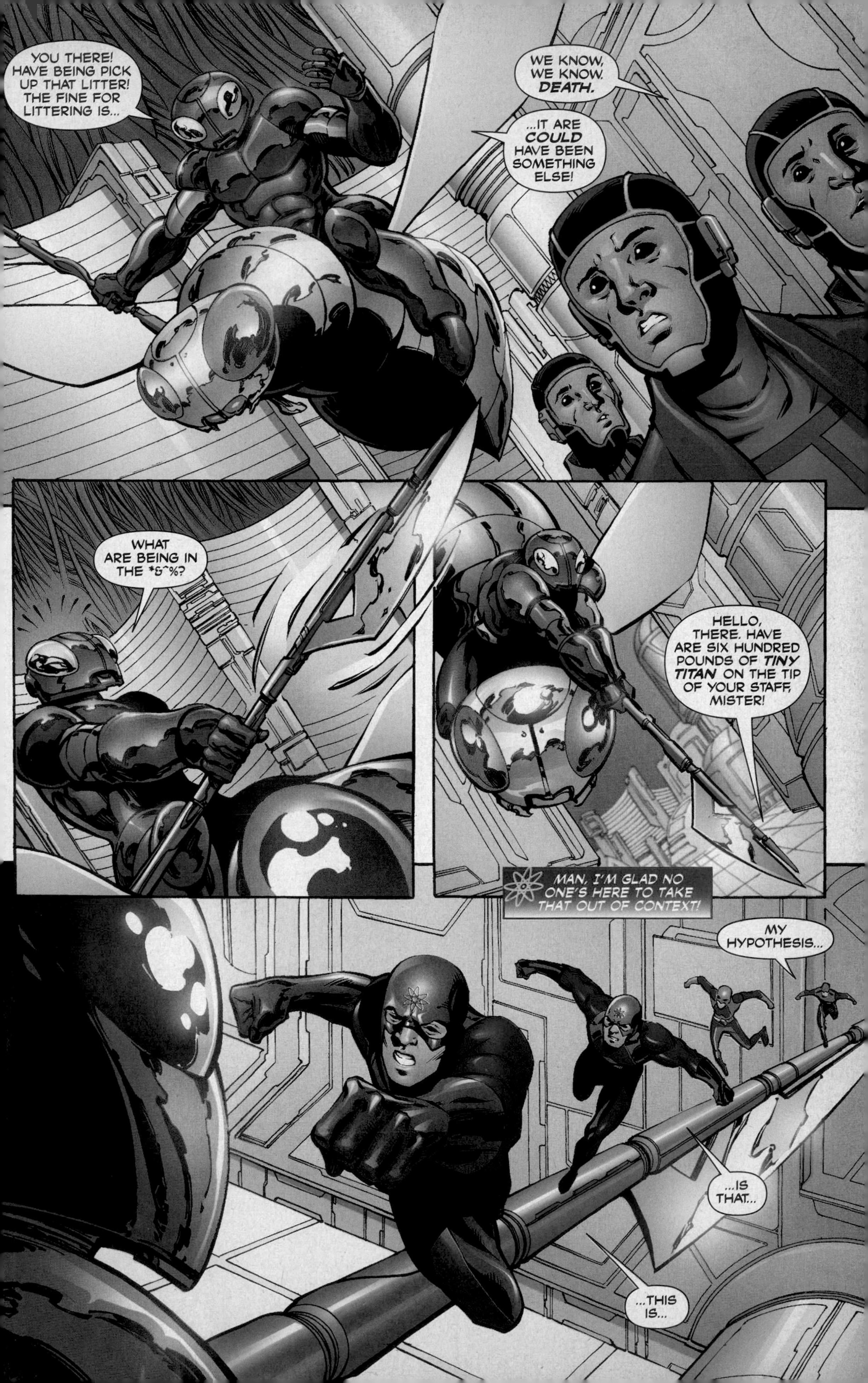
YOU THERE! HAVE BEING PICK UP THAT LITTER! THE FINE FOR LITTERING IS...
WE KNOW, WE KNOW. DEATH.
...IT ARE COULD HAVE BEEN SOMETHING ELSE!
WHAT ARE BEING IN THE *&^%?
HELLO, THERE. HAVE ARE SIX HUNDRED POUNDS OF TINY TITAN ON THE TIP OF YOUR STAFF, MISTER!
MAN, I'M GLAD NO ONE'S HERE TO TAKE THAT OUT OF CONTEXT!
MY HYPOTHESIS...
...IS THAT...
...THIS IS...

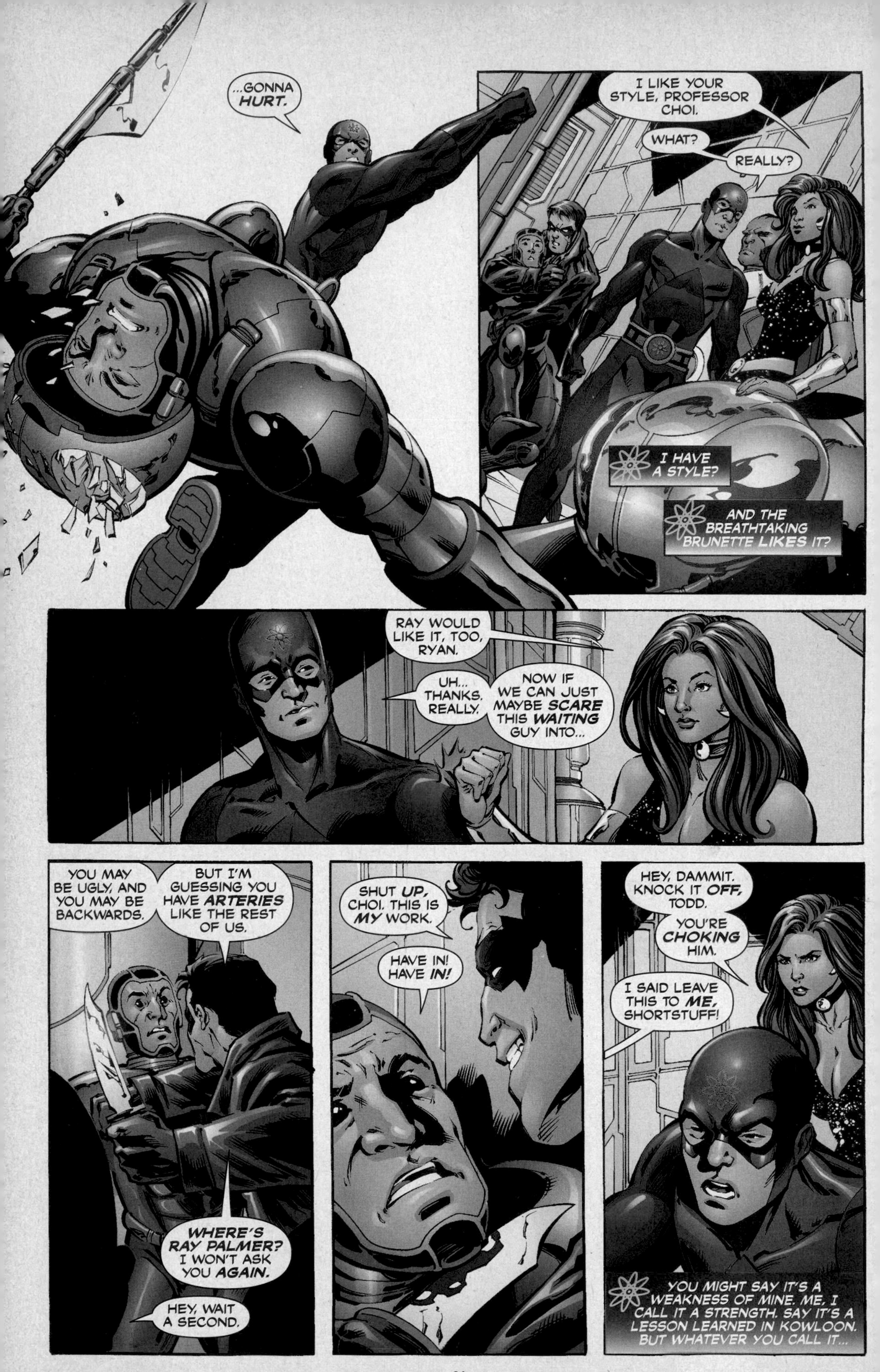
...GONNA HURT.
I LIKE YOUR STYLE, PROFESSOR CHOI.
WHAT?
REALLY?
I HAVE A STYLE?
AND THE BREATHTAKING BRUNETTE LIKES IT?
RAY WOULD LIKE IT, TOO, RYAN.
UH... THANKS. REALLY.
NOW IF WE CAN JUST MAYBE SCARE THIS WAITING GUY INTO...
YOU MAY BE UGLY, AND YOU MAY BE BACKWARDS.
BUT I'M GUESSING YOU HAVE ARTERIES LIKE THE REST OF US.
WHERE'S RAY PALMER? I WON'T ASK YOU AGAIN.
HEY, WAIT A SECOND.
SHUT UP, CHOI. THIS IS MY WORK.
HAVE IN! HAVE IN!
HEY, DAMMIT. KNOCK IT OFF, TODD.
YOU'RE CHOKING HIM.
I SAID LEAVE THIS TO ME, SHORTSTUFF!
YOU MIGHT SAY IT'S A WEAKNESS OF MINE. ME, I CALL IT A STRENGTH. SAY IT'S A LESSON LEARNED IN KOWLOON. BUT WHATEVER YOU CALL IT...

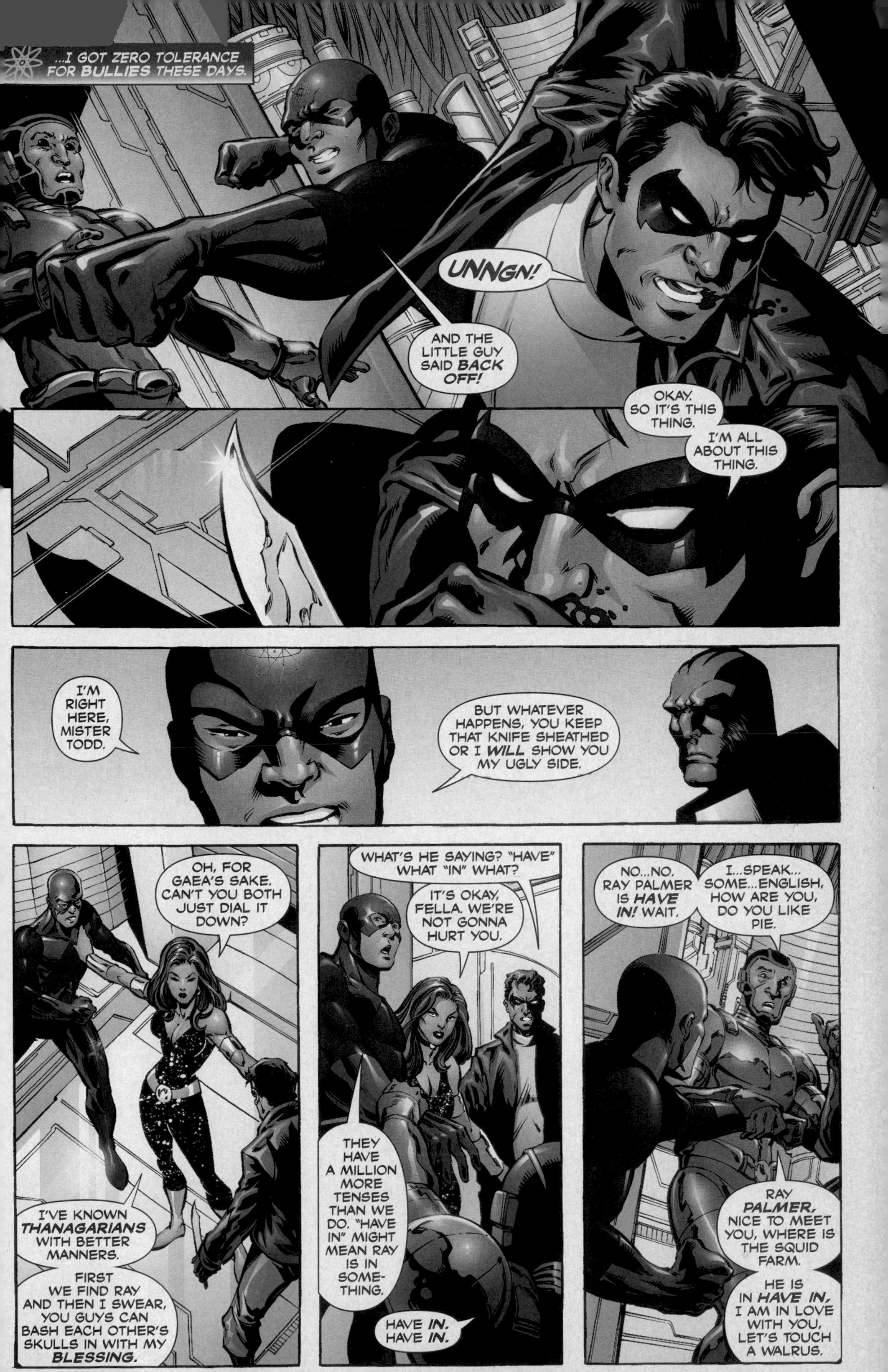
...I GOT ZERO TOLERANCE FOR BULLIES THESE DAYS.
UNNGN!
AND THE LITTLE GUY SAID BACK OFF!
OKAY. SO IT'S THIS THING.
I'M ALL ABOUT THIS THING.
I'M RIGHT HERE, MISTER TODD.
BUT WHATEVER HAPPENS, YOU KEEP THAT KNIFE SHEATHED OR I WILL SHOW YOU MY UGLY SIDE.
OH, FOR GAEA'S SAKE. CAN'T YOU BOTH JUST DIAL IT DOWN?
I'VE KNOWN THANAGARIANS WITH BETTER MANNERS.
FIRST WE FIND RAY AND THEN I SWEAR, YOU GUYS CAN BASH EACH OTHER'S SKULLS IN WITH MY BLESSING.
WHAT'S HE SAYING? "HAVE" WHAT "IN" WHAT?
IT'S OKAY, FELLA. WE'RE NOT GONNA HURT YOU.
THEY HAVE A MILLION MORE TENSES THAN WE DO. "HAVE IN" MIGHT MEAN RAY IS IN SOME-THING.
HAVE IN. HAVE IN.
NO...NO. RAY PALMER IS HAVE IN! WAIT.
I...SPEAK... SOME...ENGLISH, HOW ARE YOU, DO YOU LIKE PIE.
RAY PALMER, NICE TO MEET YOU, WHERE IS THE SQUID FARM.
HE IS IN HAVE IN, I AM IN LOVE WITH YOU, LET'S TOUCH A WALRUS.

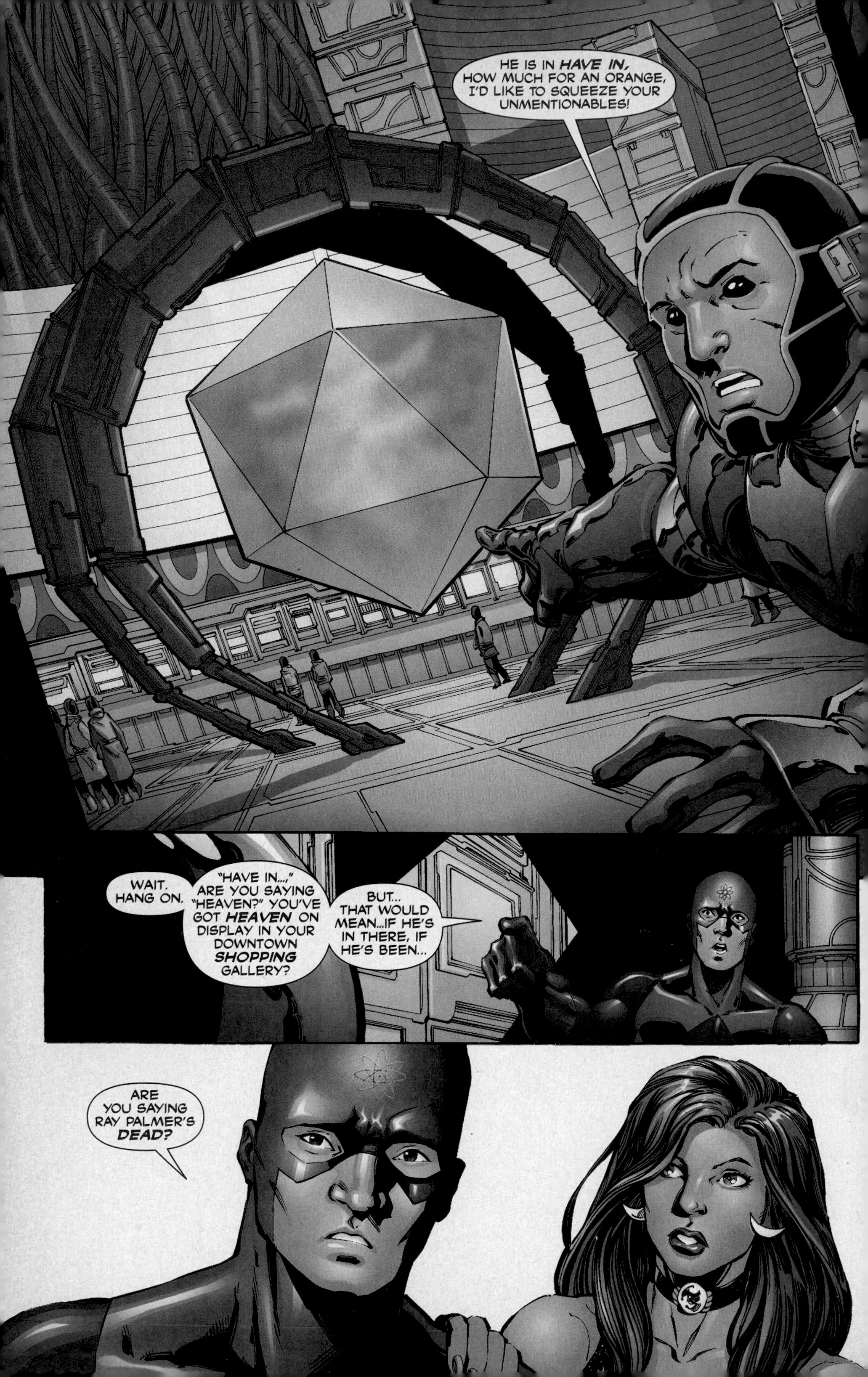
HE IS IN HAVE IN, HOW MUCH FOR AN ORANGE, I'D LIKE TO SQUEEZE YOUR UNMENTIONABLES!
WAIT. HANG ON.
"HAVE IN..." ARE YOU SAYING "HEAVEN?" YOU'VE GOT HEAVEN ON DISPLAY IN YOUR DOWNTOWN SHOPPING GALLERY?
BUT... THAT WOULD MEAN...IF HE'S IN THERE, IF HE'S BEEN...
ARE YOU SAYING RAY PALMER'S DEAD?

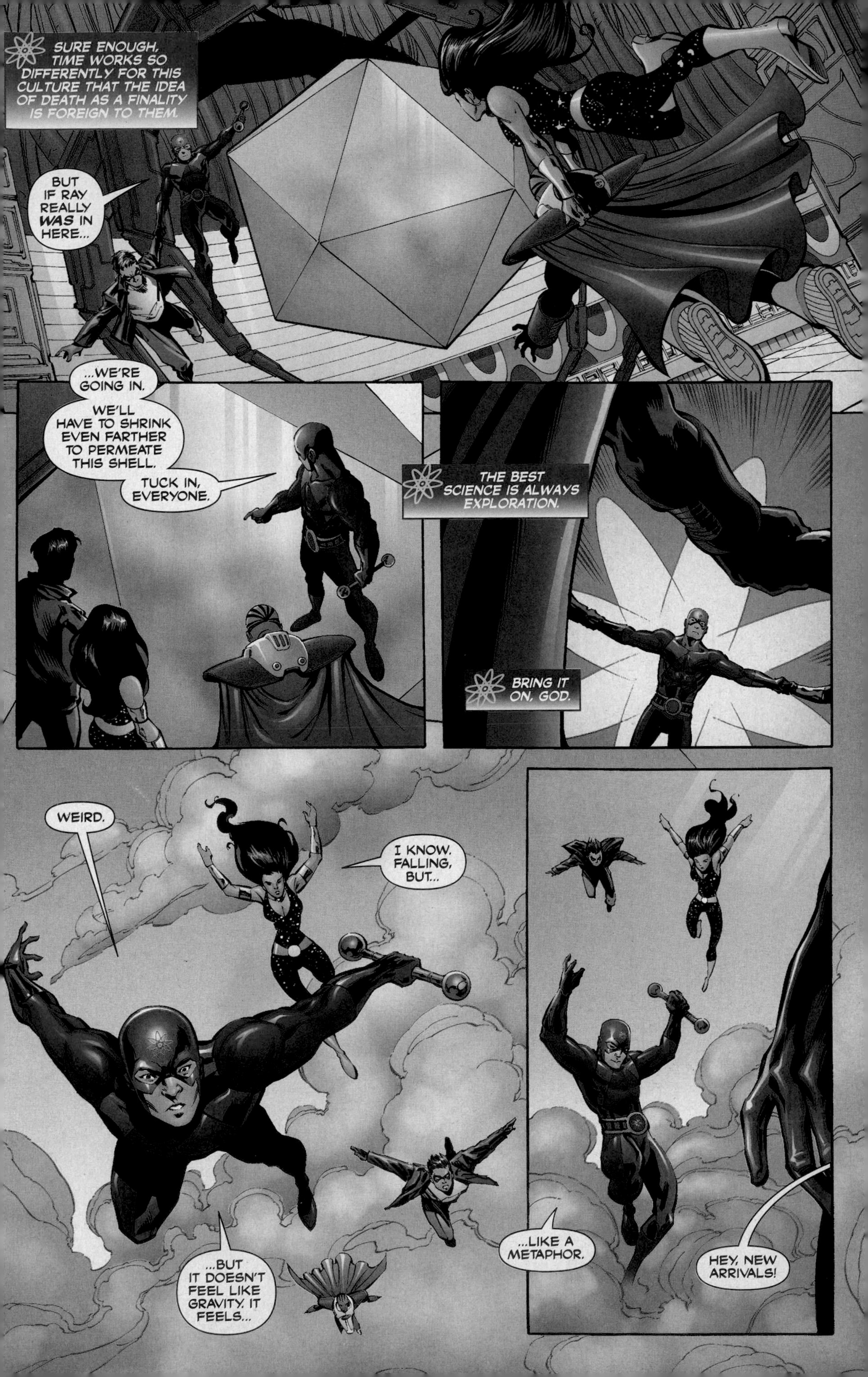
SURE ENOUGH, TIME WORKS SO DIFFERENTLY FOR THIS CULTURE THAT THE IDEA OF DEATH AS A FINALITY IS FOREIGN TO THEM.
BUT IF RAY REALLY WAS IN HERE...
...WE'RE GOING IN.
WE'LL HAVE TO SHRINK EVEN FARTHER TO PERMEATE THIS SHELL.
TUCK IN, EVERYONE.
THE BEST SCIENCE IS ALWAYS EXPLORATION.
BRING IT ON, GOD.
WEIRD.
I KNOW. FALLING, BUT...
...BUT IT DOESN'T FEEL LIKE GRAVITY. IT FEELS...
...LIKE A METAPHOR.
HEY, NEW ARRIVALS!

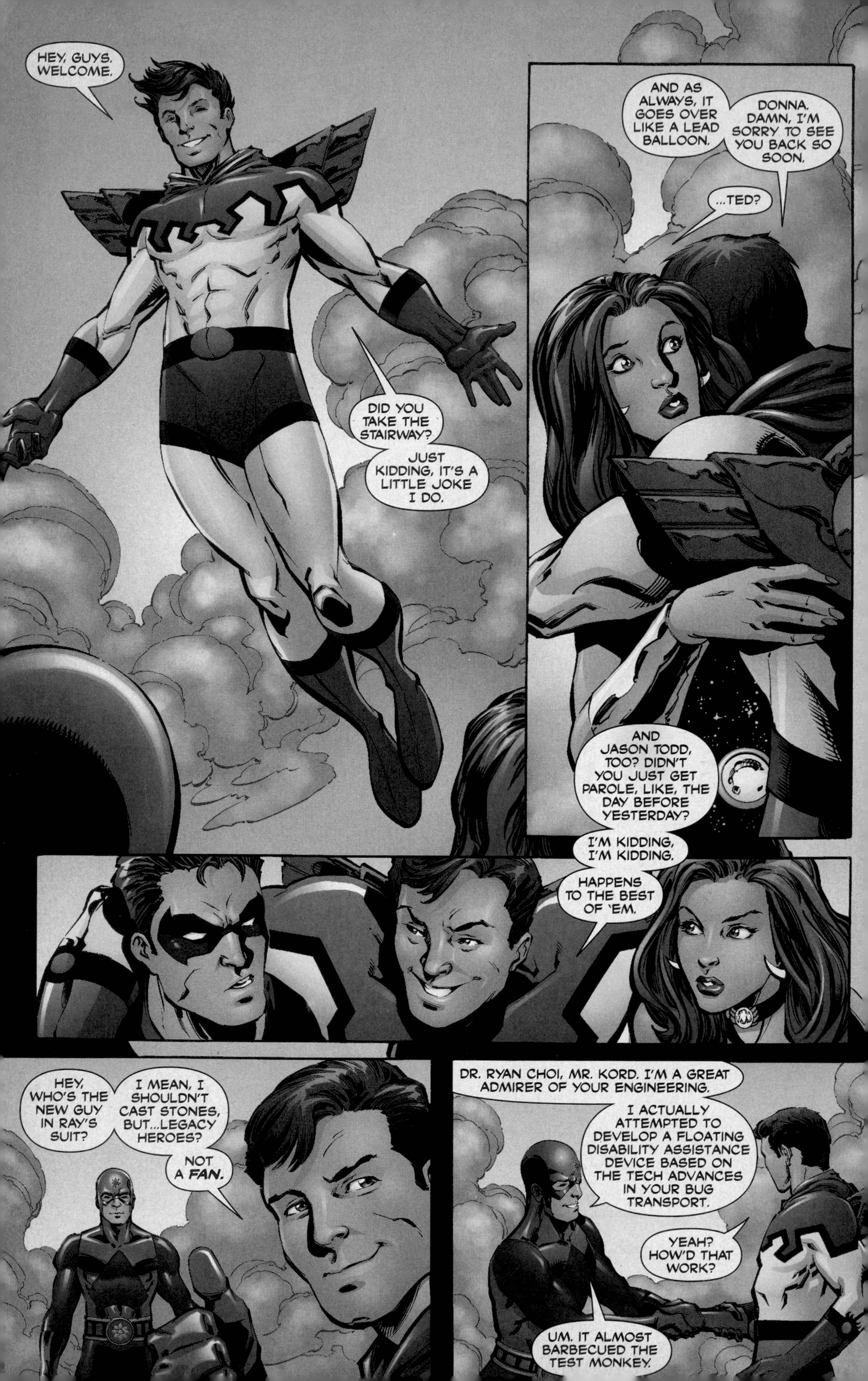
HEY, GUYS. WELCOME.
DID YOU TAKE THE STAIRWAY?
JUST KIDDING, IT'S A LITTLE JOKE I DO.
AND AS ALWAYS, IT GOES OVER LIKE A LEAD BALLOON.
DONNA. DAMN, I'M SORRY TO SEE YOU BACK SO SOON.
...TED?
AND JASON TODD, TOO? DIDN'T YOU JUST GET PAROLE, LIKE, THE DAY BEFORE YESTERDAY?
I'M KIDDING, I'M KIDDING.
HAPPENS TO THE BEST OF 'EM.
HEY, WHO'S THE NEW GUY IN RAY'S SUIT?
I MEAN, I SHOULDN'T CAST STONES, BUT...LEGACY HEROES?
NOT A FAN.
DR. RYAN CHOI, MR. KORD. I'M A GREAT ADMIRER OF YOUR ENGINEERING.
I ACTUALLY ATTEMPTED TO DEVELOP A FLOATING DISABILITY ASSISTANCE DEVICE BASED ON THE TECH ADVANCES IN YOUR BUG TRANSPORT.
YEAH? HOW'D THAT WORK?
UM. IT ALMOST BARBECUED THE TEST MONKEY.

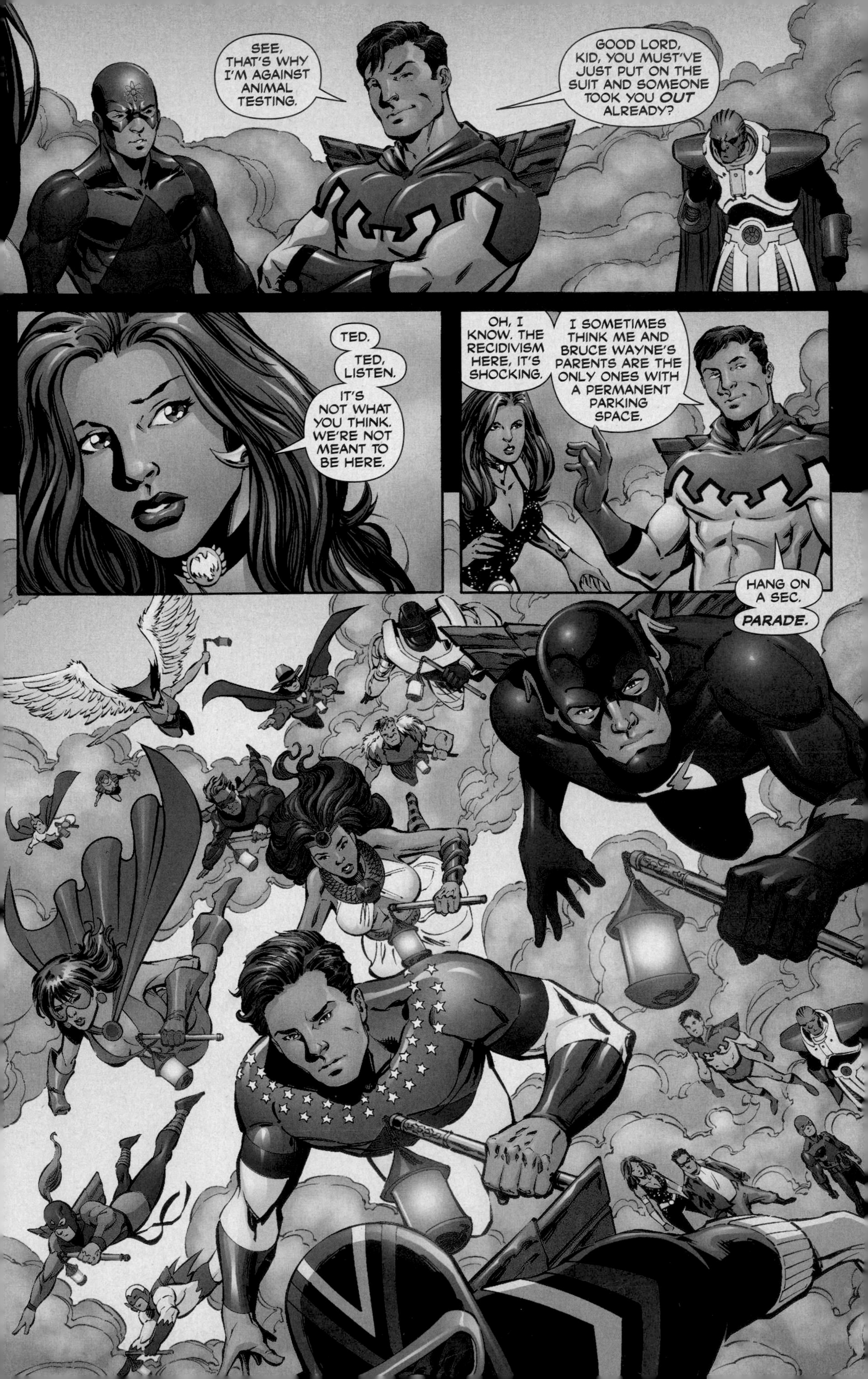
SEE, THAT'S WHY I'M AGAINST ANIMAL TESTING.
GOOD LORD, KID, YOU MUST'VE JUST PUT ON THE SUIT AND SOMEONE TOOK YOU OUT ALREADY?
TED.
TED, LISTEN.
IT'S NOT WHAT YOU THINK. WE'RE NOT MEANT TO BE HERE.
OH, I KNOW. THE RECIDIVISM HERE, IT'S SHOCKING.
I SOMETIMES THINK ME AND BRUCE WAYNE'S PARENTS ARE THE ONLY ONES WITH A PERMANENT PARKING SPACE.
HANG ON A SEC.
PARADE.

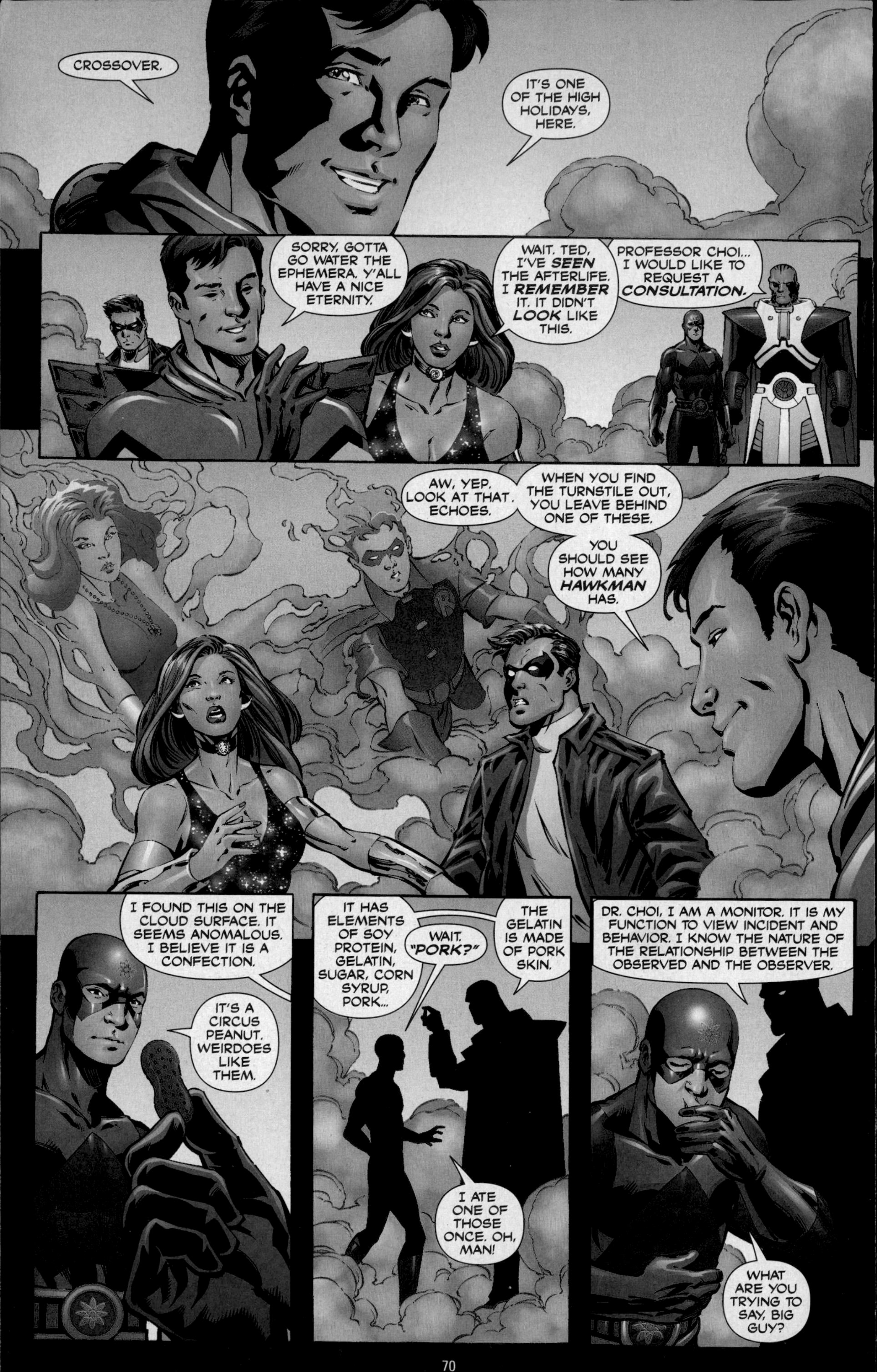
CROSSOVER.
IT'S ONE OF THE HIGH HOLIDAYS, HERE.
SORRY, GOTTA GO WATER THE EPHEMERA. Y'ALL HAVE A NICE ETERNITY.
WAIT, TED, I'VE SEEN THE AFTERLIFE. I REMEMBER IT. IT DIDN'T LOOK LIKE THIS.
PROFESSOR CHOI... I WOULD LIKE TO REQUEST A CONSULTATION.
AW, YEP, LOOK AT THAT. ECHOES.
WHEN YOU FIND THE TURNSTILE OUT, YOU LEAVE BEHIND ONE OF THESE.
YOU SHOULD SEE HOW MANY HAWKMAN HAS.
I FOUND THIS ON THE CLOUD SURFACE. IT SEEMS ANOMALOUS. I BELIEVE IT IS A CONFECTION.
IT'S A CIRCUS PEANUT. WEIRDOES LIKE THEM.
IT HAS ELEMENTS OF SOY PROTEIN, GELATIN, SUGAR, CORN SYRUP, PORK...
WAIT. "PORK?"
THE GELATIN IS MADE OF PORK SKIN.
I ATE ONE OF THOSE ONCE. OH, MAN!
DR. CHOI, I AM A MONITOR. IT IS MY FUNCTION TO VIEW INCIDENT AND BEHAVIOR. I KNOW THE NATURE OF THE RELATIONSHIP BETWEEN THE OBSERVED AND THE OBSERVER.
WHAT ARE YOU TRYING TO SAY, BIG GUY?

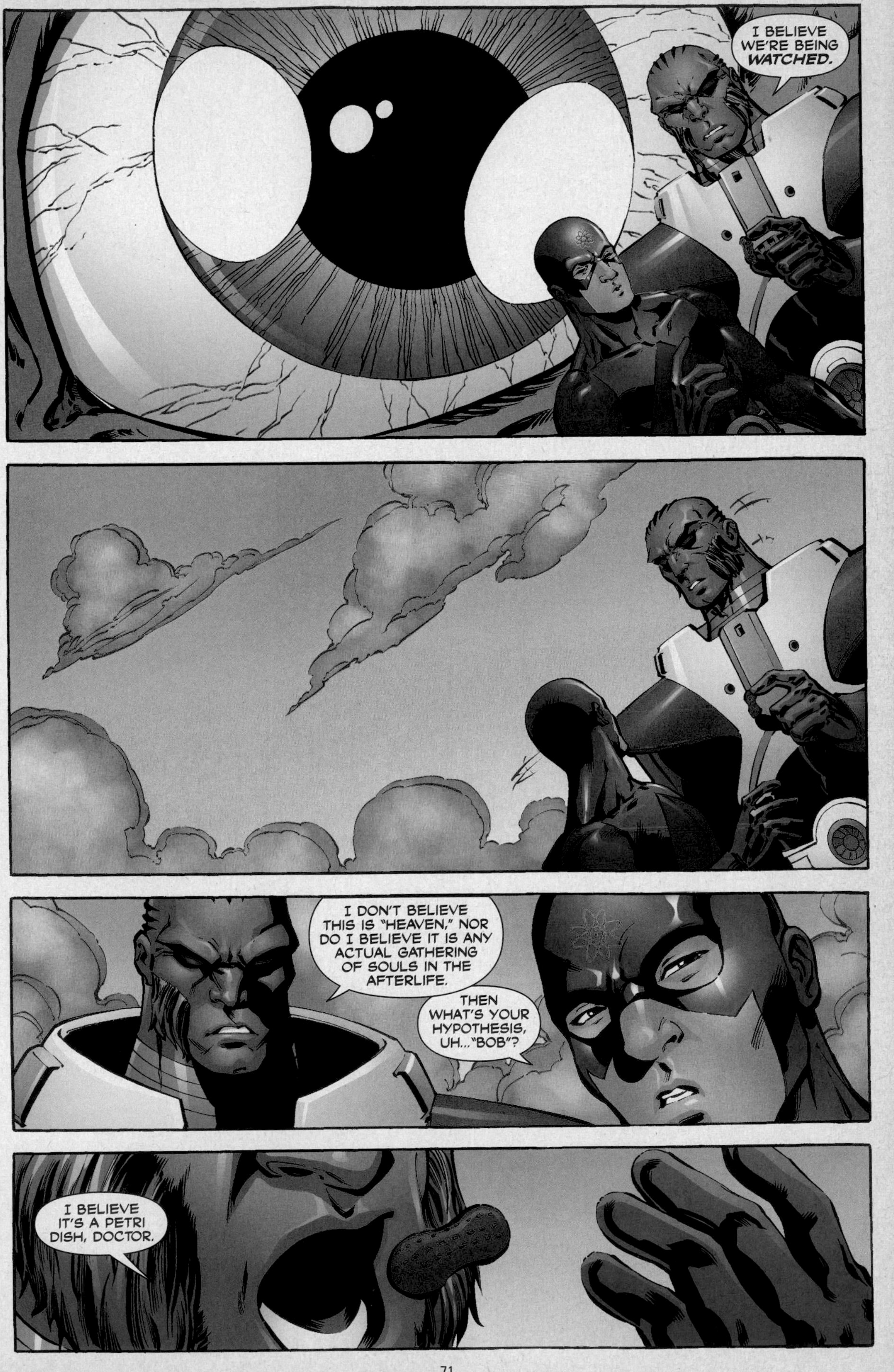
I BELIEVE WE'RE BEING WATCHED.
I DON'T BELIEVE THIS IS "HEAVEN," NOR DO I BELIEVE IT IS ANY ACTUAL GATHERING OF SOULS IN THE AFTERLIFE.
THEN WHAT'S YOUR HYPOTHESIS, UH..."BOB"?
I BELIEVE IT'S A PETRI DISH, DOCTOR.

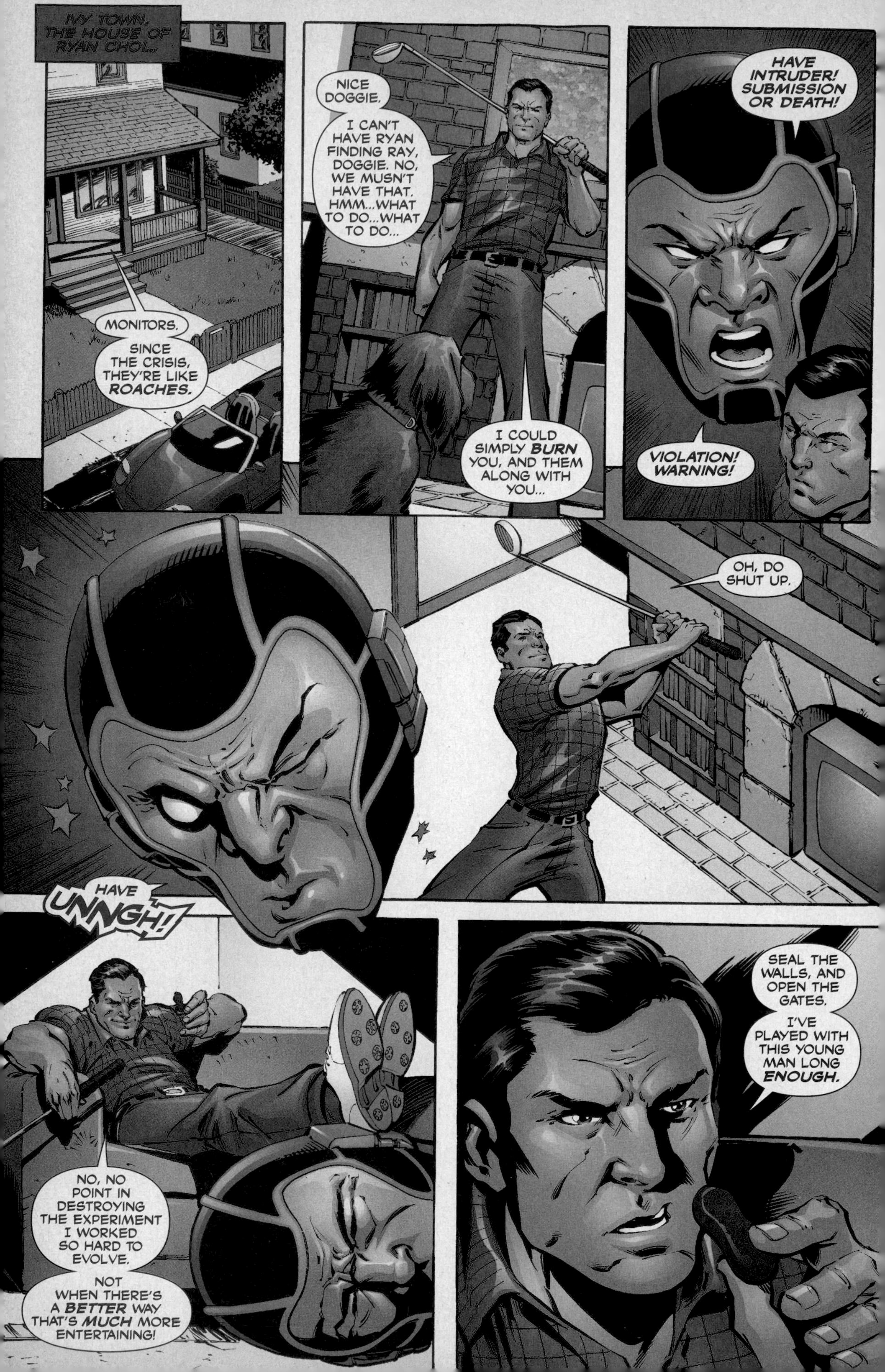
IVY TOWN, THE HOUSE OF RYAN CHOI...
MONITORS.
SINCE THE CRISIS, THEY'RE LIKE ROACHES.
NICE DOGGIE.
I CAN'T HAVE RYAN FINDING RAY, DOGGIE. NO, WE MUSN'T HAVE THAT. HMM...WHAT TO DO...WHAT TO DO...
I COULD SIMPLY BURN YOU, AND THEM ALONG WITH YOU...
HAVE INTRUDER! SUBMISSION OR DEATH!
VIOLATION! WARNING!
OH, DO SHUT UP.
HAVE UNNGH!!
NO, NO POINT IN DESTROYING THE EXPERIMENT I WORKED SO HARD TO EVOLVE.
NOT WHEN THERE'S A BETTER WAY THAT'S MUCH MORE ENTERTAINING!
SEAL THE WALLS, AND OPEN THE GATES.
I'VE PLAYED WITH THIS YOUNG MAN LONG ENOUGH.

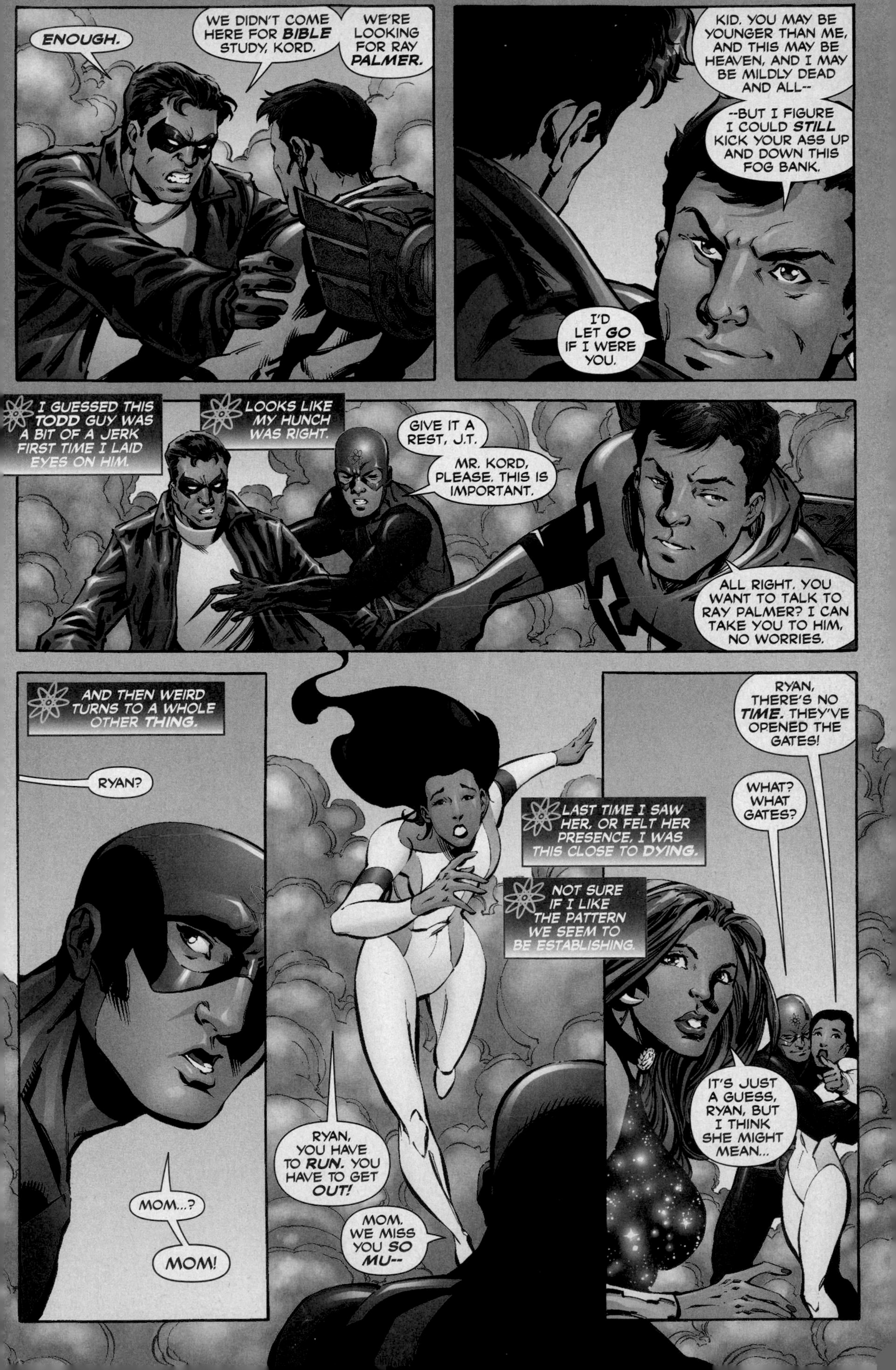
ENOUGH.
WE DIDN'T COME HERE FOR BIBLE STUDY, KORD.
WE'RE LOOKING FOR RAY PALMER.
KID, YOU MAY BE YOUNGER THAN ME, AND THIS MAY BE HEAVEN, AND I MAY BE MILDLY DEAD AND ALL--
--BUT I FIGURE I COULD STILL KICK YOUR ASS UP AND DOWN THIS FOG BANK.
I'D LET GO IF I WERE YOU.
I GUESSED THIS TODD GUY WAS A BIT OF A JERK FIRST TIME I LAID EYES ON HIM.
LOOKS LIKE MY HUNCH WAS RIGHT.
GIVE IT A REST, J.T.
MR. KORD, PLEASE. THIS IS IMPORTANT.
ALL RIGHT. YOU WANT TO TALK TO RAY PALMER? I CAN TAKE YOU TO HIM, NO WORRIES.
AND THEN WEIRD TURNS TO A WHOLE OTHER THING.
RYAN?
MOM...?
MOM!
RYAN, YOU HAVE TO RUN. YOU HAVE TO GET OUT!
MOM. WE MISS YOU SO MU--
LAST TIME I SAW HER, OR FELT HER PRESENCE, I WAS THIS CLOSE TO DYING.
NOT SURE IF I LIKE THE PATTERN WE SEEM TO BE ESTABLISHING.
RYAN, THERE'S NO TIME. THEY'VE OPENED THE GATES!
WHAT? WHAT GATES?
IT'S JUST A GUESS, RYAN, BUT I THINK SHE MIGHT MEAN...

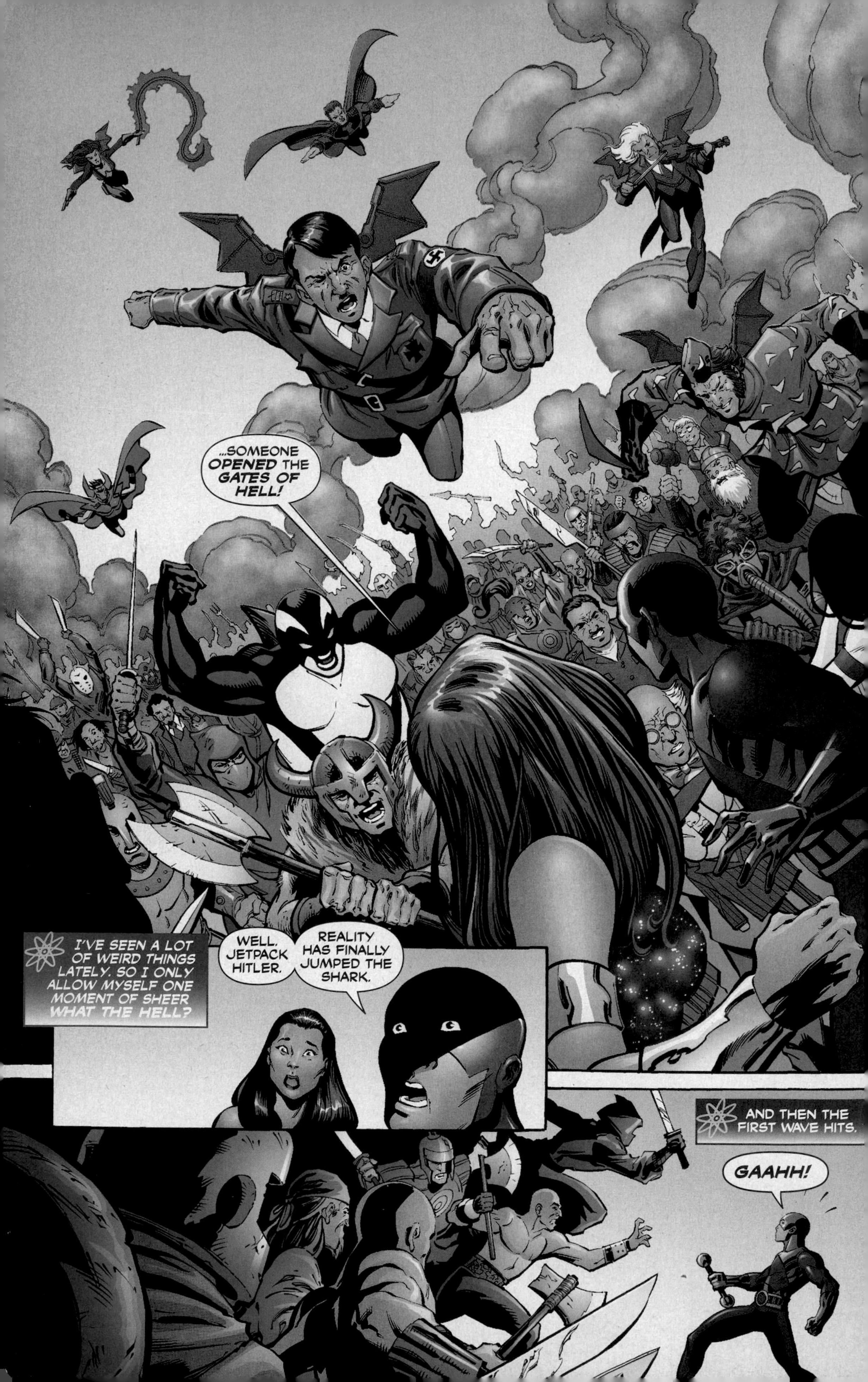
...SOMEONE OPENED THE GATES OF HELL!
I'VE SEEN A LOT OF WEIRD THINGS LATELY. SO I ONLY ALLOW MYSELF ONE MOMENT OF SHEER WHAT THE HELL?
WELL. JETPACK HITLER.
REALITY HAS FINALLY JUMPED THE SHARK.
AND THEN THE FIRST WAVE HITS.
GAAHH!

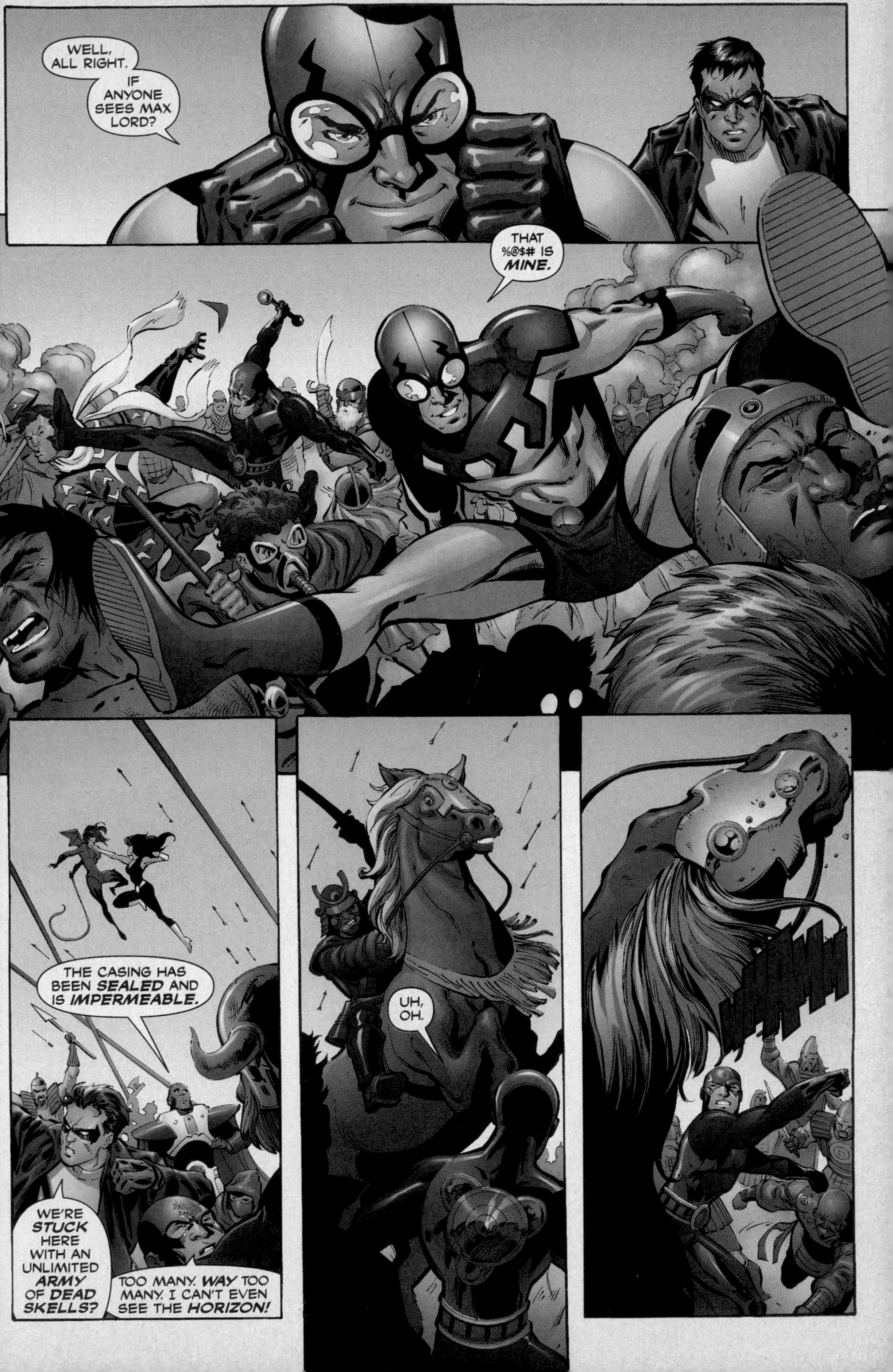
WELL, ALL RIGHT.
IF ANYONE SEES MAX LORD?
THAT %@$# IS MINE.
THE CASING HAS BEEN SEALED AND IS IMPERMEABLE.
WE'RE STUCK HERE WITH AN UNLIMITED ARMY OF DEAD SKELLS?
TOO MANY. WAY TOO MANY. I CAN'T EVEN SEE THE HORIZON!
UH, OH.

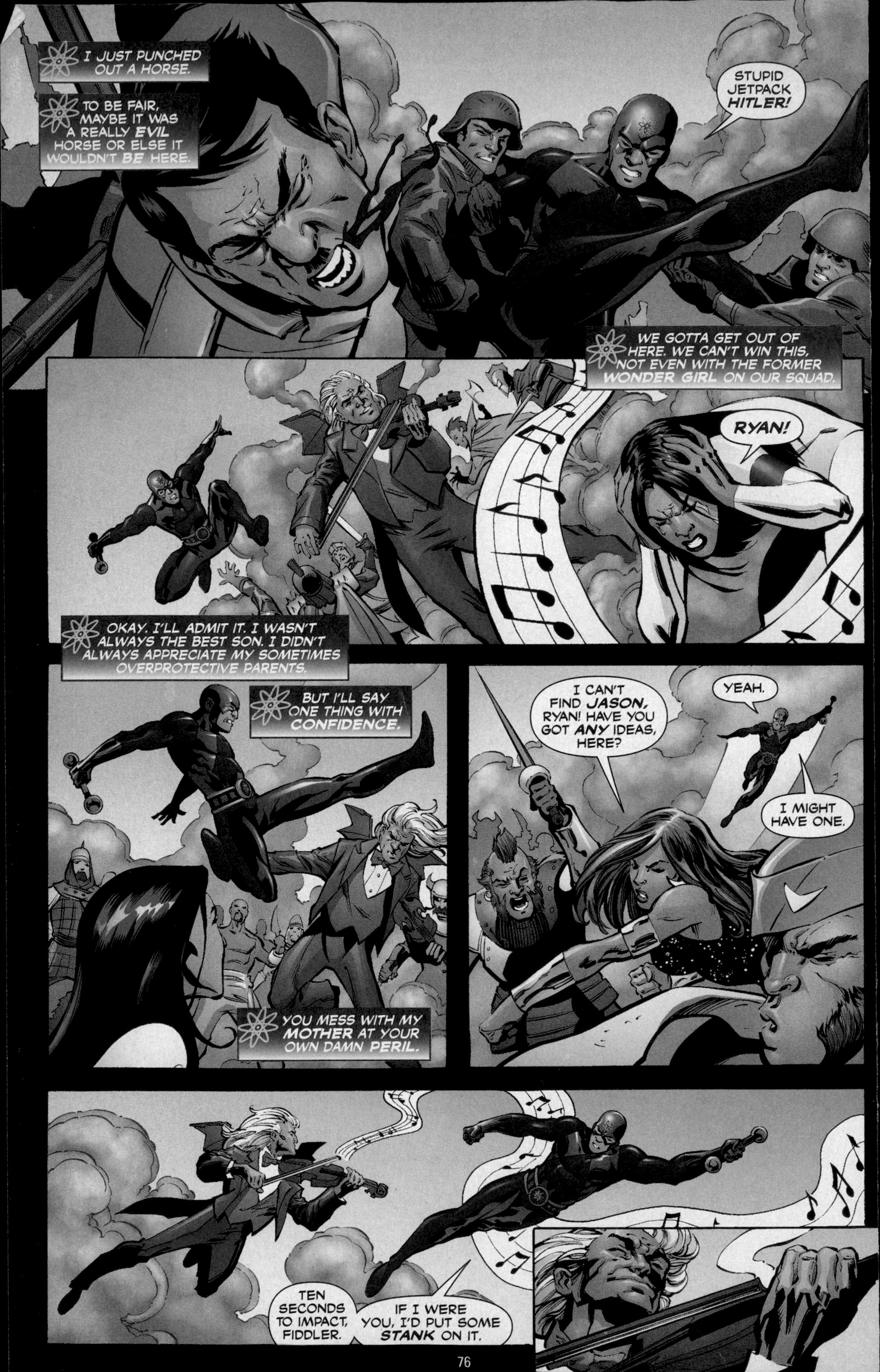

I JUST PUNCHED OUT A HORSE.
TO BE FAIR, MAYBE IT WAS A REALLY EVIL HORSE OR ELSE IT WOULDN'T BE HERE.
STUPID JETPACK HITLER!
WE GOTTA GET OUT OF HERE. WE CAN'T WIN THIS, NOT EVEN WITH THE FORMER WONDER GIRL ON OUR SQUAD.
RYAN!
OKAY. I'LL ADMIT IT. I WASN'T ALWAYS THE BEST SON. I DIDN'T ALWAYS APPRECIATE MY SOMETIMES OVERPROTECTIVE PARENTS.
BUT I'LL SAY ONE THING WITH CONFIDENCE.
YOU MESS WITH MY MOTHER AT YOUR OWN DAMN PERIL.
I CAN'T FIND JASON, RYAN! HAVE YOU GOT ANY IDEAS, HERE?
YEAH.
I MIGHT HAVE ONE.
TEN SECONDS TO IMPACT, FIDDLER.
IF I WERE YOU, I'D PUT SOME STANK ON IT.

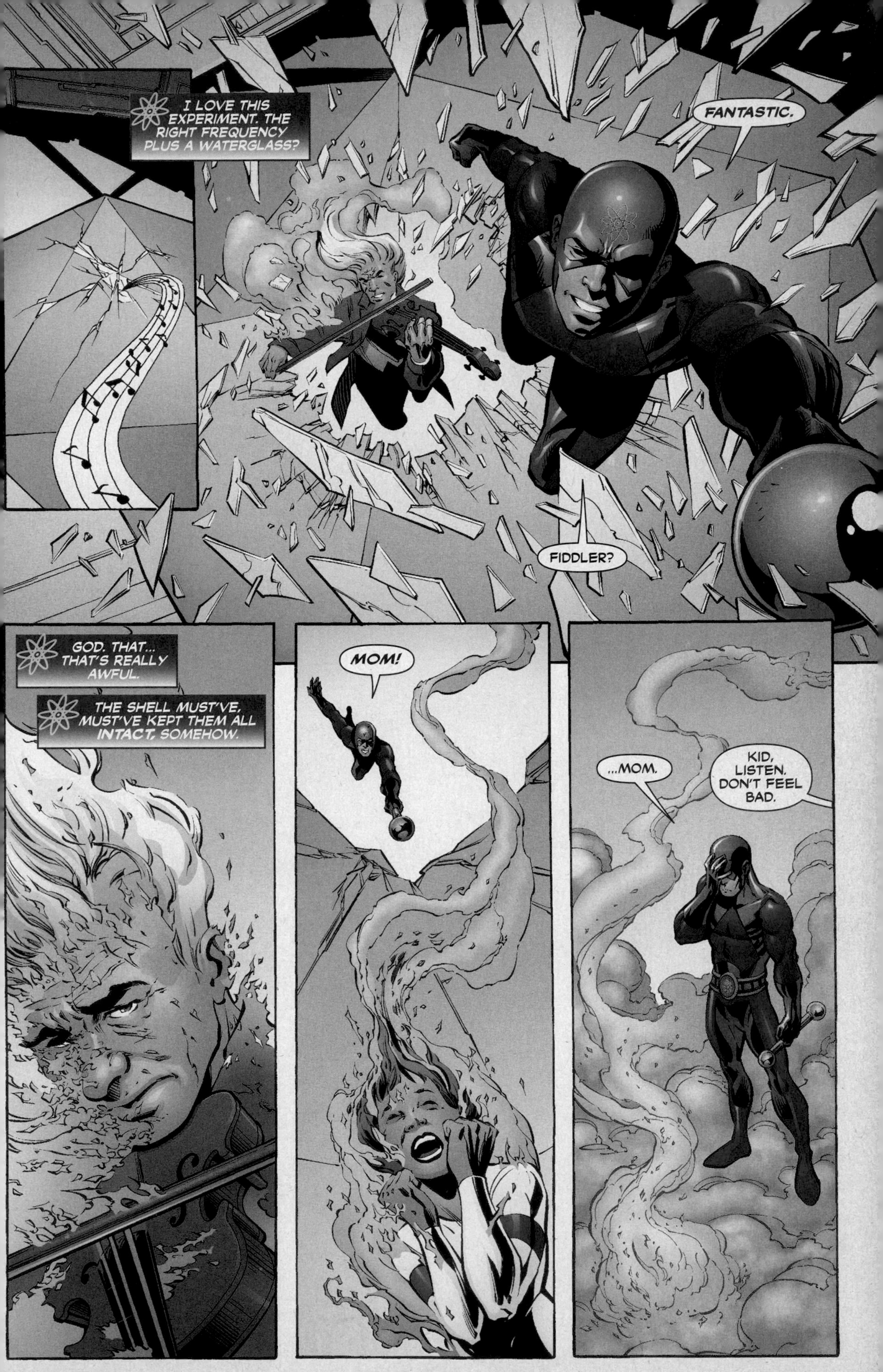
I LOVE THIS EXPERIMENT. THE RIGHT FREQUENCY PLUS A WATERGLASS?
FANTASTIC.
FIDDLER?
GOD. THAT... THAT'S REALLY AWFUL.
THE SHELL MUST'VE, MUST'VE KEPT THEM ALL INTACT, SOMEHOW.
MOM!
...MOM.
KID, LISTEN. DON'T FEEL BAD.

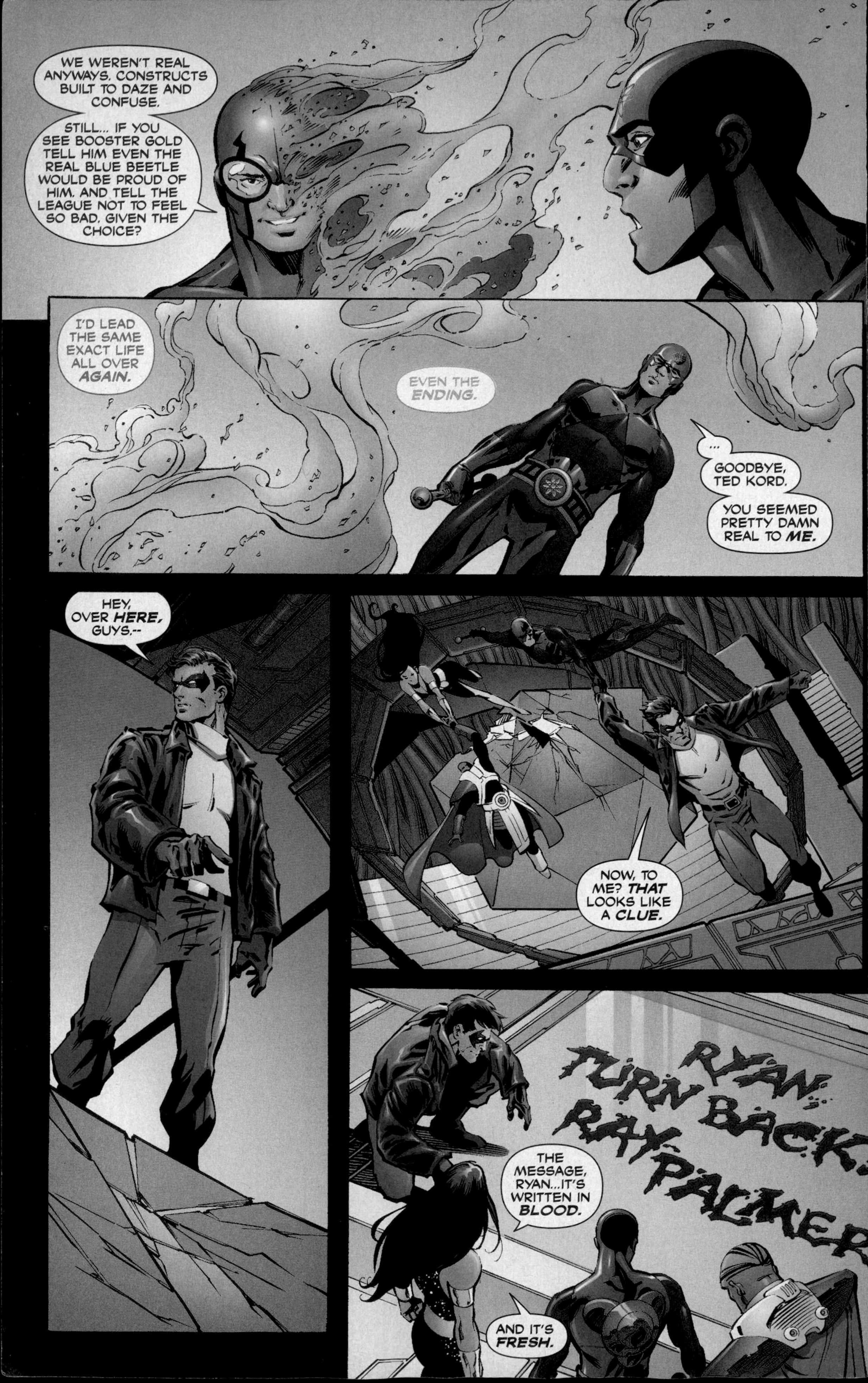

WE WEREN'T REAL ANYWAYS. CONSTRUCTS BUILT TO DAZE AND CONFUSE.
STILL... IF YOU SEE BOOSTER GOLD TELL HIM EVEN THE REAL BLUE BEETLE WOULD BE PROUD OF HIM. AND TELL THE LEAGUE NOT TO FEEL SO BAD. GIVEN THE CHOICE?
I'D LEAD THE SAME EXACT LIFE ALL OVER AGAIN.
EVEN THE ENDING.
...
GOODBYE, TED KORD.
YOU SEEMED PRETTY DAMN REAL TO ME.
HEY, OVER HERE, GUYS,--
NOW, TO ME? THAT LOOKS LIKE A CLUE.
RYAN. TURN BACK. RAY PALMER
THE MESSAGE, RYAN...IT'S WRITTEN IN BLOOD.
AND IT'S FRESH.

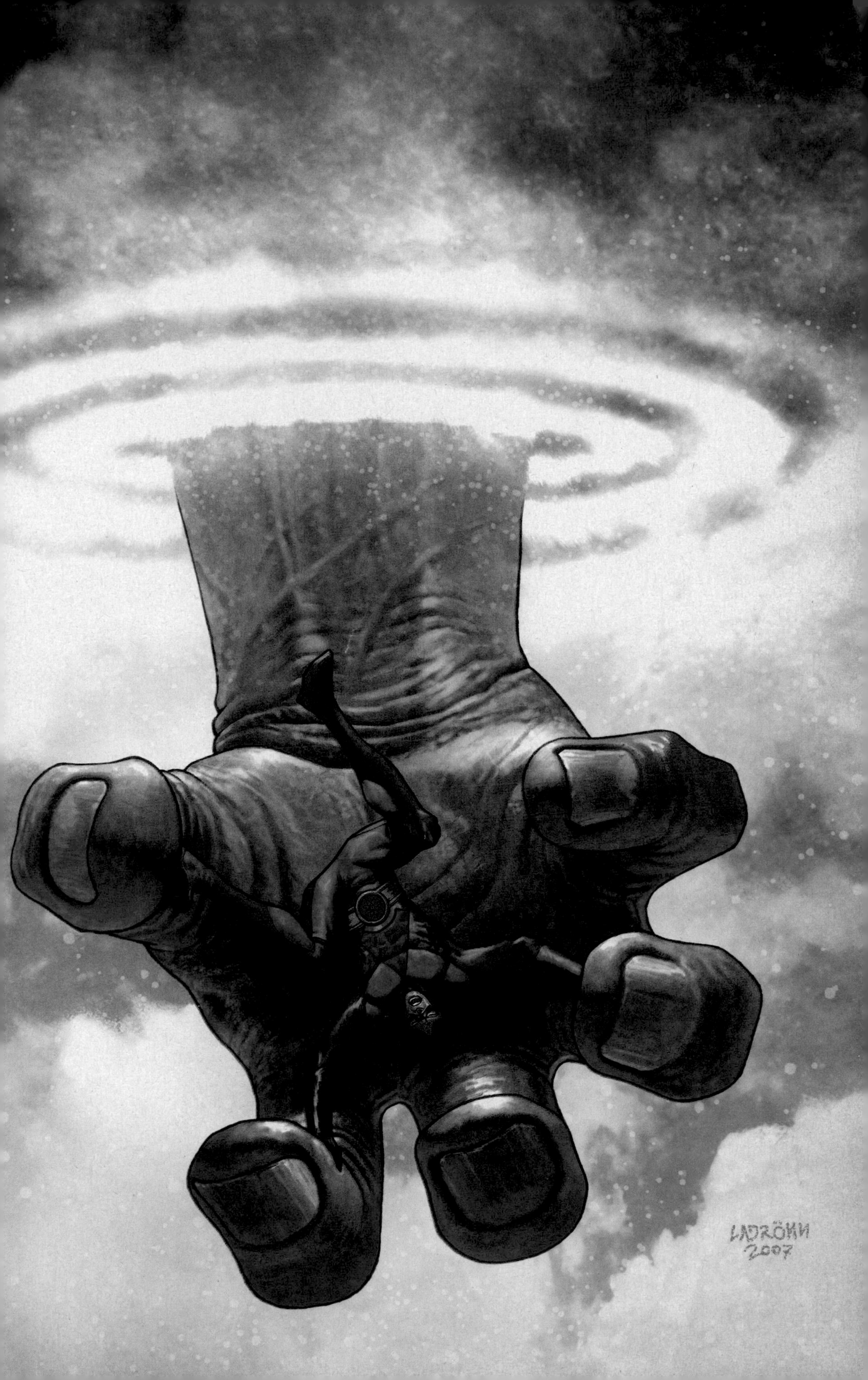
LADRÖNN
2007

HUNT FOR RAY PALMER: PART FOUR
LOSS LEADER

from **THE ALL NEW ATOM #15**

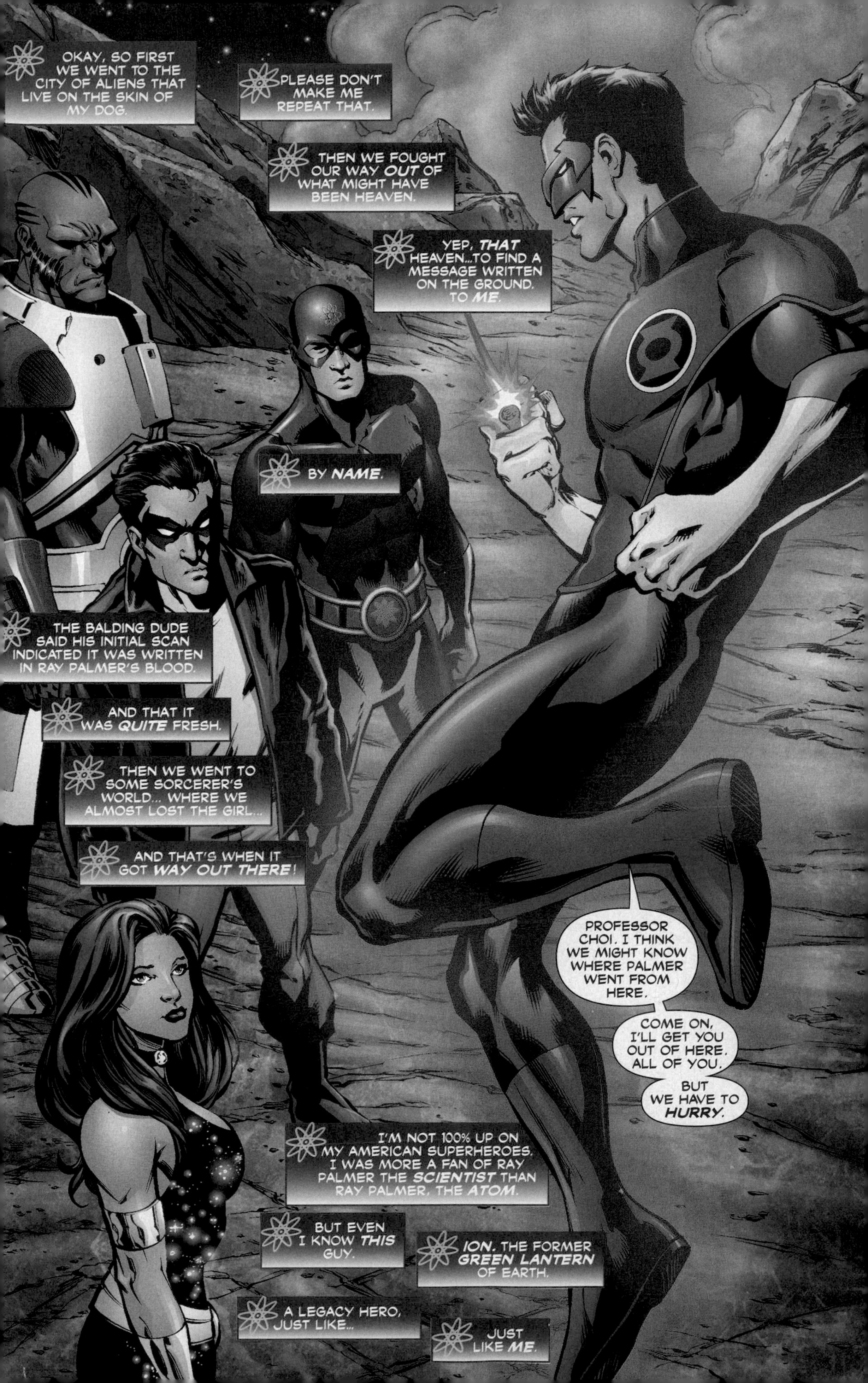
OKAY, SO FIRST WE WENT TO THE CITY OF ALIENS THAT LIVE ON THE SKIN OF MY DOG.
PLEASE DON'T MAKE ME REPEAT THAT.
THEN WE FOUGHT OUR WAY OUT OF WHAT MIGHT HAVE BEEN HEAVEN.
YEP, THAT HEAVEN...TO FIND A MESSAGE WRITTEN ON THE GROUND. TO ME.
BY NAME.
THE BALDING DUDE SAID HIS INITIAL SCAN INDICATED IT WAS WRITTEN IN RAY PALMER'S BLOOD.
AND THAT IT WAS QUITE FRESH.
THEN WE WENT TO SOME SORCERER'S WORLD... WHERE WE ALMOST LOST THE GIRL...
AND THAT'S WHEN IT GOT WAY OUT THERE!
PROFESSOR CHOI. I THINK WE MIGHT KNOW WHERE PALMER WENT FROM HERE.
COME ON, I'LL GET YOU OUT OF HERE. ALL OF YOU.
BUT WE HAVE TO HURRY.
I'M NOT 100% UP ON MY AMERICAN SUPERHEROES. I WAS MORE A FAN OF RAY PALMER THE SCIENTIST THAN RAY PALMER, THE ATOM.
BUT EVEN I KNOW THIS GUY.
ION. THE FORMER GREEN LANTERN OF EARTH.
A LEGACY HERO, JUST LIKE...
JUST LIKE ME.

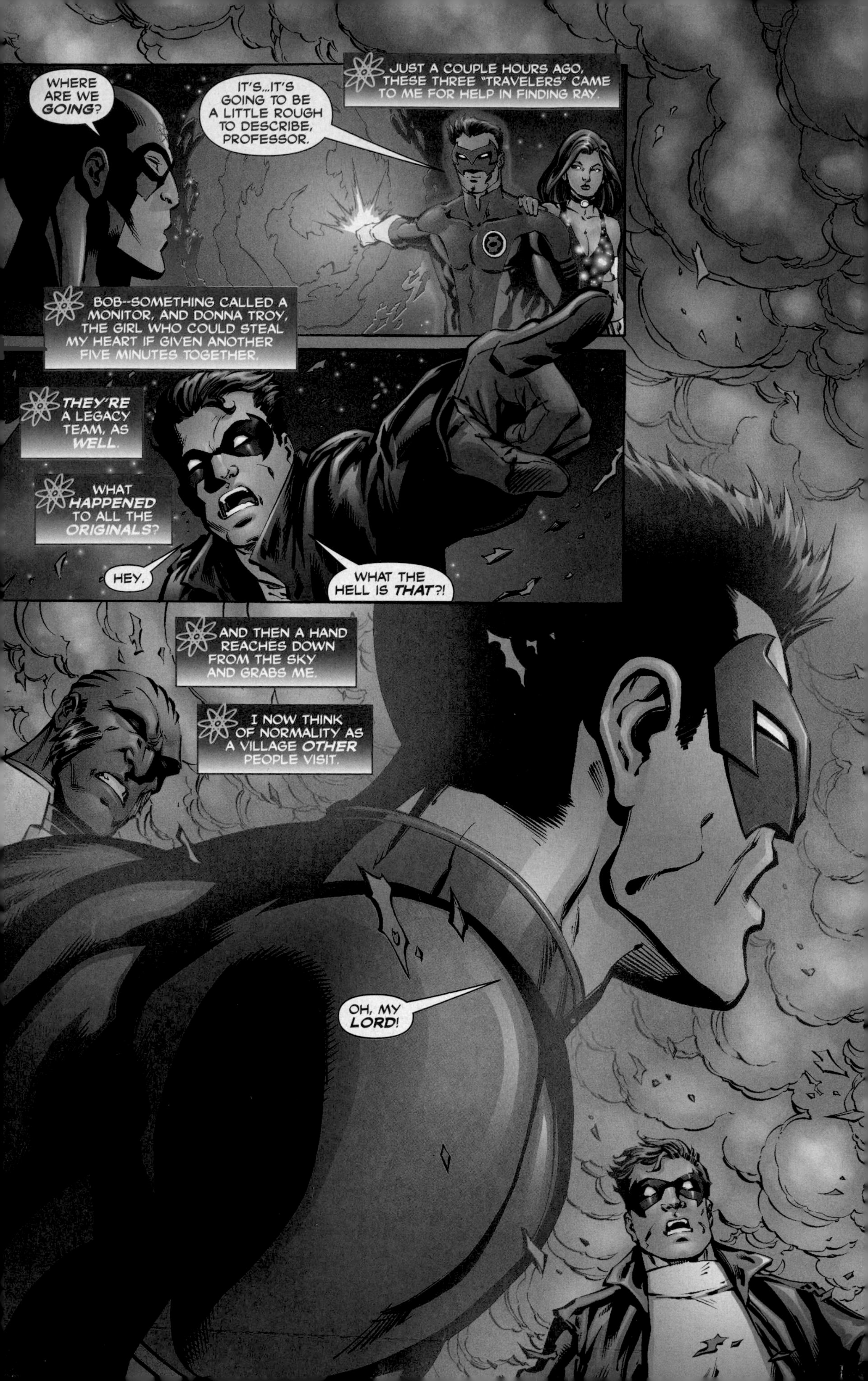

WHERE ARE WE *GOING*?
IT'S...IT'S GOING TO BE A LITTLE ROUGH TO DESCRIBE, PROFESSOR.
JUST A COUPLE HOURS AGO, THESE THREE "TRAVELERS" CAME TO ME FOR HELP IN FINDING RAY.
BOB--SOMETHING CALLED A MONITOR, AND DONNA TROY, THE GIRL WHO COULD STEAL MY HEART IF GIVEN ANOTHER FIVE MINUTES TOGETHER.
THEY'RE A LEGACY TEAM, AS *WELL*.
WHAT *HAPPENED* TO ALL THE *ORIGINALS*?
HEY.
WHAT THE HELL IS *THAT*?!
AND THEN A HAND REACHES DOWN FROM THE SKY AND GRABS ME.
I NOW THINK OF NORMALITY AS A VILLAGE *OTHER* PEOPLE VISIT.
OH, MY *LORD*!

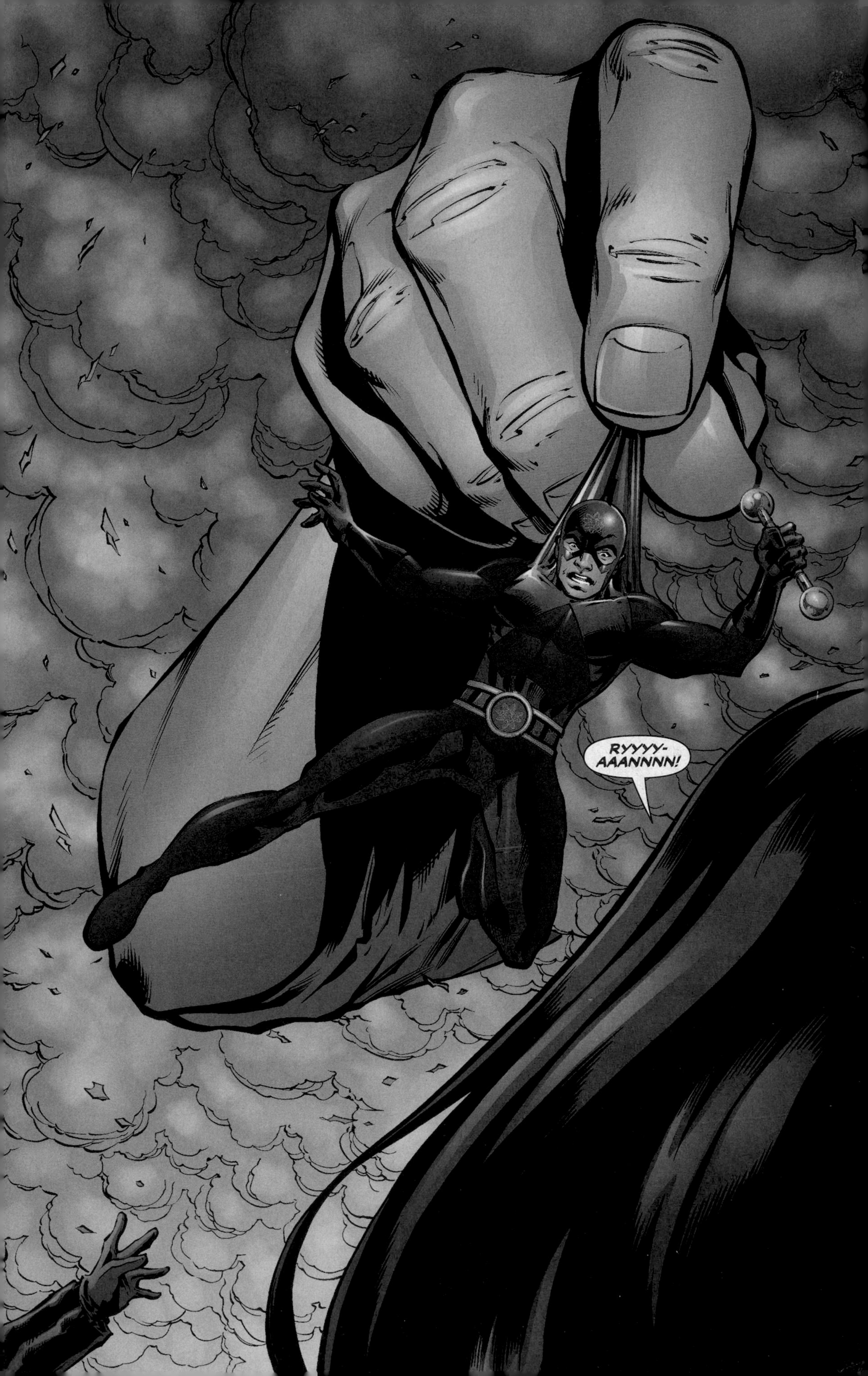
RYYYY-
AAANNNN!

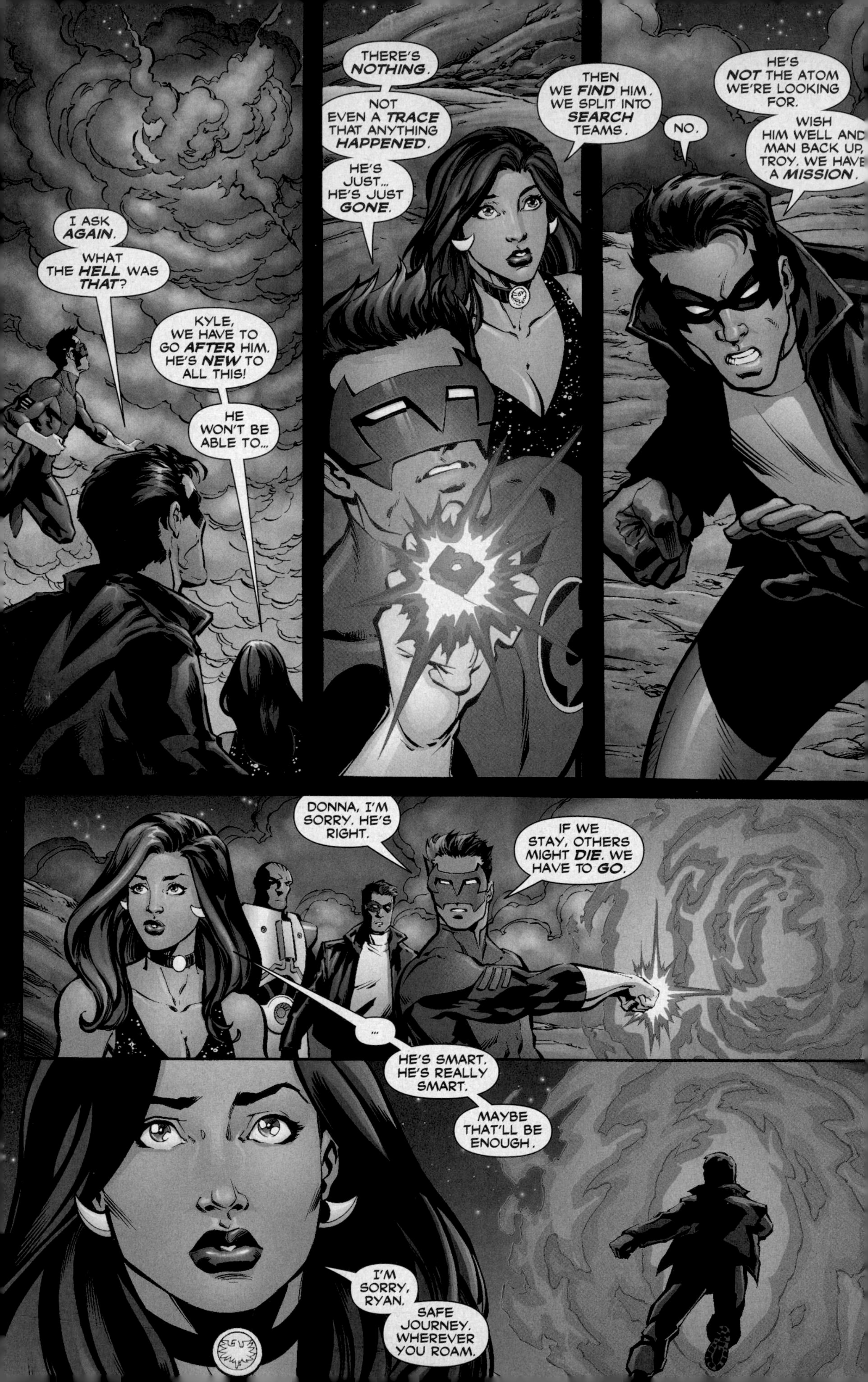
I ASK AGAIN.
WHAT THE HELL WAS THAT?
KYLE, WE HAVE TO GO AFTER HIM. HE'S NEW TO ALL THIS!
HE WON'T BE ABLE TO...
THERE'S NOTHING.
NOT EVEN A TRACE THAT ANYTHING HAPPENED.
HE'S JUST... HE'S JUST GONE.
THEN WE FIND HIM. WE SPLIT INTO SEARCH TEAMS.
NO.
HE'S NOT THE ATOM WE'RE LOOKING FOR.
WISH HIM WELL AND MAN BACK UP, TROY. WE HAVE A MISSION.
DONNA, I'M SORRY. HE'S RIGHT.
IF WE STAY, OTHERS MIGHT DIE. WE HAVE TO GO.
...
HE'S SMART. HE'S REALLY SMART.
MAYBE THAT'LL BE ENOUGH.
I'M SORRY, RYAN.
SAFE JOURNEY. WHEREVER YOU ROAM.

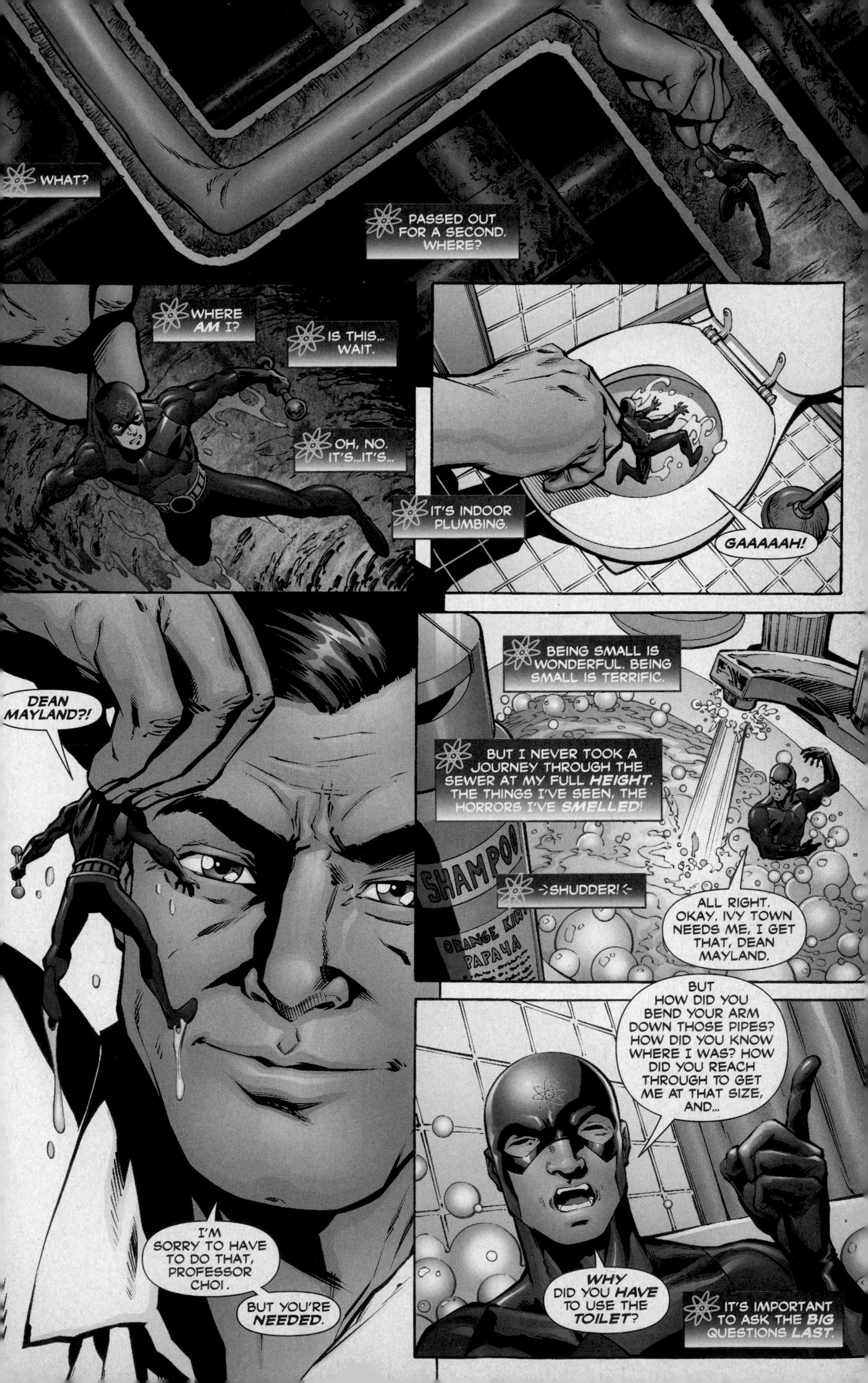
WHAT?
PASSED OUT FOR A SECOND. WHERE?
WHERE AM I?
IS THIS... WAIT.
OH, NO. IT'S...IT'S...
IT'S INDOOR PLUMBING.
GAAAAAH!
DEAN MAYLAND?!
I'M SORRY TO HAVE TO DO THAT, PROFESSOR CHOI.
BUT YOU'RE NEEDED.
BEING SMALL IS WONDERFUL. BEING SMALL IS TERRIFIC.
BUT I NEVER TOOK A JOURNEY THROUGH THE SEWER AT MY FULL HEIGHT. THE THINGS I'VE SEEN, THE HORRORS I'VE SMELLED!
SHAMPOO
ORANGE KIWI PAPAYA
>SHUDDER!<
ALL RIGHT. OKAY. IVY TOWN NEEDS ME, I GET THAT, DEAN MAYLAND.
BUT HOW DID YOU BEND YOUR ARM DOWN THOSE PIPES? HOW DID YOU KNOW WHERE I WAS? HOW DID YOU REACH THROUGH TO GET ME AT THAT SIZE, AND...
WHY DID YOU HAVE TO USE THE TOILET?
IT'S IMPORTANT TO ASK THE BIG QUESTIONS LAST.

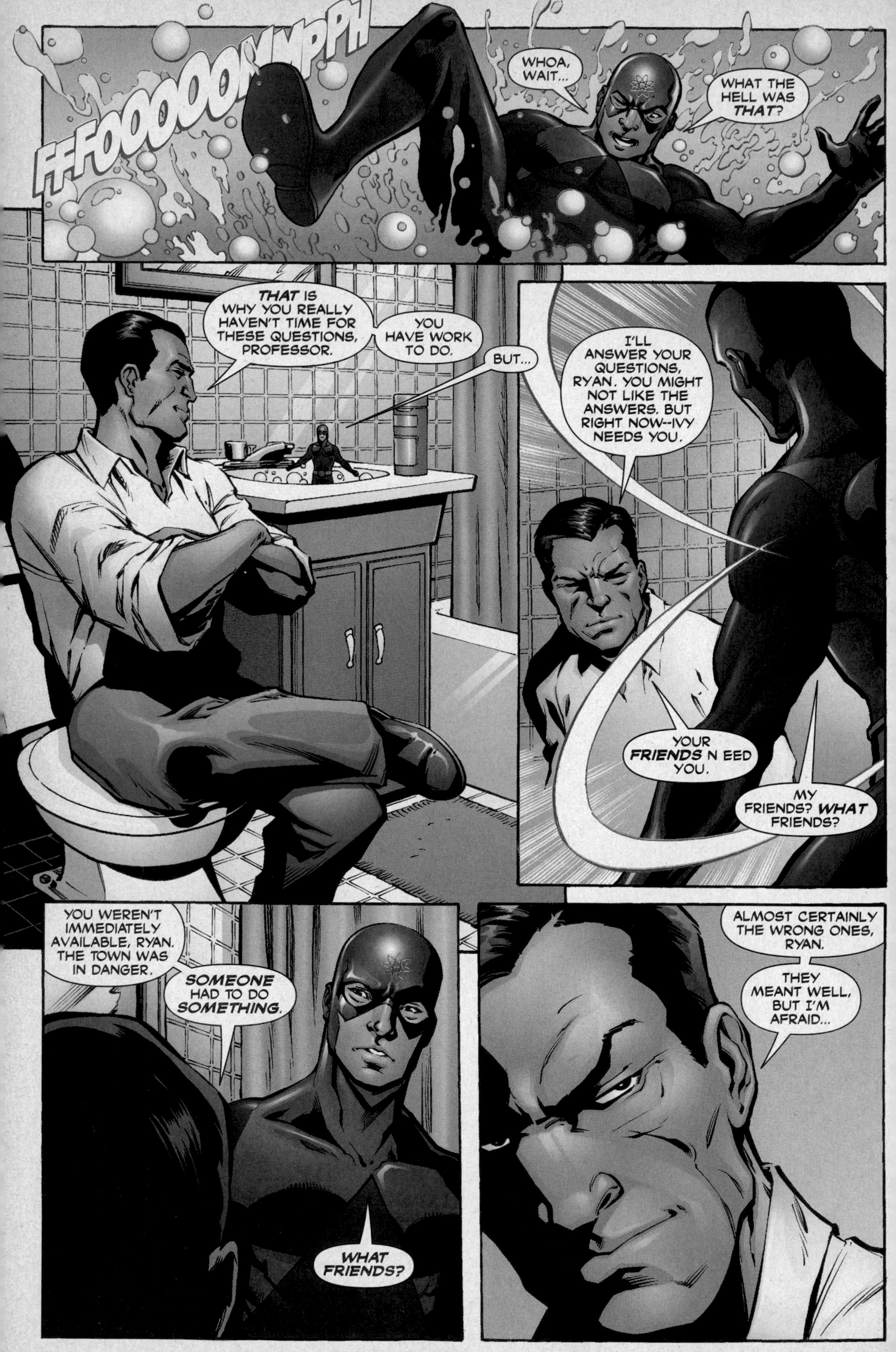
FFFOOOOOMMMPPH
WHOA, WAIT...
WHAT THE HELL WAS THAT?
THAT IS WHY YOU REALLY HAVEN'T TIME FOR THESE QUESTIONS, PROFESSOR.
YOU HAVE WORK TO DO.
BUT...
I'LL ANSWER YOUR QUESTIONS, RYAN. YOU MIGHT NOT LIKE THE ANSWERS. BUT RIGHT NOW--IVY NEEDS YOU.
YOUR FRIENDS N EED YOU.
MY FRIENDS? WHAT FRIENDS?
YOU WEREN'T IMMEDIATELY AVAILABLE, RYAN. THE TOWN WAS IN DANGER.
SOMEONE HAD TO DO SOMETHING.
WHAT FRIENDS?
ALMOST CERTAINLY THE WRONG ONES, RYAN.
THEY MEANT WELL, BUT I'M AFRAID...

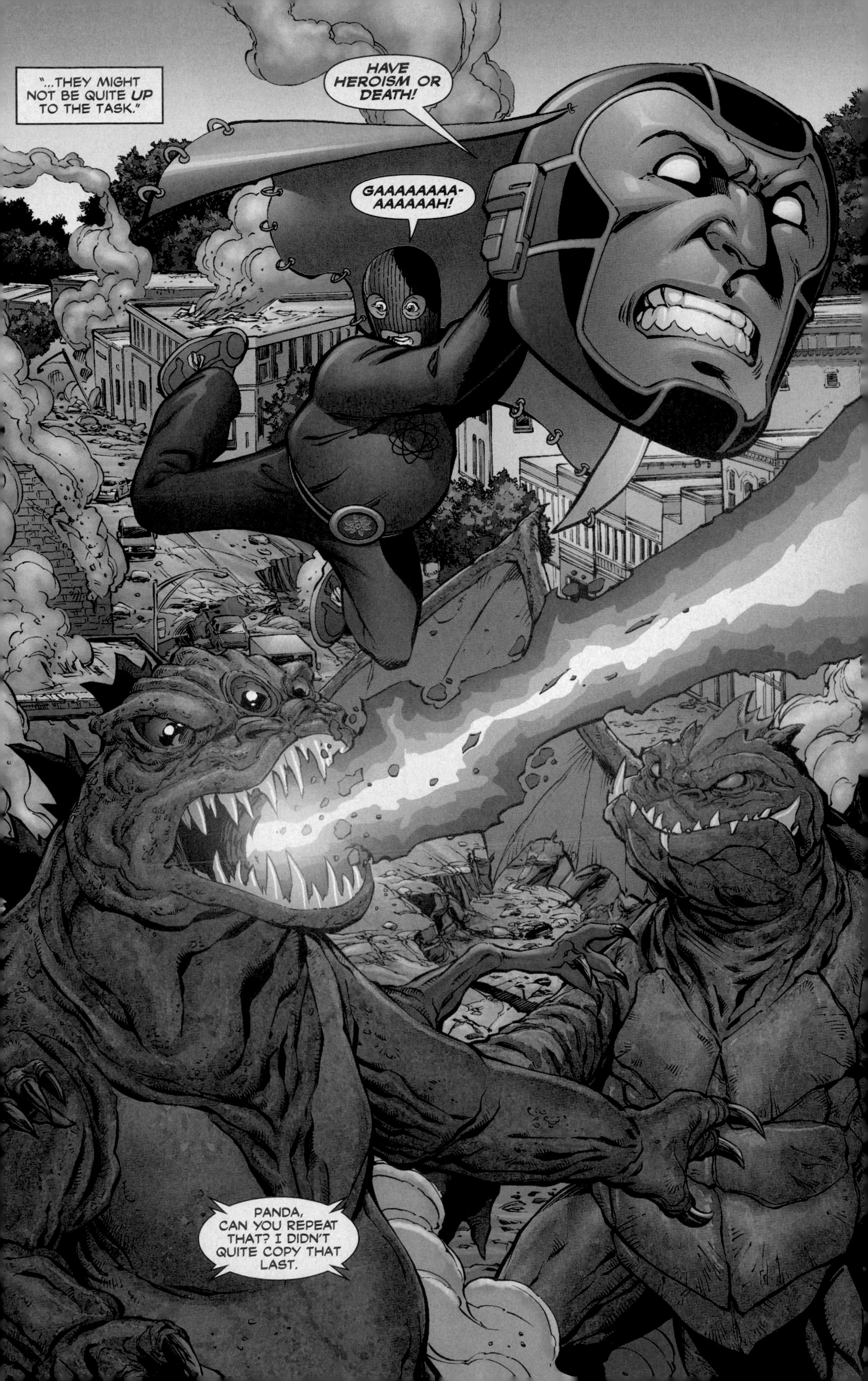
"...THEY MIGHT NOT BE QUITE UP TO THE TASK."
HAVE HEROISM OR DEATH!
GAAAAAAAA-AAAAAAH!
PANDA, CAN YOU REPEAT THAT? I DIDN'T QUITE COPY THAT LAST.

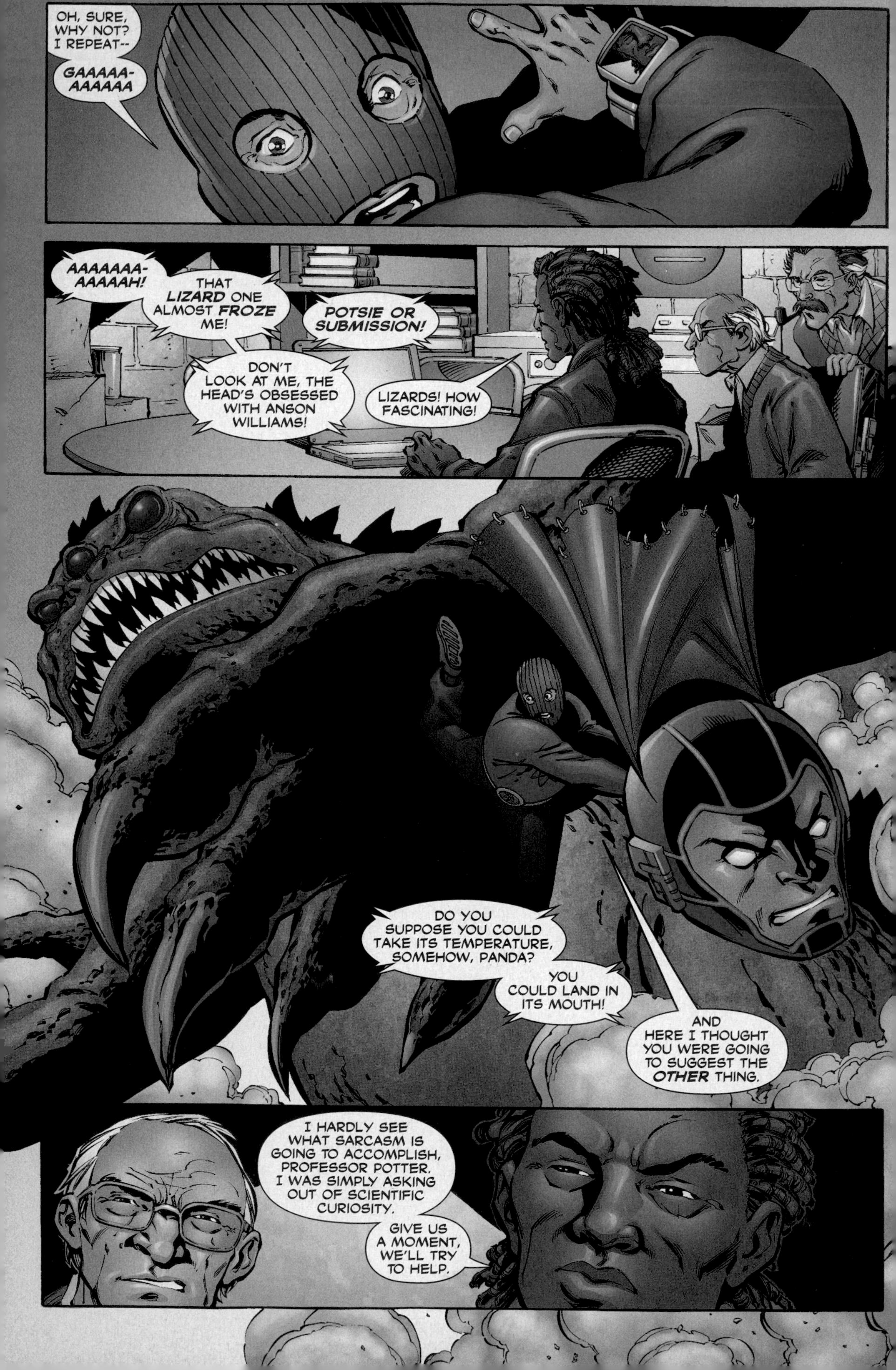
OH, SURE, WHY NOT? I REPEAT--
GAAAAA-AAAAAA
AAAAAAA-AAAAAH!
THAT LIZARD ONE ALMOST FROZE ME!
POTSIE OR SUBMISSION!
DON'T LOOK AT ME, THE HEAD'S OBSESSED WITH ANSON WILLIAMS!
LIZARDS! HOW FASCINATING!
DO YOU SUPPOSE YOU COULD TAKE ITS TEMPERATURE, SOMEHOW, PANDA?
YOU COULD LAND IN ITS MOUTH!
AND HERE I THOUGHT YOU WERE GOING TO SUGGEST THE OTHER THING.
I HARDLY SEE WHAT SARCASM IS GOING TO ACCOMPLISH, PROFESSOR POTTER. I WAS SIMPLY ASKING OUT OF SCIENTIFIC CURIOSITY.
GIVE US A MOMENT, WE'LL TRY TO HELP.

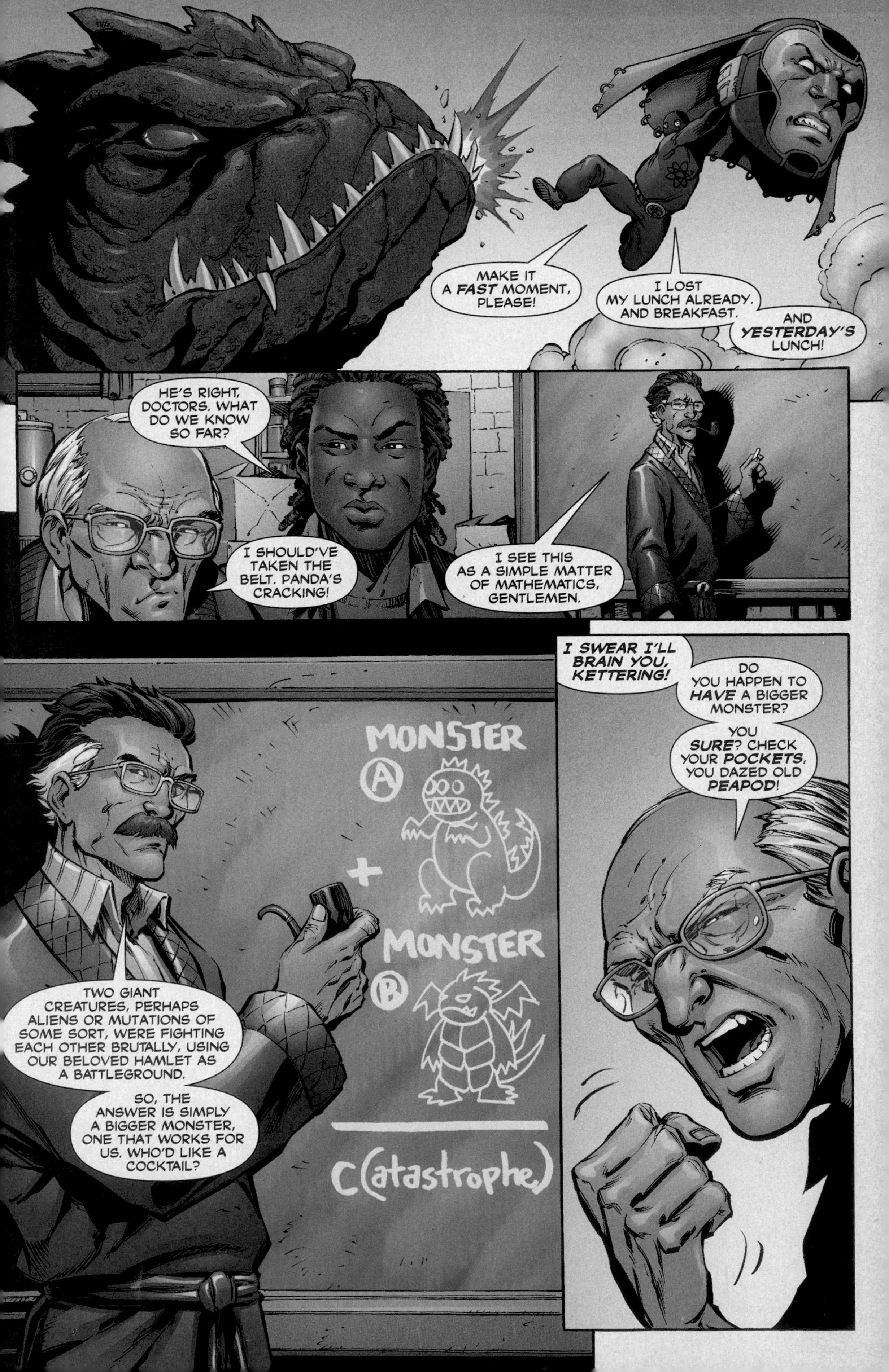
MAKE IT A FAST MOMENT, PLEASE!
I LOST MY LUNCH ALREADY. AND BREAKFAST.
AND YESTERDAY'S LUNCH!
HE'S RIGHT, DOCTORS. WHAT DO WE KNOW SO FAR?
I SHOULD'VE TAKEN THE BELT. PANDA'S CRACKING!
I SEE THIS AS A SIMPLE MATTER OF MATHEMATICS, GENTLEMEN.
MONSTER
A
+
MONSTER
B
C(atastrophe)
TWO GIANT CREATURES, PERHAPS ALIENS OR MUTATIONS OF SOME SORT, WERE FIGHTING EACH OTHER BRUTALLY, USING OUR BELOVED HAMLET AS A BATTLEGROUND.
SO, THE ANSWER IS SIMPLY A BIGGER MONSTER, ONE THAT WORKS FOR US. WHO'D LIKE A COCKTAIL?
I SWEAR I'LL BRAIN YOU, KETTERING!
DO YOU HAPPEN TO HAVE A BIGGER MONSTER?
YOU SURE? CHECK YOUR POCKETS, YOU DAZED OLD PEAPOD!

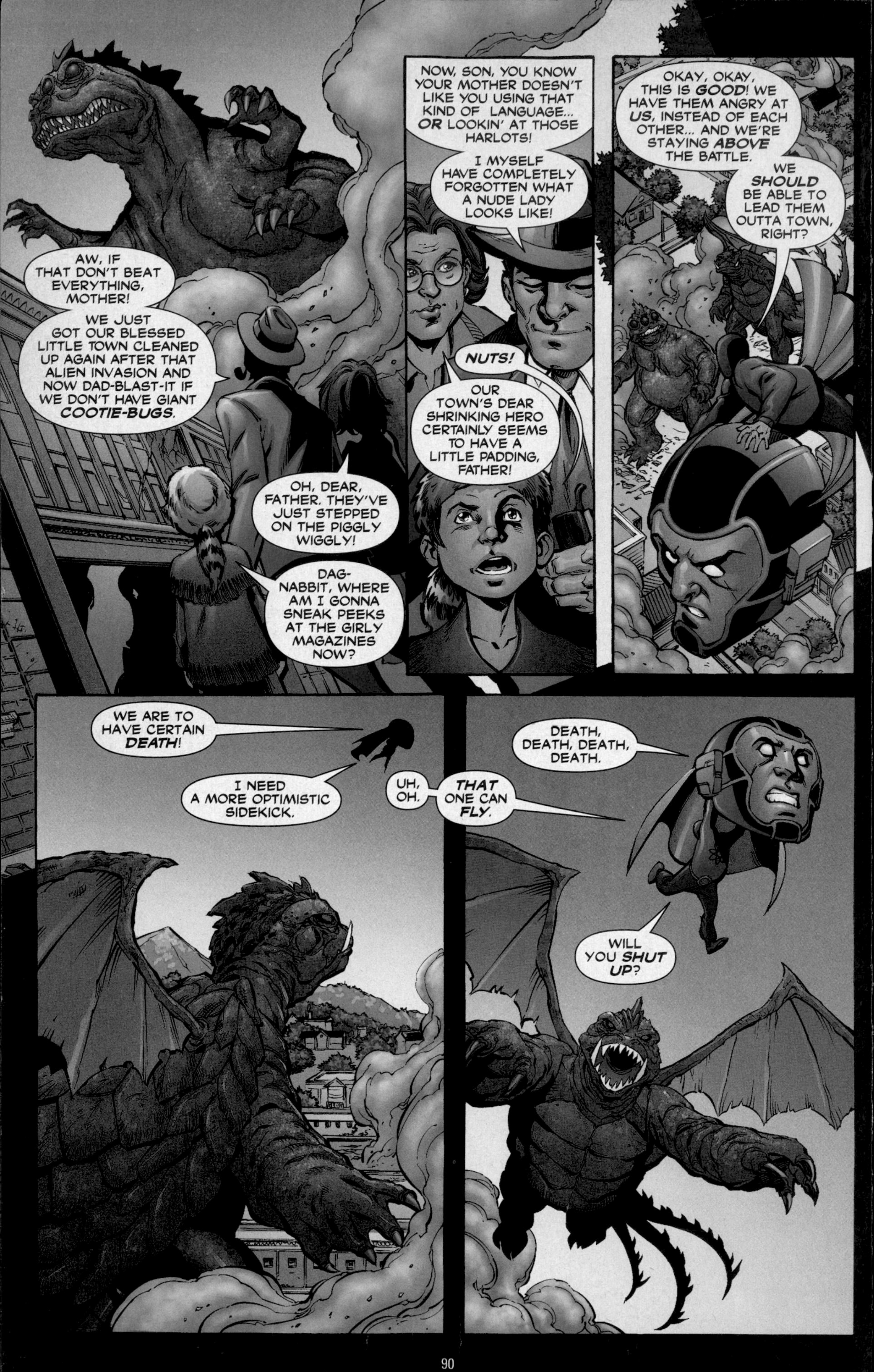
AW, IF THAT DON'T BEAT EVERYTHING, MOTHER!
WE JUST GOT OUR BLESSED LITTLE TOWN CLEANED UP AGAIN AFTER THAT ALIEN INVASION AND NOW DAD-BLAST-IT IF WE DON'T HAVE GIANT COOTIE-BUGS.
OH, DEAR, FATHER. THEY'VE JUST STEPPED ON THE PIGGLY WIGGLY!
DAG-NABBIT, WHERE AM I GONNA SNEAK PEEKS AT THE GIRLY MAGAZINES NOW?
NOW, SON, YOU KNOW YOUR MOTHER DOESN'T LIKE YOU USING THAT KIND OF LANGUAGE... OR LOOKIN' AT THOSE HARLOTS!
I MYSELF HAVE COMPLETELY FORGOTTEN WHAT A NUDE LADY LOOKS LIKE!
NUTS!
OUR TOWN'S DEAR SHRINKING HERO CERTAINLY SEEMS TO HAVE A LITTLE PADDING, FATHER!
OKAY, OKAY, THIS IS GOOD! WE HAVE THEM ANGRY AT US, INSTEAD OF EACH OTHER... AND WE'RE STAYING ABOVE THE BATTLE.
WE SHOULD BE ABLE TO LEAD THEM OUTTA TOWN, RIGHT?
WE ARE TO HAVE CERTAIN DEATH!
I NEED A MORE OPTIMISTIC SIDEKICK.
UH, OH.
THAT ONE CAN FLY.
DEATH, DEATH, DEATH, DEATH.
WILL YOU SHUT UP?

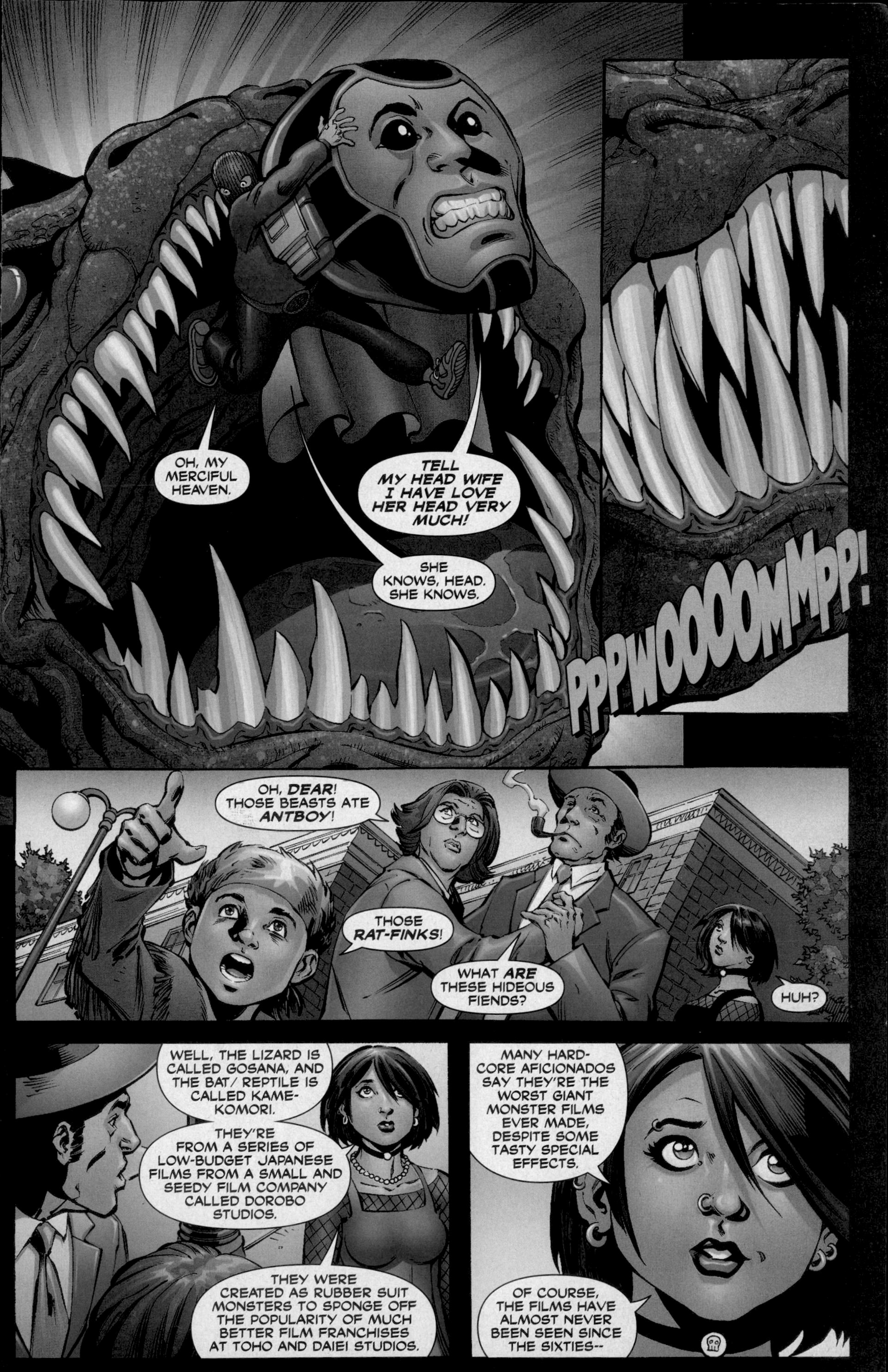
OH, MY MERCIFUL HEAVEN.
TELL MY HEAD WIFE I HAVE LOVE HER HEAD VERY MUCH!
SHE KNOWS, HEAD. SHE KNOWS.
PPPWOOOOMMPP!
OH, DEAR! THOSE BEASTS ATE ANTBOY!
THOSE RAT-FINKS!
WHAT ARE THESE HIDEOUS FIENDS?
HUH?
WELL, THE LIZARD IS CALLED GOSANA, AND THE BAT/ REPTILE IS CALLED KAME-KOMORI.
THEY'RE FROM A SERIES OF LOW-BUDGET JAPANESE FILMS FROM A SMALL AND SEEDY FILM COMPANY CALLED DOROBO STUDIOS.
THEY WERE CREATED AS RUBBER SUIT MONSTERS TO SPONGE OFF THE POPULARITY OF MUCH BETTER FILM FRANCHISES AT TOHO AND DAIEI STUDIOS.
MANY HARD-CORE AFICIONADOS SAY THEY'RE THE WORST GIANT MONSTER FILMS EVER MADE, DESPITE SOME TASTY SPECIAL EFFECTS.
OF COURSE, THE FILMS HAVE ALMOST NEVER BEEN SEEN SINCE THE SIXTIES--

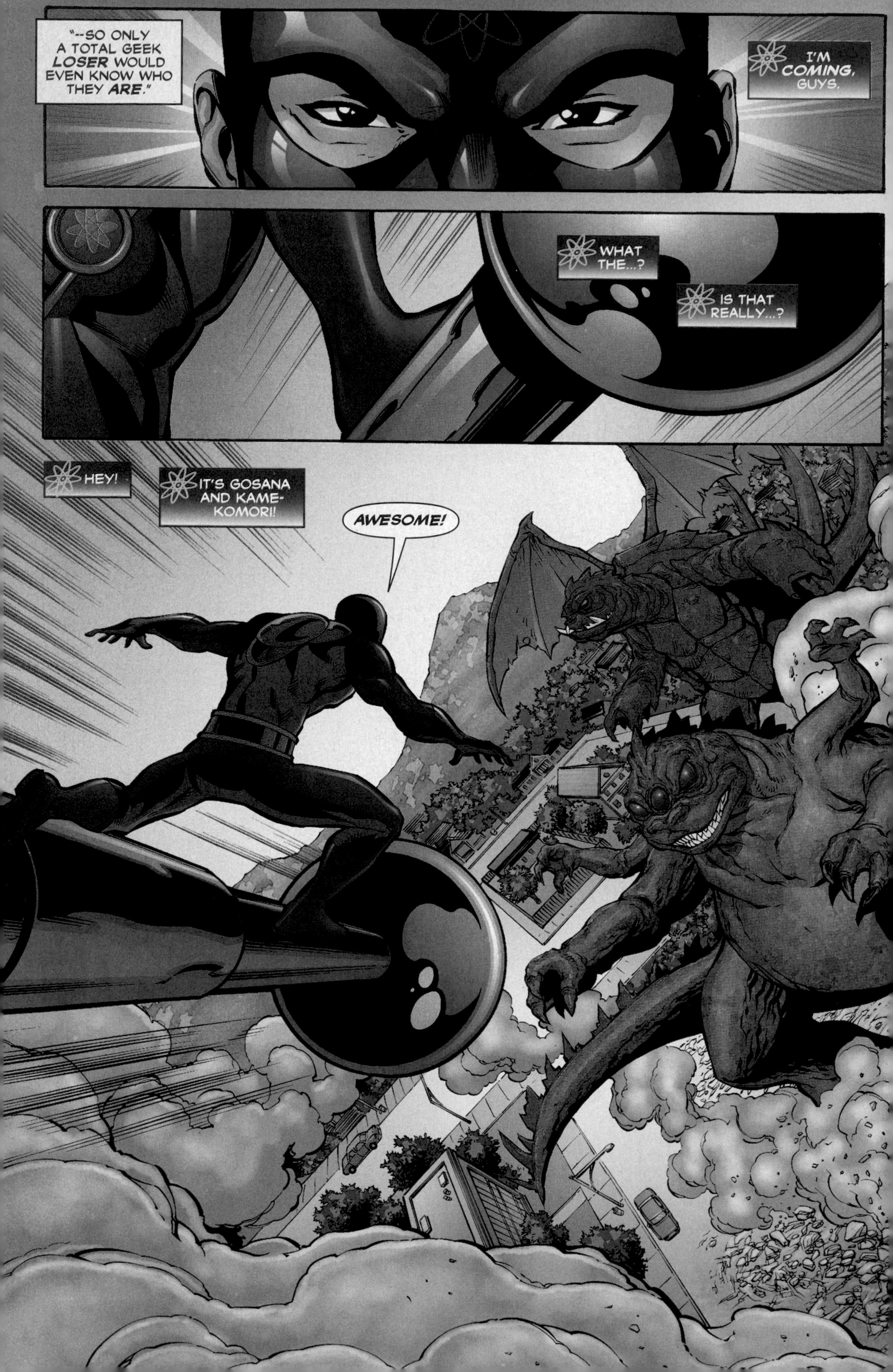
"--SO ONLY A TOTAL GEEK LOSER WOULD EVEN KNOW WHO THEY ARE."
I'M COMING, GUYS.
WHAT THE...?
IS THAT REALLY...?
HEY!
IT'S GOSANA AND KAME-KOMORI!
AWESOME!

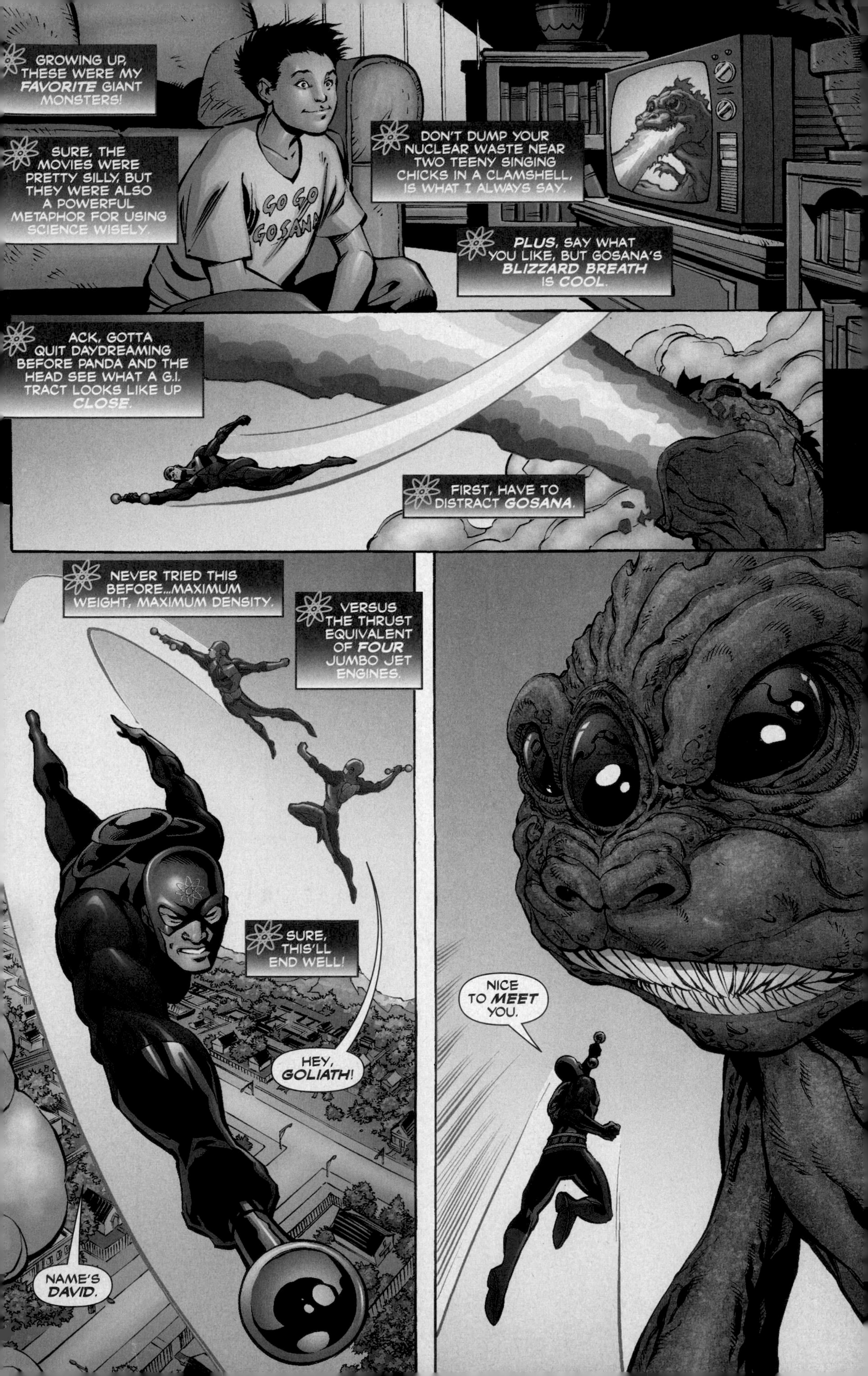
GROWING UP, THESE WERE MY FAVORITE GIANT MONSTERS!
SURE, THE MOVIES WERE PRETTY SILLY, BUT THEY WERE ALSO A POWERFUL METAPHOR FOR USING SCIENCE WISELY.
GO GO GOSANA
DON'T DUMP YOUR NUCLEAR WASTE NEAR TWO TEENY SINGING CHICKS IN A CLAMSHELL, IS WHAT I ALWAYS SAY.
PLUS, SAY WHAT YOU LIKE, BUT GOSANA'S BLIZZARD BREATH IS COOL.
ACK, GOTTA QUIT DAYDREAMING BEFORE PANDA AND THE HEAD SEE WHAT A G.I. TRACT LOOKS LIKE UP CLOSE.
FIRST, HAVE TO DISTRACT GOSANA.
NEVER TRIED THIS BEFORE...MAXIMUM WEIGHT, MAXIMUM DENSITY.
VERSUS THE THRUST EQUIVALENT OF FOUR JUMBO JET ENGINES.
SURE, THIS'LL END WELL!
HEY, GOLIATH!
NAME'S DAVID.
NICE TO MEET YOU.

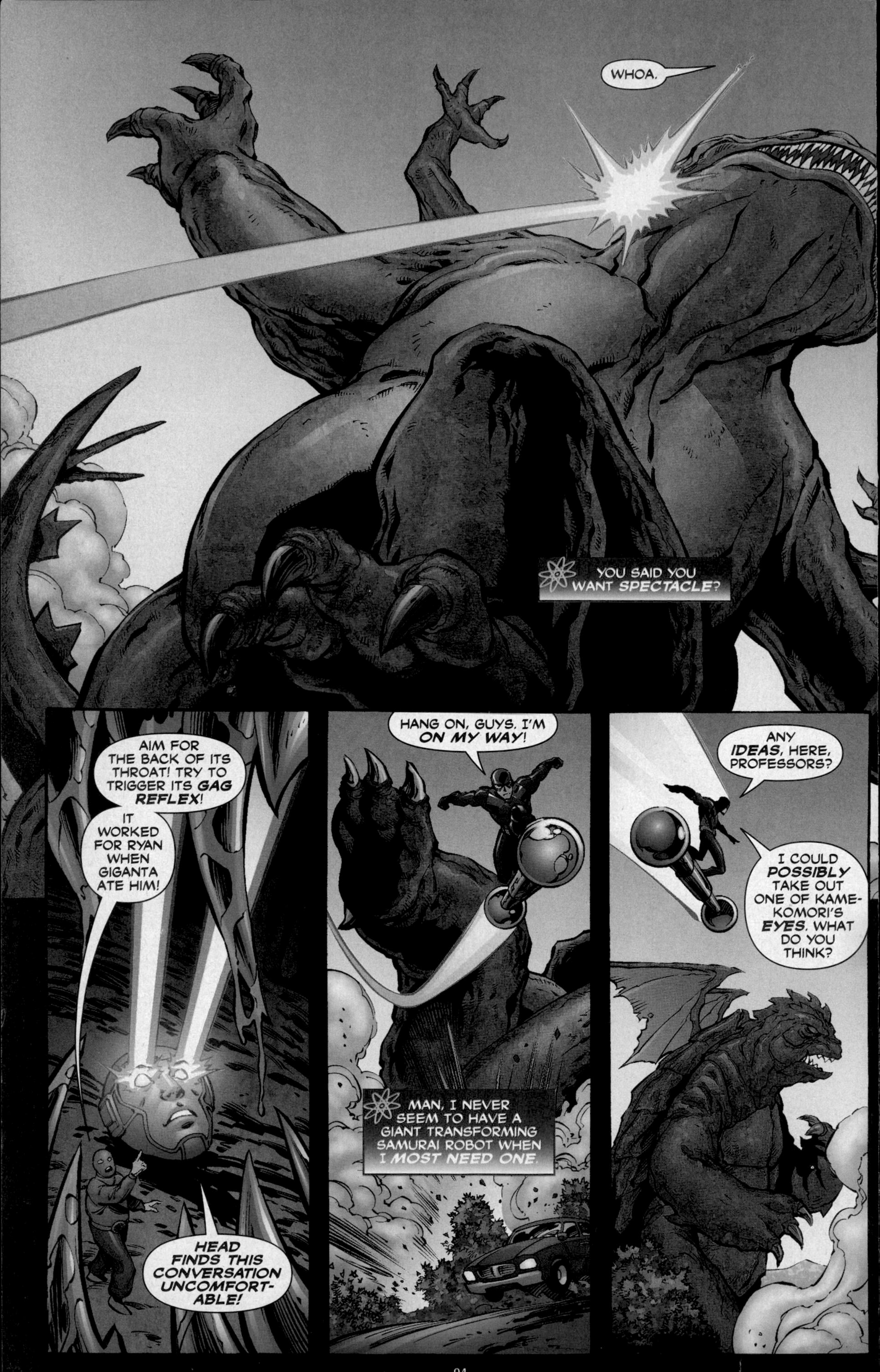
WHOA.
YOU SAID YOU WANT SPECTACLE?
AIM FOR THE BACK OF ITS THROAT! TRY TO TRIGGER ITS GAG REFLEX!
IT WORKED FOR RYAN WHEN GIGANTA ATE HIM!
HEAD FINDS THIS CONVERSATION UNCOMFORT-ABLE!
HANG ON, GUYS. I'M ON MY WAY!
MAN, I NEVER SEEM TO HAVE A GIANT TRANSFORMING SAMURAI ROBOT WHEN I MOST NEED ONE.
ANY IDEAS, HERE, PROFESSORS?
I COULD POSSIBLY TAKE OUT ONE OF KAME-KOMORI'S EYES. WHAT DO YOU THINK?

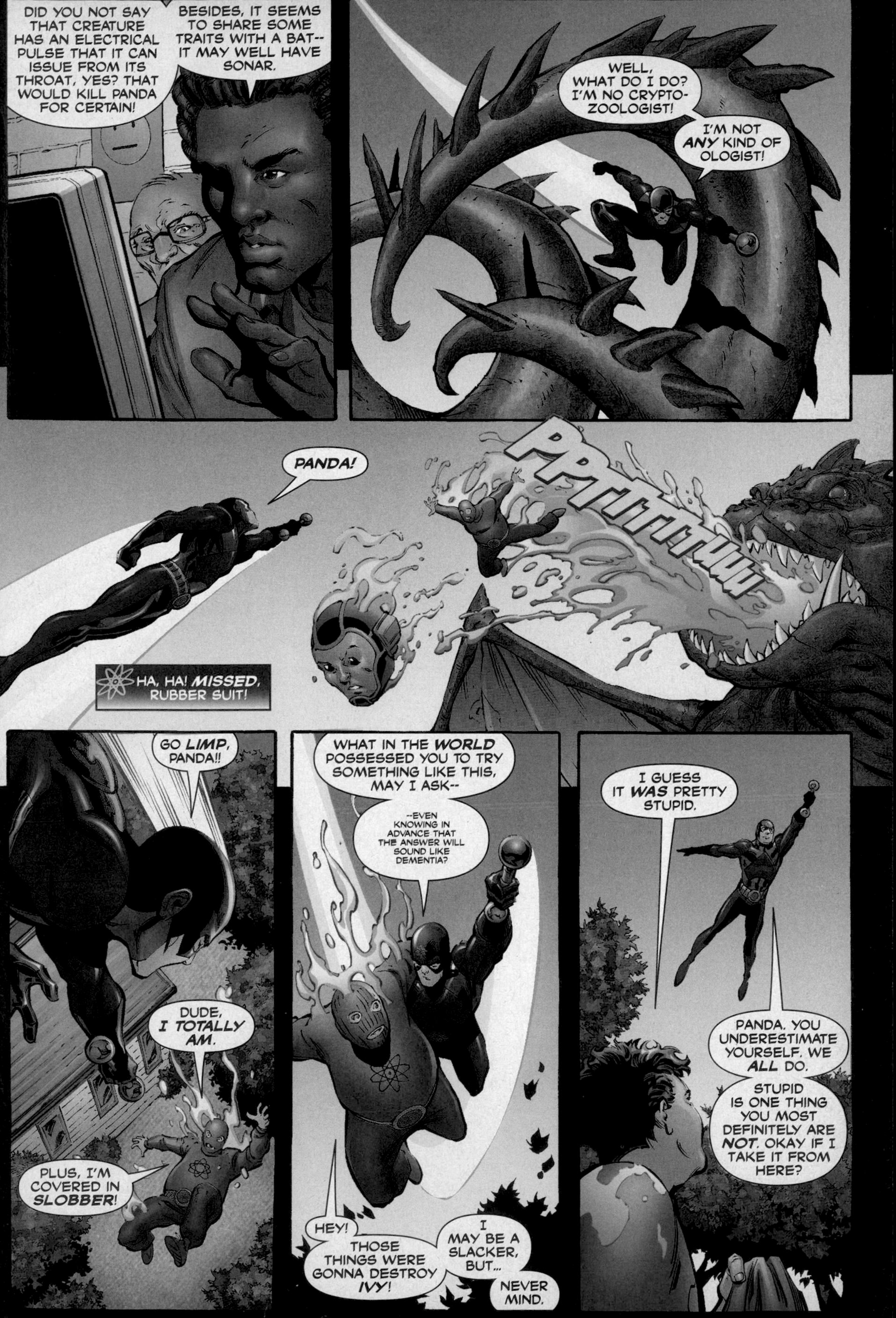
DID YOU NOT SAY THAT CREATURE HAS AN ELECTRICAL PULSE THAT IT CAN ISSUE FROM ITS THROAT, YES? THAT WOULD KILL PANDA FOR CERTAIN!
BESIDES, IT SEEMS TO SHARE SOME TRAITS WITH A BAT-- IT MAY WELL HAVE SONAR.
WELL, WHAT DO I DO? I'M NO CRYPTO-ZOOLOGIST!
I'M NOT ANY KIND OF OLOGIST!
PANDA!
PPTHTHTHTHWW
HA, HA! MISSED, RUBBER SUIT!
GO LIMP, PANDA!!
DUDE, I TOTALLY AM.
PLUS, I'M COVERED IN SLOBBER!
WHAT IN THE WORLD POSSESSED YOU TO TRY SOMETHING LIKE THIS, MAY I ASK--
--EVEN KNOWING IN ADVANCE THAT THE ANSWER WILL SOUND LIKE DEMENTIA?
HEY!
THOSE THINGS WERE GONNA DESTROY IVY!
I MAY BE A SLACKER, BUT...
NEVER MIND.
I GUESS IT WAS PRETTY STUPID.
PANDA, YOU UNDERESTIMATE YOURSELF. WE ALL DO.
STUPID IS ONE THING YOU MOST DEFINITELY ARE NOT. OKAY IF I TAKE IT FROM HERE?

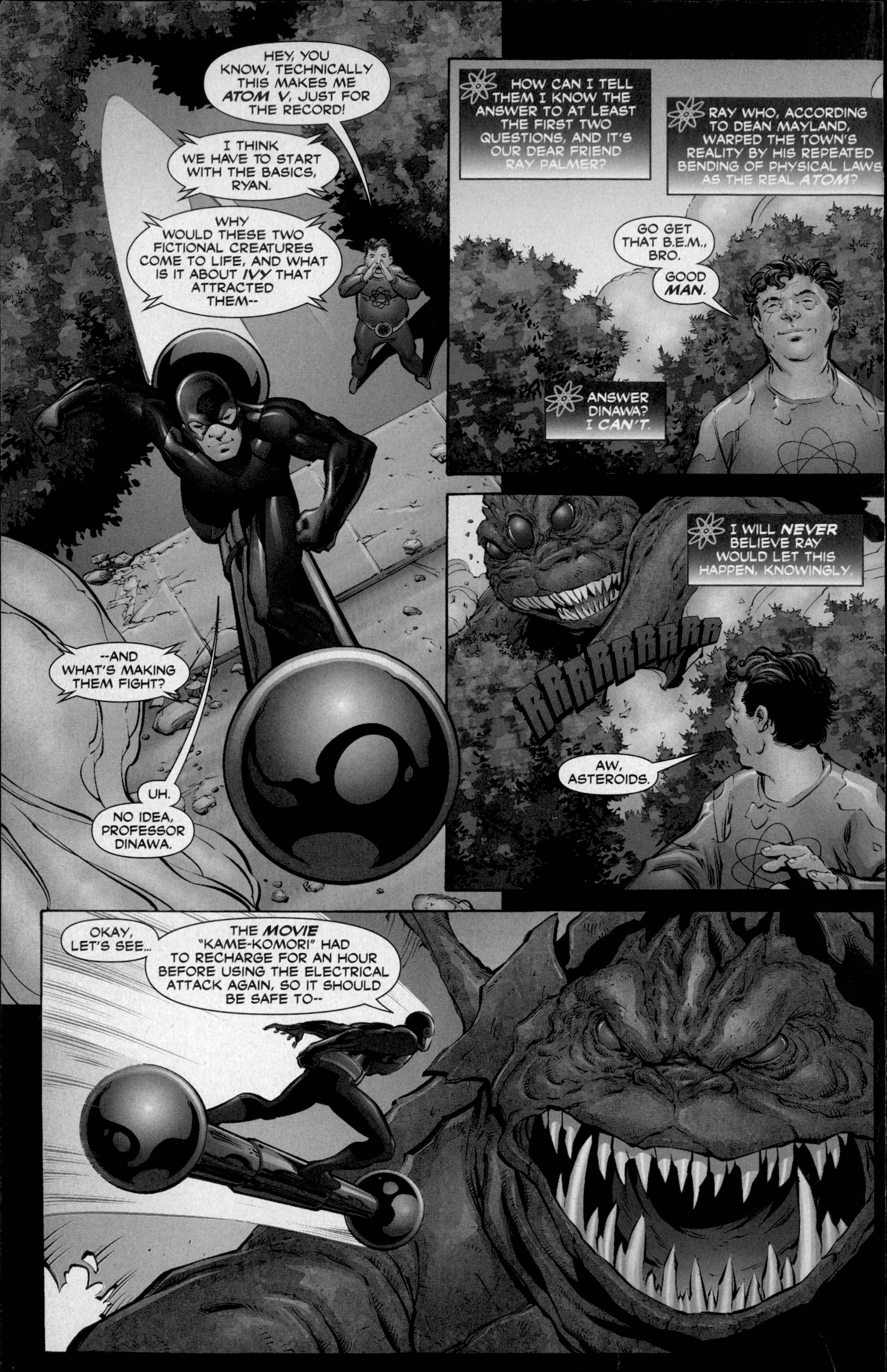
HEY, YOU KNOW, TECHNICALLY THIS MAKES ME ATOM V, JUST FOR THE RECORD!
I THINK WE HAVE TO START WITH THE BASICS, RYAN.
WHY WOULD THESE TWO FICTIONAL CREATURES COME TO LIFE, AND WHAT IS IT ABOUT IVY THAT ATTRACTED THEM--
--AND WHAT'S MAKING THEM FIGHT?
UH.
NO IDEA, PROFESSOR DINAWA.
HOW CAN I TELL THEM I KNOW THE ANSWER TO AT LEAST THE FIRST TWO QUESTIONS, AND IT'S OUR DEAR FRIEND RAY PALMER?
RAY WHO, ACCORDING TO DEAN MAYLAND, WARPED THE TOWN'S REALITY BY HIS REPEATED BENDING OF PHYSICAL LAWS AS THE REAL ATOM?
GO GET THAT B.E.M., BRO.
GOOD MAN.
ANSWER DINAWA? I CAN'T.
I WILL NEVER BELIEVE RAY WOULD LET THIS HAPPEN, KNOWINGLY.
RRRRRRRRRR
AW, ASTEROIDS.
OKAY, LET'S SEE...
THE MOVIE "KAME-KOMORI" HAD TO RECHARGE FOR AN HOUR BEFORE USING THE ELECTRICAL ATTACK AGAIN, SO IT SHOULD BE SAFE TO--

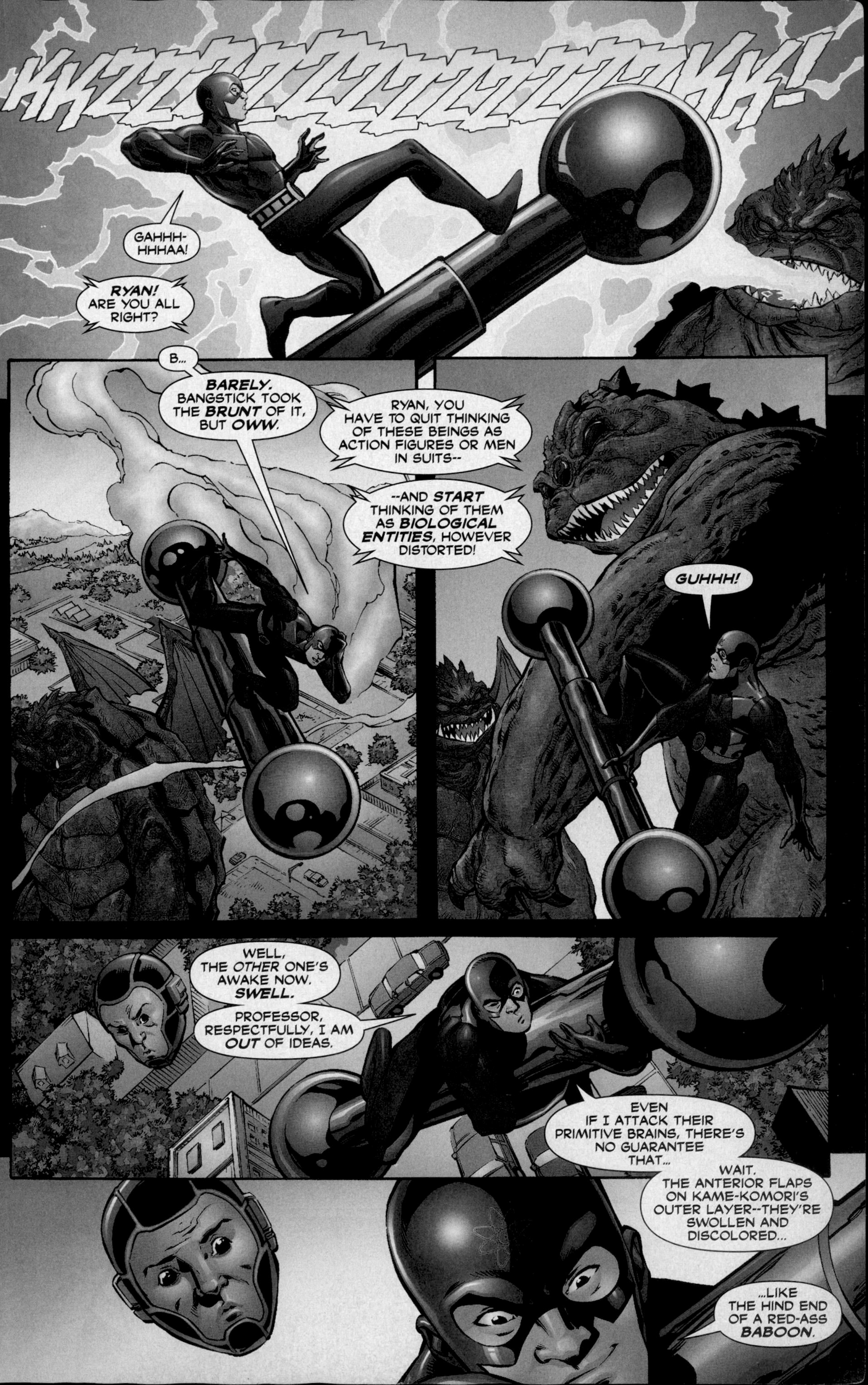
KKZZRRZZZZZZZZZZZAKK!
GAHHH-HHHAA!
RYAN! ARE YOU ALL RIGHT?
B...
BARELY. BANGSTICK TOOK THE BRUNT OF IT, BUT OWW.
RYAN, YOU HAVE TO QUIT THINKING OF THESE BEINGS AS ACTION FIGURES OR MEN IN SUITS--
--AND START THINKING OF THEM AS BIOLOGICAL ENTITIES, HOWEVER DISTORTED!
GUHHH!
WELL, THE OTHER ONE'S AWAKE NOW. SWELL.
PROFESSOR, RESPECTFULLY, I AM OUT OF IDEAS.
EVEN IF I ATTACK THEIR PRIMITIVE BRAINS, THERE'S NO GUARANTEE THAT...
WAIT. THE ANTERIOR FLAPS ON KAME-KOMORI'S OUTER LAYER--THEY'RE SWOLLEN AND DISCOLORED...
...LIKE THE HIND END OF A RED-ASS BABOON.

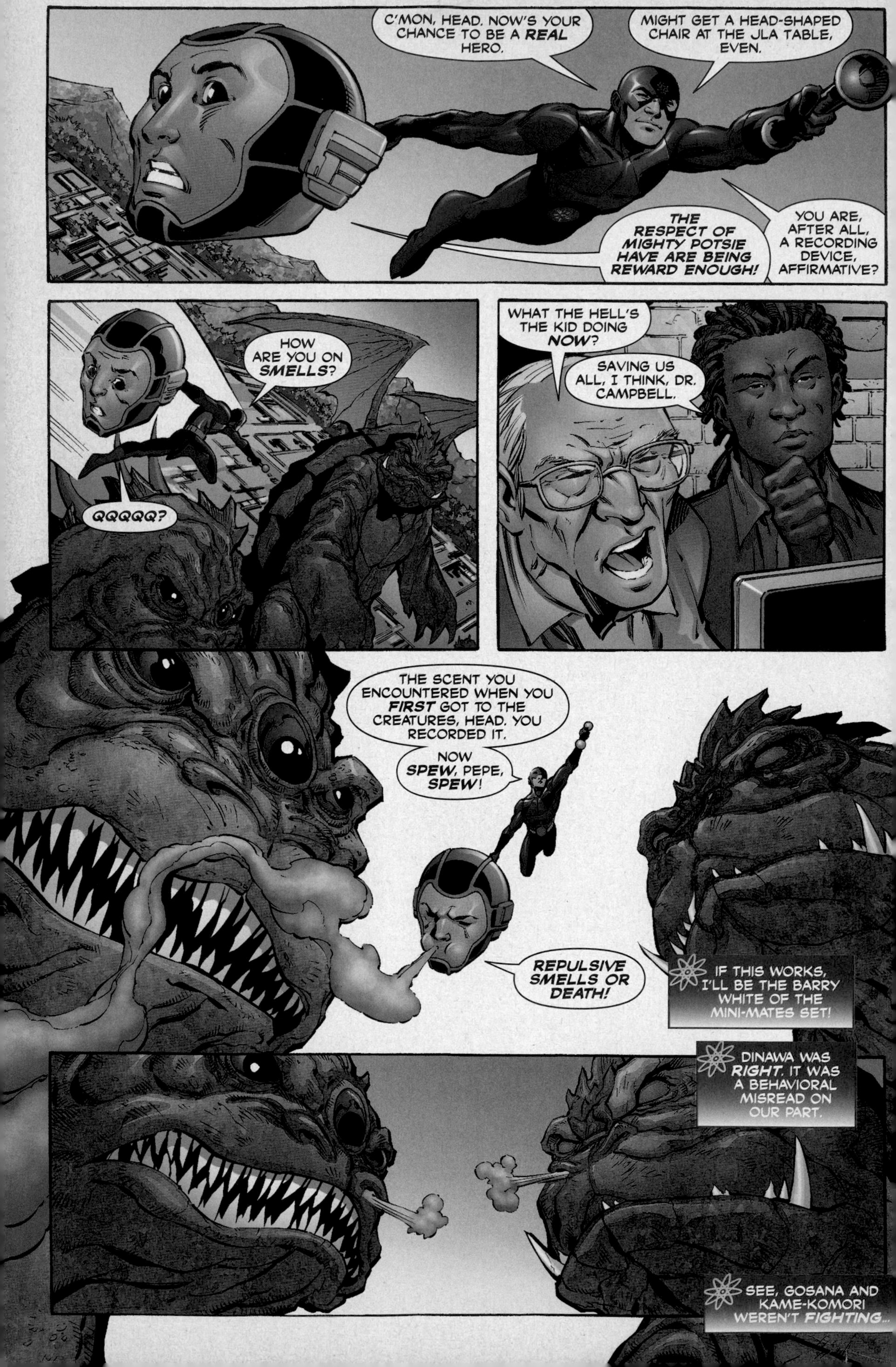
C'MON, HEAD. NOW'S YOUR CHANCE TO BE A *REAL* HERO.
MIGHT GET A HEAD-SHAPED CHAIR AT THE JLA TABLE, EVEN.
THE RESPECT OF MIGHTY POTSIE HAVE ARE BEING REWARD ENOUGH!
YOU ARE, AFTER ALL, A RECORDING DEVICE, AFFIRMATIVE?
HOW ARE YOU ON *SMELLS*?
QQQQQ?
WHAT THE HELL'S THE KID DOING *NOW*?
SAVING US ALL, I THINK, DR. CAMPBELL.
THE SCENT YOU ENCOUNTERED WHEN YOU *FIRST* GOT TO THE CREATURES, HEAD. YOU RECORDED IT.
NOW *SPEW*, PEPE, *SPEW*!
REPULSIVE SMELLS OR DEATH!
IF THIS WORKS, I'LL BE THE BARRY WHITE OF THE MINI-MATES SET!
DINAWA WAS *RIGHT*. IT WAS A BEHAVIORAL MISREAD ON OUR PART.
SEE, GOSANA AND KAME-KOMORI WEREN'T *FIGHTING*...

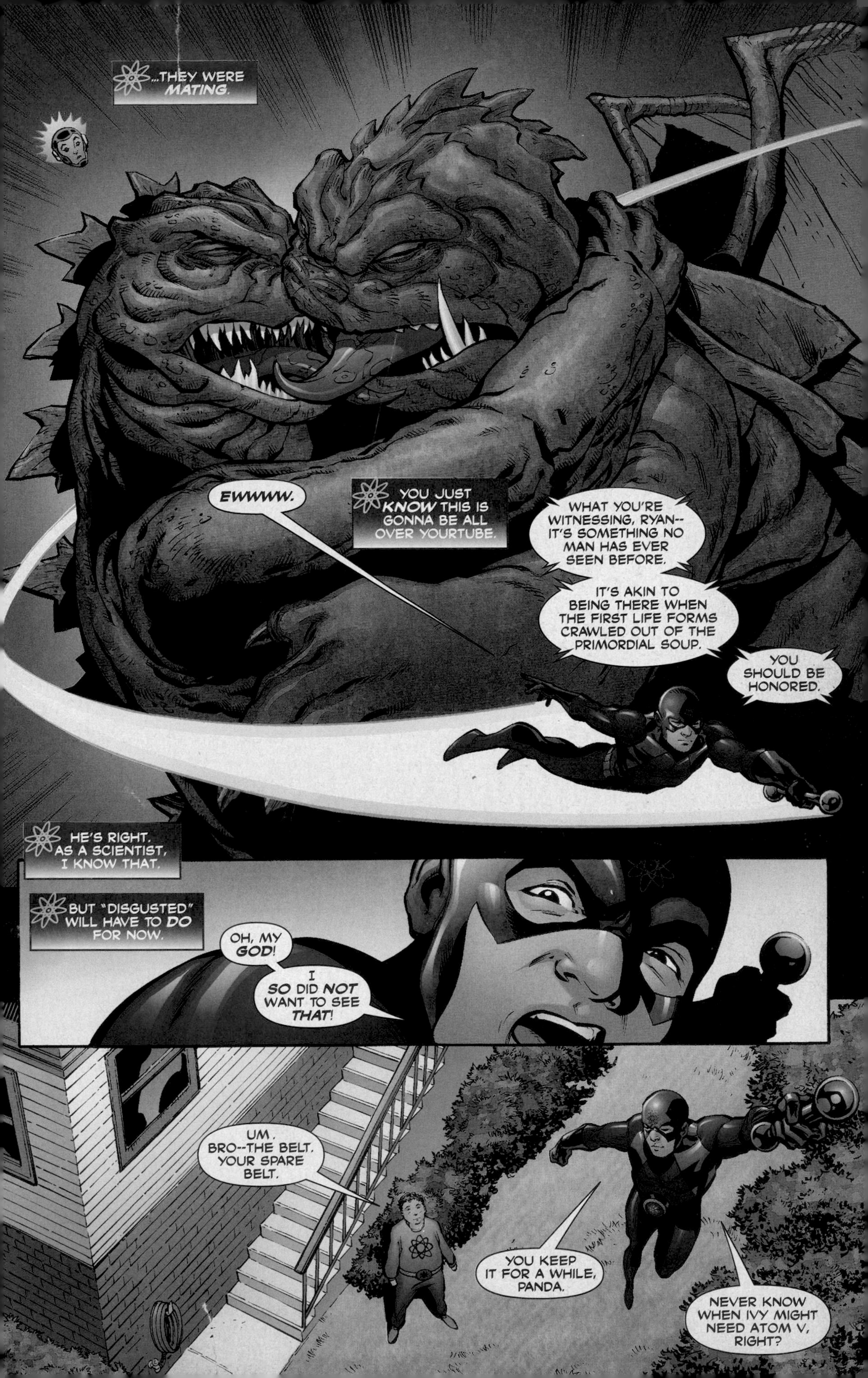
...THEY WERE MATING.
EWWWW.
YOU JUST KNOW THIS IS GONNA BE ALL OVER YOURTUBE.
WHAT YOU'RE WITNESSING, RYAN-- IT'S SOMETHING NO MAN HAS EVER SEEN BEFORE.
IT'S AKIN TO BEING THERE WHEN THE FIRST LIFE FORMS CRAWLED OUT OF THE PRIMORDIAL SOUP.
YOU SHOULD BE HONORED.
HE'S RIGHT. AS A SCIENTIST, I KNOW THAT.
BUT "DISGUSTED" WILL HAVE TO DO FOR NOW.
OH, MY GOD!
I SO DID NOT WANT TO SEE THAT!
UM, BRO--THE BELT. YOUR SPARE BELT.
YOU KEEP IT FOR A WHILE, PANDA.
NEVER KNOW WHEN IVY MIGHT NEED ATOM V, RIGHT?

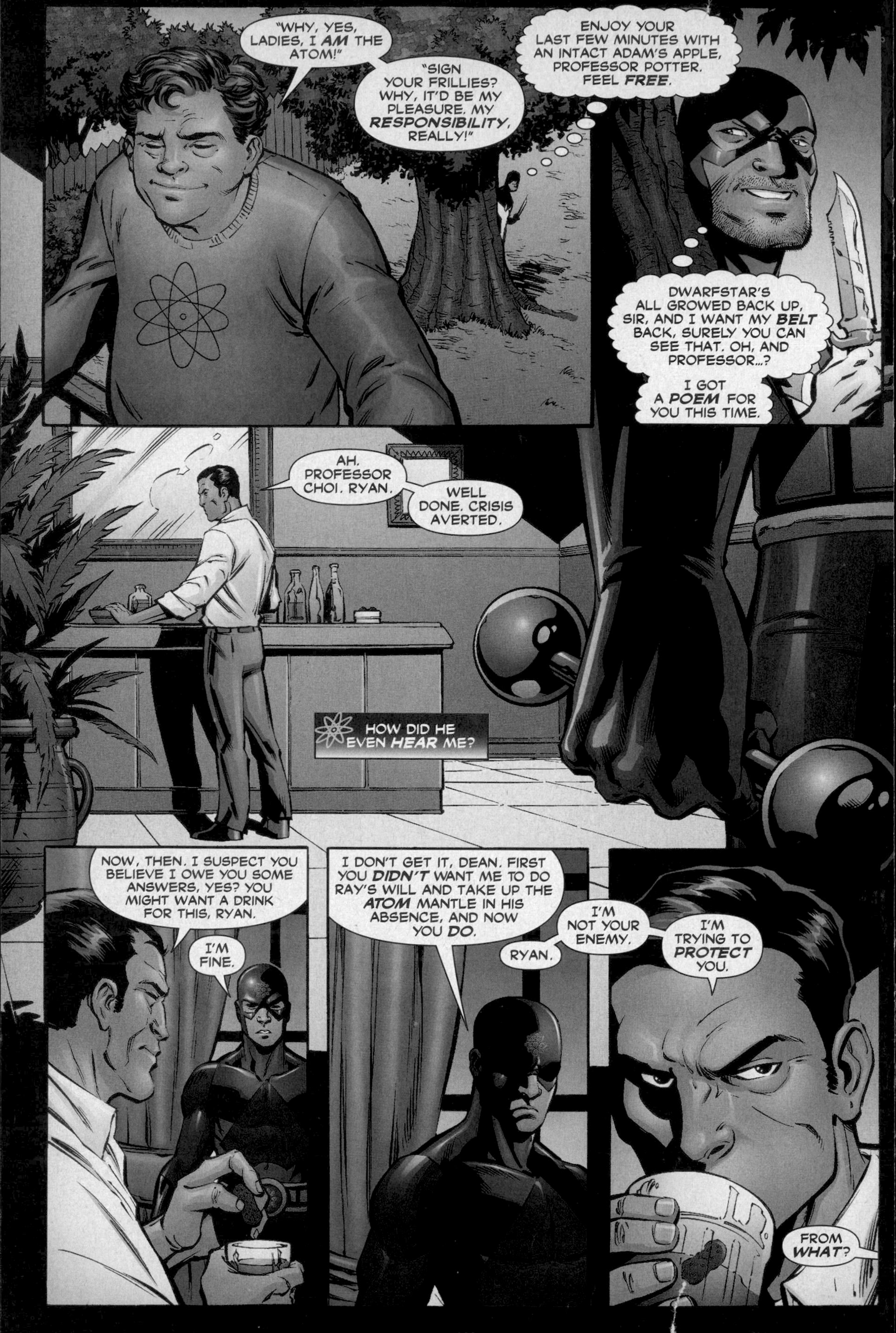
"WHY, YES, LADIES, I AM THE ATOM!"
"SIGN YOUR FRILLIES? WHY, IT'D BE MY PLEASURE, MY RESPONSIBILITY, REALLY!"
ENJOY YOUR LAST FEW MINUTES WITH AN INTACT ADAM'S APPLE, PROFESSOR POTTER. FEEL FREE.
DWARFSTAR'S ALL GROWED BACK UP, SIR, AND I WANT MY BELT BACK, SURELY YOU CAN SEE THAT. OH, AND PROFESSOR...?
I GOT A POEM FOR YOU THIS TIME.
AH. PROFESSOR CHOI. RYAN.
WELL DONE. CRISIS AVERTED.
HOW DID HE EVEN HEAR ME?
NOW, THEN. I SUSPECT YOU BELIEVE I OWE YOU SOME ANSWERS, YES? YOU MIGHT WANT A DRINK FOR THIS, RYAN.
I'M FINE.
I DON'T GET IT, DEAN. FIRST YOU DIDN'T WANT ME TO DO RAY'S WILL AND TAKE UP THE ATOM MANTLE IN HIS ABSENCE, AND NOW YOU DO.
RYAN.
I'M NOT YOUR ENEMY.
I'M TRYING TO PROTECT YOU.
FROM WHAT?

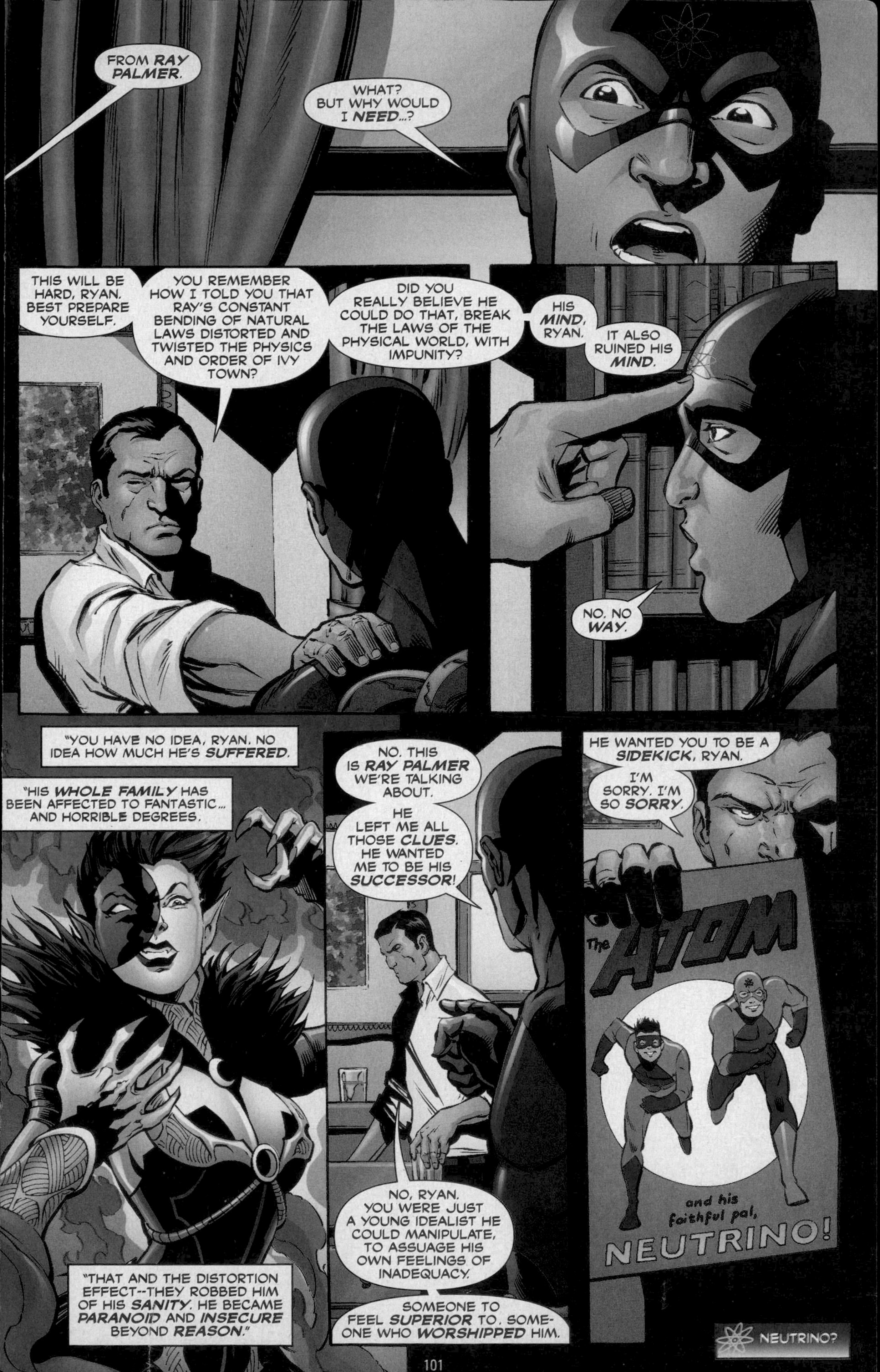
FROM RAY PALMER.
WHAT? BUT WHY WOULD I NEED...?
THIS WILL BE HARD, RYAN. BEST PREPARE YOURSELF.
YOU REMEMBER HOW I TOLD YOU THAT RAY'S CONSTANT BENDING OF NATURAL LAWS DISTORTED AND TWISTED THE PHYSICS AND ORDER OF IVY TOWN?
DID YOU REALLY BELIEVE HE COULD DO THAT, BREAK THE LAWS OF THE PHYSICAL WORLD, WITH IMPUNITY?
HIS MIND, RYAN.
IT ALSO RUINED HIS MIND.
NO. NO WAY.
"YOU HAVE NO IDEA, RYAN. NO IDEA HOW MUCH HE'S SUFFERED.
"HIS WHOLE FAMILY HAS BEEN AFFECTED TO FANTASTIC... AND HORRIBLE DEGREES.
"THAT AND THE DISTORTION EFFECT--THEY ROBBED HIM OF HIS SANITY. HE BECAME PARANOID AND INSECURE BEYOND REASON."
NO. THIS IS RAY PALMER WE'RE TALKING ABOUT.
HE LEFT ME ALL THOSE CLUES. HE WANTED ME TO BE HIS SUCCESSOR!
NO, RYAN. YOU WERE JUST A YOUNG IDEALIST HE COULD MANIPULATE, TO ASSUAGE HIS OWN FEELINGS OF INADEQUACY.
SOMEONE TO FEEL SUPERIOR TO. SOME-ONE WHO WORSHIPPED HIM.
HE WANTED YOU TO BE A SIDEKICK, RYAN.
I'M SORRY. I'M SO SORRY.
The ATOM
and his faithful pal,
NEUTRINO!
NEUTRINO?

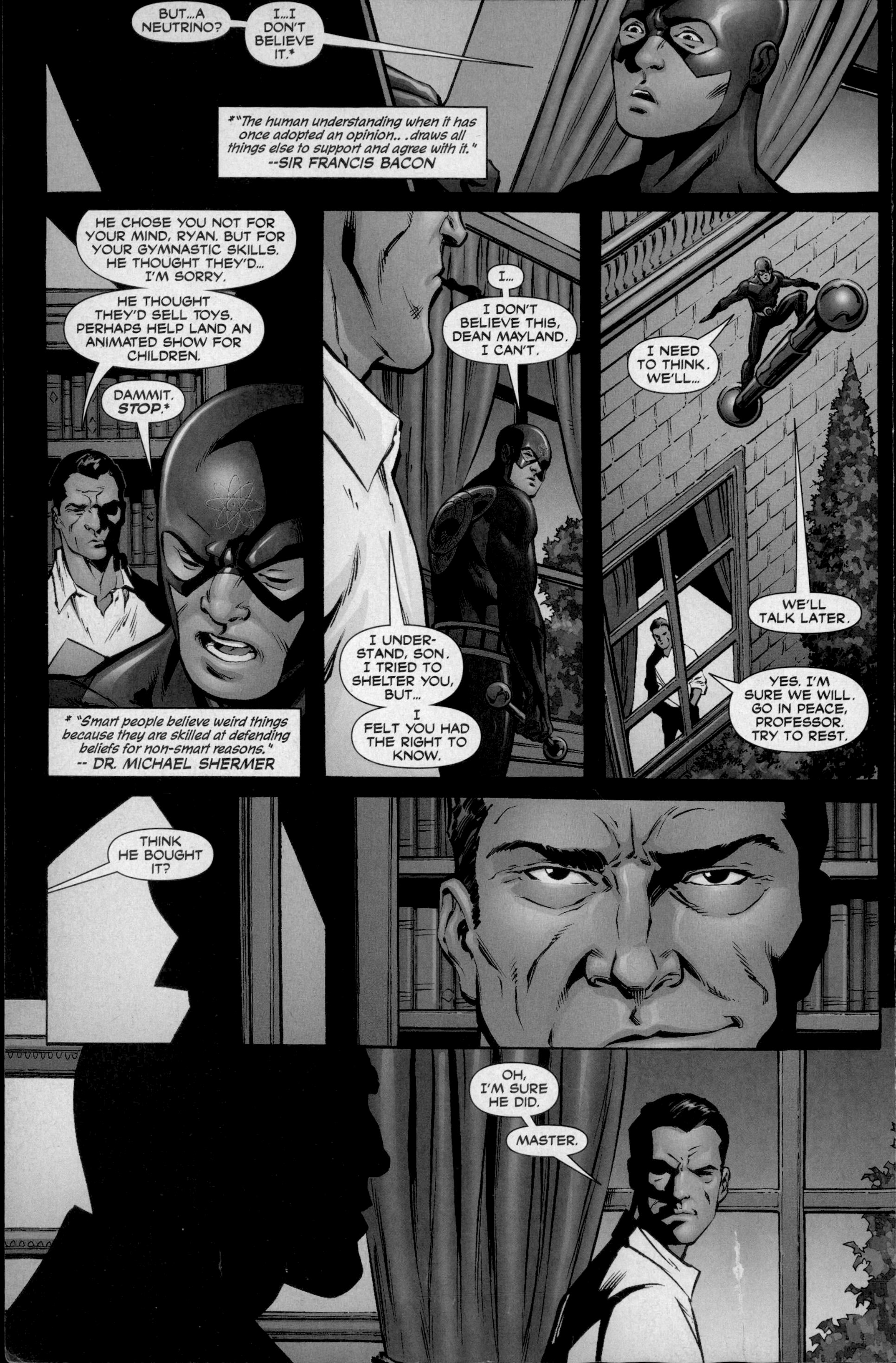

BUT...A NEUTRINO?
I...I DON'T BELIEVE IT.*
*"The human understanding when it has once adopted an opinion.. .draws all things else to support and agree with it." --SIR FRANCIS BACON
HE CHOSE YOU NOT FOR YOUR MIND, RYAN. BUT FOR YOUR GYMNASTIC SKILLS. HE THOUGHT THEY'D... I'M SORRY.
HE THOUGHT THEY'D SELL TOYS. PERHAPS HELP LAND AN ANIMATED SHOW FOR CHILDREN.
DAMMIT. STOP.*
* "Smart people believe weird things because they are skilled at defending beliefs for non-smart reasons." -- DR. MICHAEL SHERMER
I...
I DON'T BELIEVE THIS, DEAN MAYLAND. I CAN'T.
I UNDER-STAND, SON. I TRIED TO SHELTER YOU, BUT...
I FELT YOU HAD THE RIGHT TO KNOW.
I NEED TO THINK. WE'LL...
WE'LL TALK LATER.
YES. I'M SURE WE WILL. GO IN PEACE, PROFESSOR. TRY TO REST.
THINK HE BOUGHT IT?
OH, I'M SURE HE DID.
MASTER.

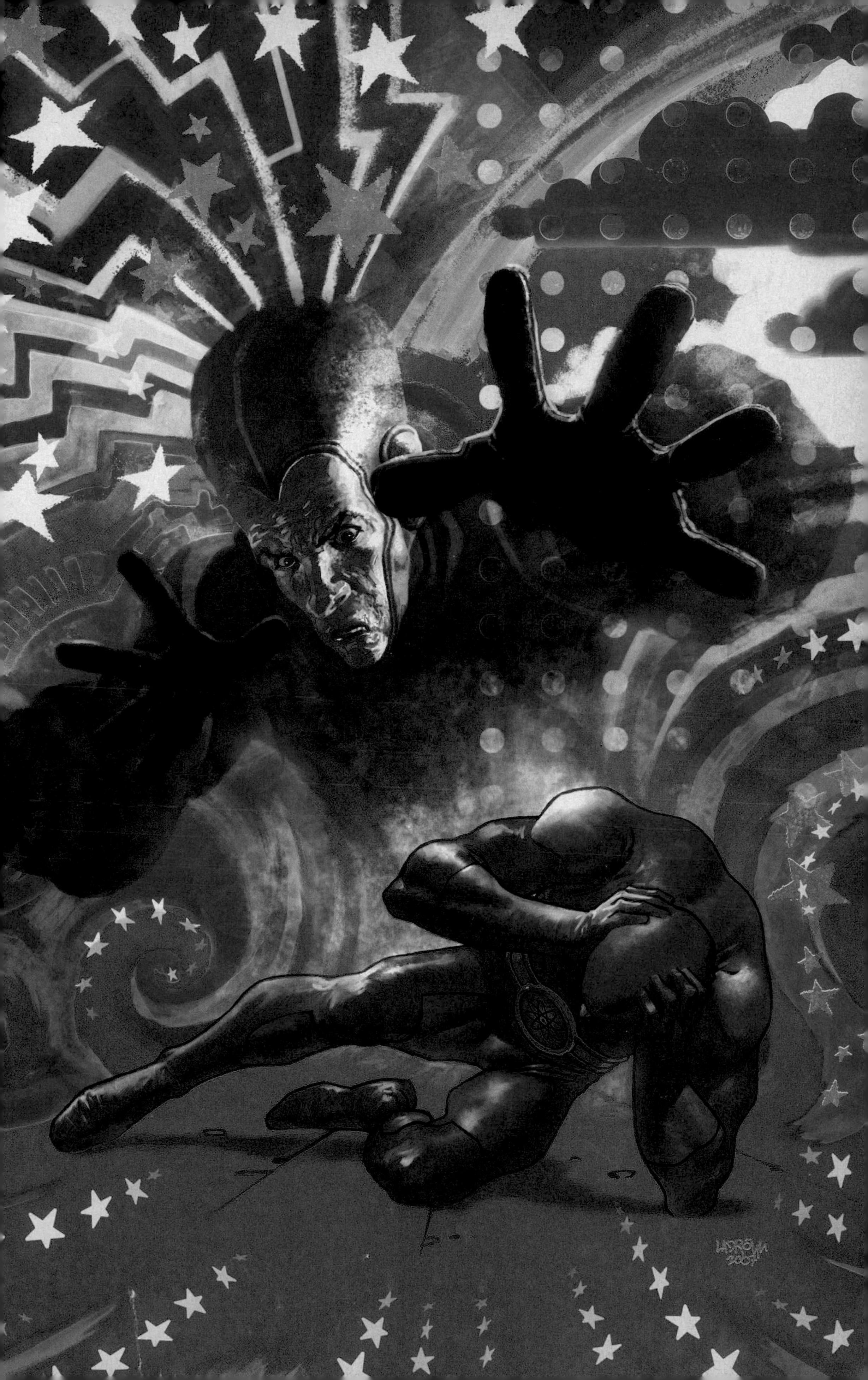

FORWARD! INTO THE PAST!

from **THE ALL NEW ATOM #16**

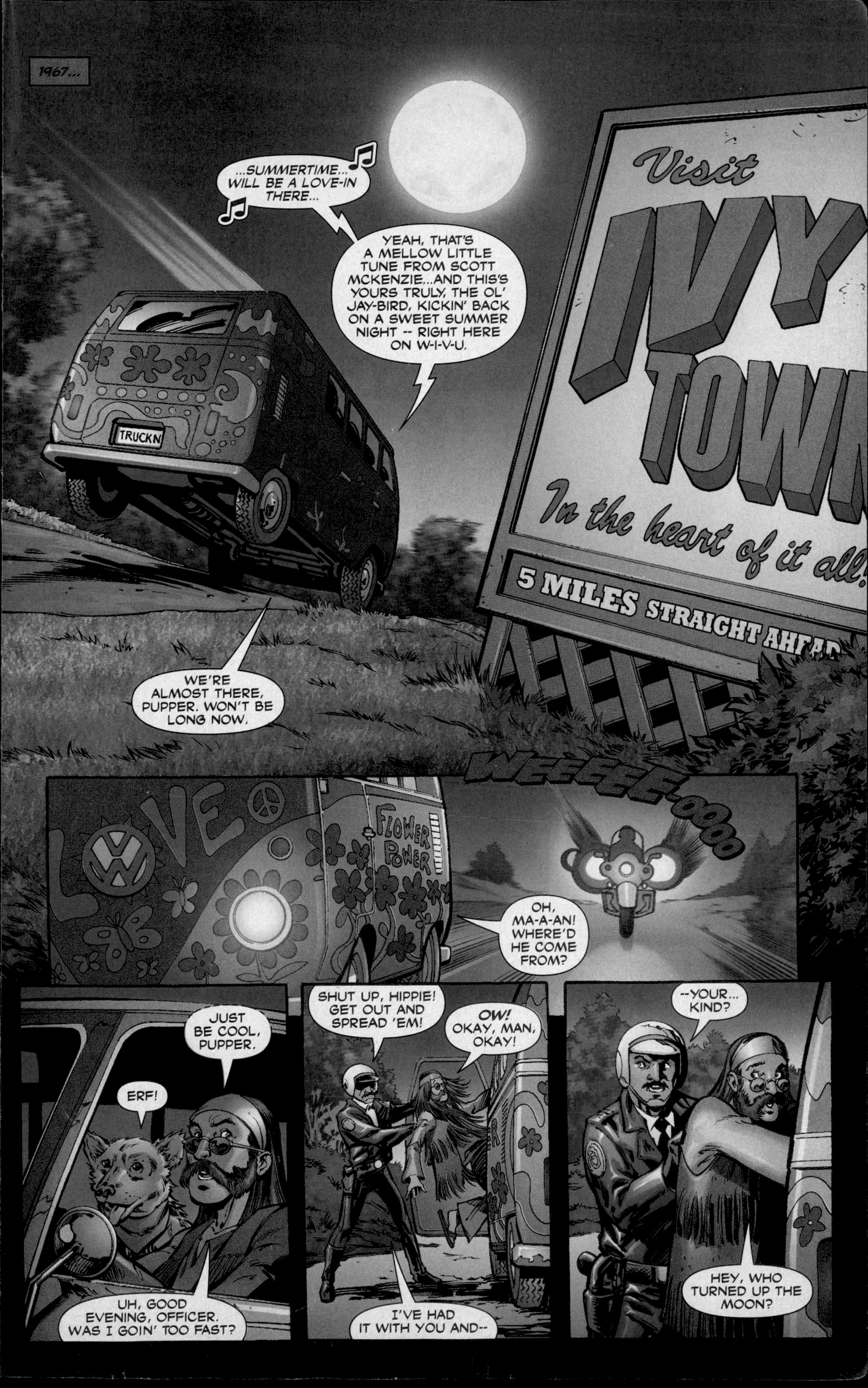
1967...
...SUMMERTIME... WILL BE A LOVE-IN THERE...
YEAH, THAT'S A MELLOW LITTLE TUNE FROM SCOTT MCKENZIE...AND THIS'S YOURS TRULY, THE OL' JAY-BIRD, KICKIN' BACK ON A SWEET SUMMER NIGHT -- RIGHT HERE ON W-I-V-U.
TRUCKN
Visit IVY TOWN In the heart of it all!
5 MILES STRAIGHT AHEAD
WE'RE ALMOST THERE, PUPPER. WON'T BE LONG NOW.
WEEEEE-OOOO
LOVE
FLOWER POWER
OH, MA-A-AN! WHERE'D HE COME FROM?
JUST BE COOL, PUPPER.
ERF!
UH, GOOD EVENING, OFFICER. WAS I GOIN' TOO FAST?
SHUT UP, HIPPIE! GET OUT AND SPREAD 'EM!
OW! OKAY, MAN, OKAY!
I'VE HAD IT WITH YOU AND--
--YOUR... KIND?
HEY, WHO TURNED UP THE MOON?

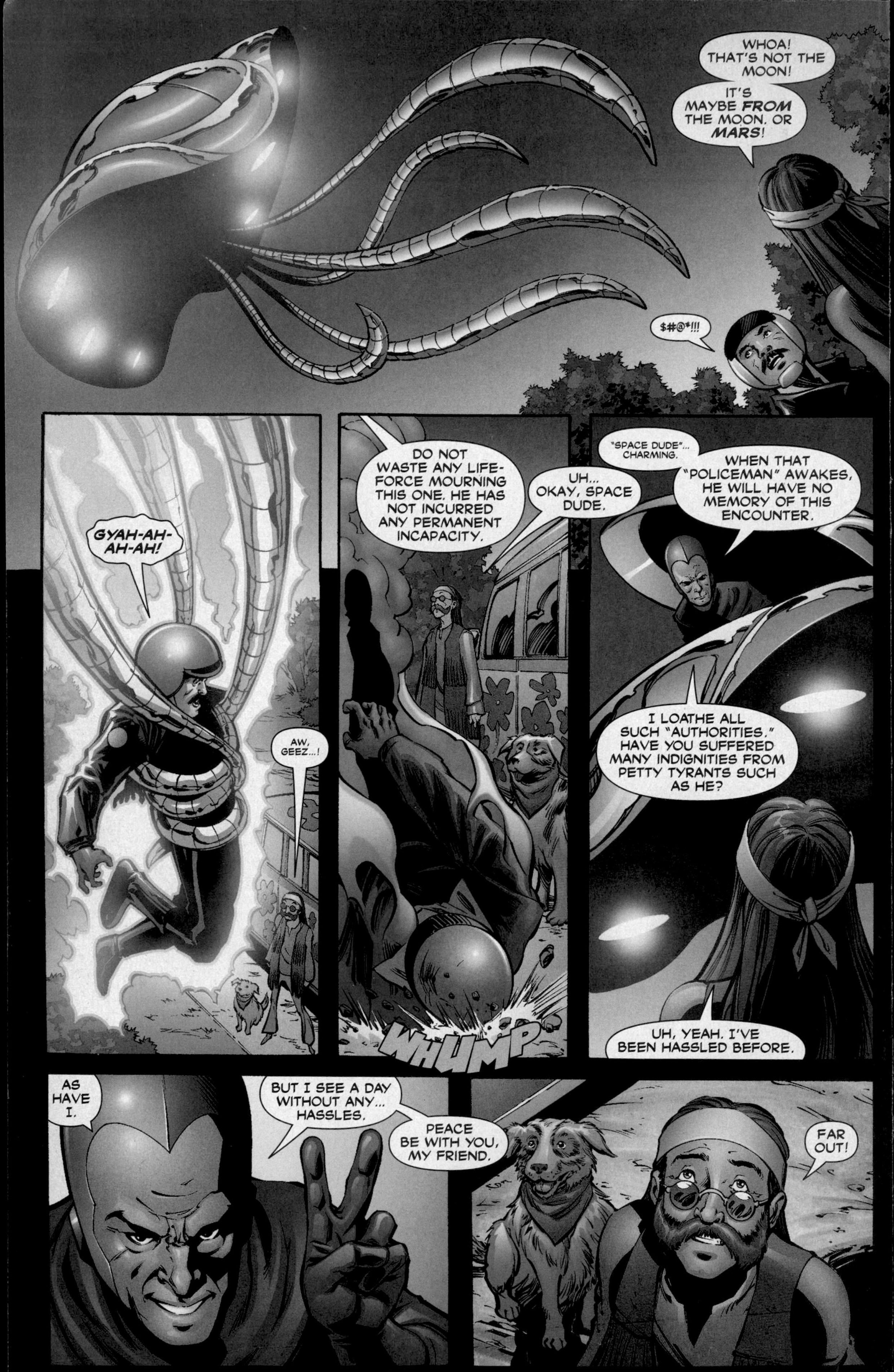
WHOA! THAT'S NOT THE MOON!
IT'S MAYBE FROM THE MOON. OR MARS!
$#@*!!!
GYAH-AH-AH-AH!
AW, GEEZ...!
DO NOT WASTE ANY LIFE-FORCE MOURNING THIS ONE. HE HAS NOT INCURRED ANY PERMANENT INCAPACITY.
UH... OKAY, SPACE DUDE.
WHUMP
"SPACE DUDE"... CHARMING.
WHEN THAT "POLICEMAN" AWAKES, HE WILL HAVE NO MEMORY OF THIS ENCOUNTER.
I LOATHE ALL SUCH "AUTHORITIES." HAVE YOU SUFFERED MANY INDIGNITIES FROM PETTY TYRANTS SUCH AS HE?
UH, YEAH. I'VE BEEN HASSLED BEFORE.
AS HAVE I.
BUT I SEE A DAY WITHOUT ANY... HASSLES.
PEACE BE WITH YOU, MY FRIEND.
FAR OUT!

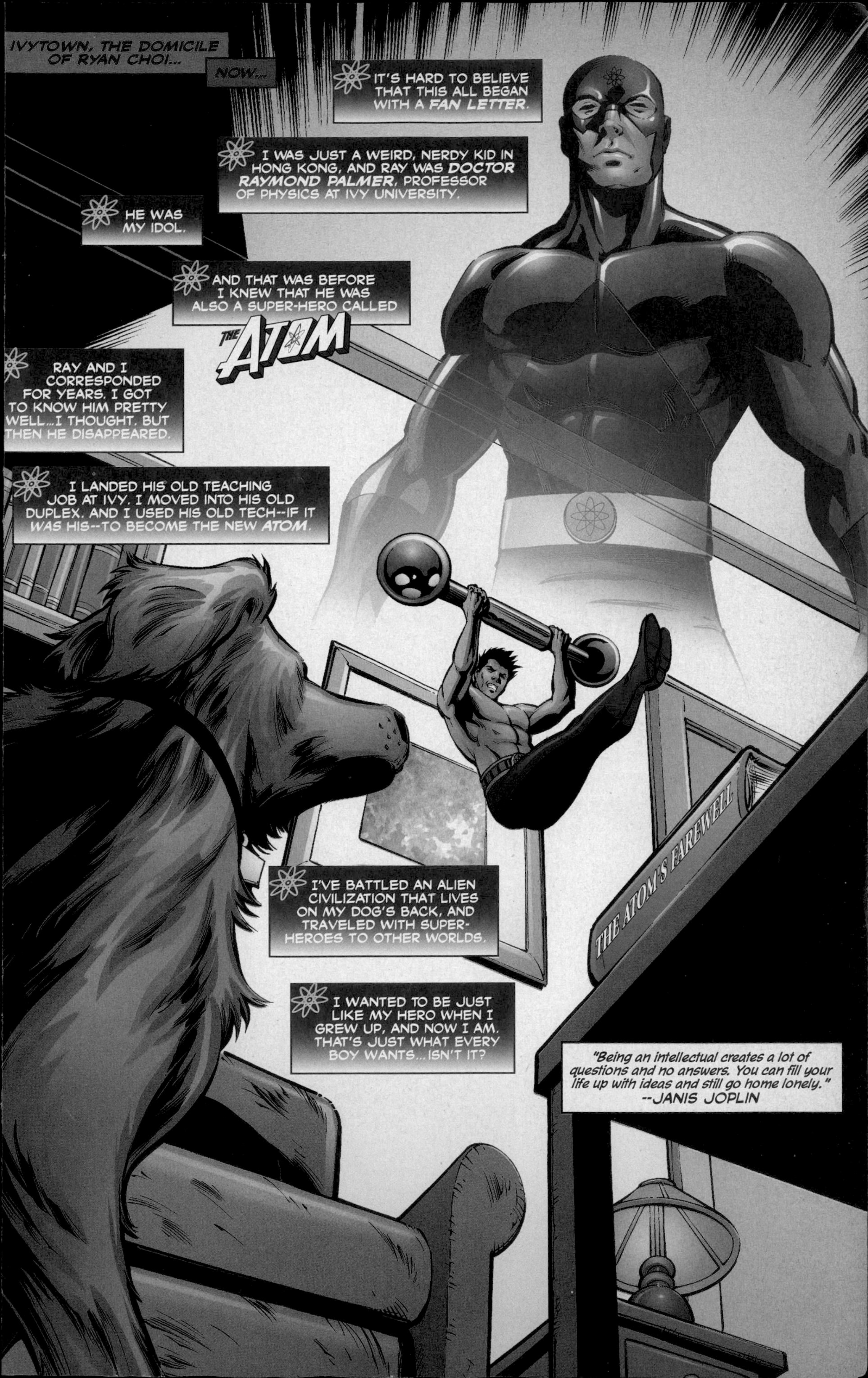
IVYTOWN, THE DOMICILE OF RYAN CHOI...
NOW...
IT'S HARD TO BELIEVE THAT THIS ALL BEGAN WITH A FAN LETTER.
I WAS JUST A WEIRD, NERDY KID IN HONG KONG, AND RAY WAS DOCTOR RAYMOND PALMER, PROFESSOR OF PHYSICS AT IVY UNIVERSITY.
HE WAS MY IDOL.
AND THAT WAS BEFORE I KNEW THAT HE WAS ALSO A SUPER-HERO CALLED
THE ATOM
RAY AND I CORRESPONDED FOR YEARS. I GOT TO KNOW HIM PRETTY WELL...I THOUGHT. BUT THEN HE DISAPPEARED.
I LANDED HIS OLD TEACHING JOB AT IVY. I MOVED INTO HIS OLD DUPLEX. AND I USED HIS OLD TECH--IF IT WAS HIS--TO BECOME THE NEW ATOM.
I'VE BATTLED AN ALIEN CIVILIZATION THAT LIVES ON MY DOG'S BACK, AND TRAVELED WITH SUPER-HEROES TO OTHER WORLDS.
THE ATOM'S FAREWELL
I WANTED TO BE JUST LIKE MY HERO WHEN I GREW UP, AND NOW I AM. THAT'S JUST WHAT EVERY BOY WANTS...ISN'T IT?
"Being an intellectual creates a lot of questions and no answers. You can fill your life up with ideas and still go home lonely."
--JANIS JOPLIN

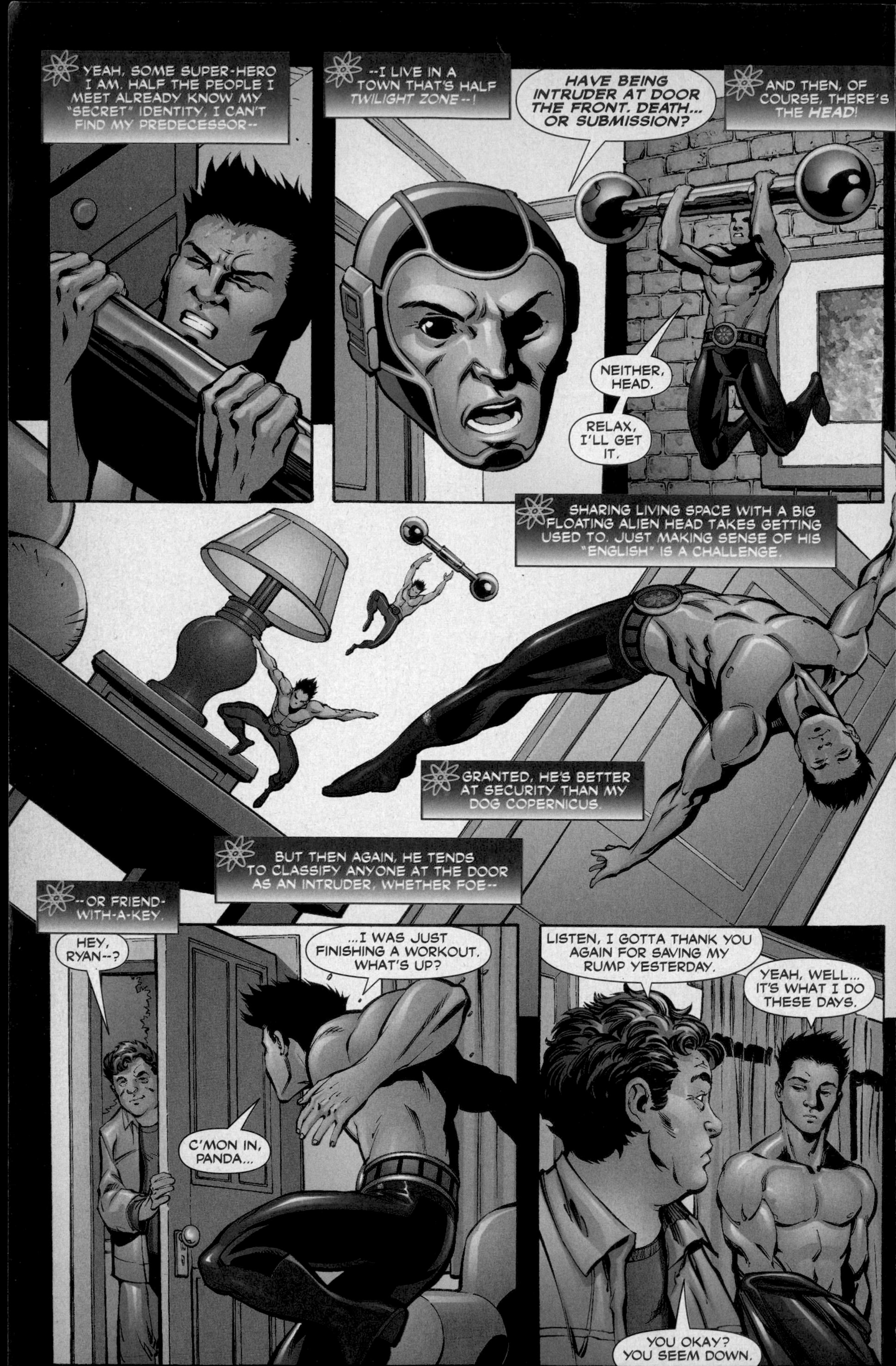
YEAH, SOME SUPER-HERO I AM. HALF THE PEOPLE I MEET ALREADY KNOW MY "SECRET" IDENTITY, I CAN'T FIND MY PREDECESSOR--
--I LIVE IN A TOWN THAT'S HALF TWILIGHT ZONE--!
HAVE BEING INTRUDER AT DOOR THE FRONT. DEATH... OR SUBMISSION?
AND THEN, OF COURSE, THERE'S THE HEAD!
NEITHER, HEAD.
RELAX, I'LL GET IT.
SHARING LIVING SPACE WITH A BIG FLOATING ALIEN HEAD TAKES GETTING USED TO. JUST MAKING SENSE OF HIS "ENGLISH" IS A CHALLENGE.
GRANTED, HE'S BETTER AT SECURITY THAN MY DOG COPERNICUS.
BUT THEN AGAIN, HE TENDS TO CLASSIFY ANYONE AT THE DOOR AS AN INTRUDER, WHETHER FOE--
--OR FRIEND-WITH-A-KEY.
HEY, RYAN--?
...I WAS JUST FINISHING A WORKOUT. WHAT'S UP?
C'MON IN, PANDA...
LISTEN, I GOTTA THANK YOU AGAIN FOR SAVING MY RUMP YESTERDAY.
YEAH, WELL... IT'S WHAT I DO THESE DAYS.
YOU OKAY? YOU SEEM DOWN.

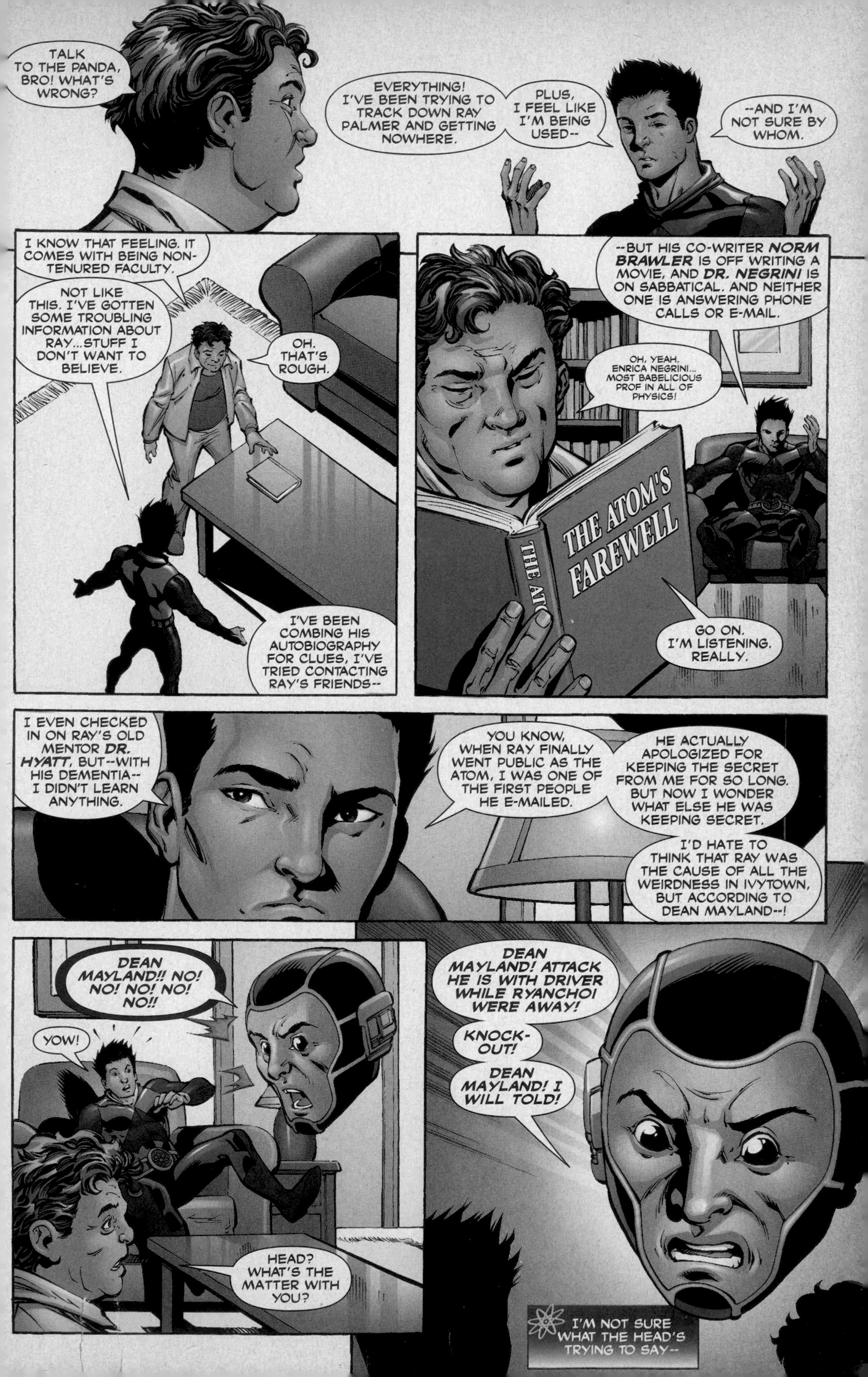

TALK TO THE PANDA, BRO! WHAT'S WRONG?
EVERYTHING! I'VE BEEN TRYING TO TRACK DOWN RAY PALMER AND GETTING NOWHERE.
PLUS, I FEEL LIKE I'M BEING USED--
--AND I'M NOT SURE BY WHOM.
I KNOW THAT FEELING. IT COMES WITH BEING NON-TENURED FACULTY.
NOT LIKE THIS. I'VE GOTTEN SOME TROUBLING INFORMATION ABOUT RAY...STUFF I DON'T WANT TO BELIEVE.
OH. THAT'S ROUGH.
I'VE BEEN COMBING HIS AUTOBIOGRAPHY FOR CLUES, I'VE TRIED CONTACTING RAY'S FRIENDS--
--BUT HIS CO-WRITER NORM BRAWLER IS OFF WRITING A MOVIE, AND DR. NEGRINI IS ON SABBATICAL. AND NEITHER ONE IS ANSWERING PHONE CALLS OR E-MAIL.
OH, YEAH. ENRICA NEGRINI... MOST BABELICIOUS PROF IN ALL OF PHYSICS!
THE ATOM'S FAREWELL
THE ATO
GO ON. I'M LISTENING. REALLY.
I EVEN CHECKED IN ON RAY'S OLD MENTOR DR. HYATT, BUT--WITH HIS DEMENTIA--I DIDN'T LEARN ANYTHING.
YOU KNOW, WHEN RAY FINALLY WENT PUBLIC AS THE ATOM, I WAS ONE OF THE FIRST PEOPLE HE E-MAILED.
HE ACTUALLY APOLOGIZED FOR KEEPING THE SECRET FROM ME FOR SO LONG. BUT NOW I WONDER WHAT ELSE HE WAS KEEPING SECRET.
I'D HATE TO THINK THAT RAY WAS THE CAUSE OF ALL THE WEIRDNESS IN IVYTOWN, BUT ACCORDING TO DEAN MAYLAND--!
DEAN MAYLAND!! NO! NO! NO! NO! NO!!
YOW!
HEAD? WHAT'S THE MATTER WITH YOU?
DEAN MAYLAND! ATTACK HE IS WITH DRIVER WHILE RYANCHOI WERE AWAY!
KNOCK-OUT!
DEAN MAYLAND! I WILL TOLD!
I'M NOT SURE WHAT THE HEAD'S TRYING TO SAY--

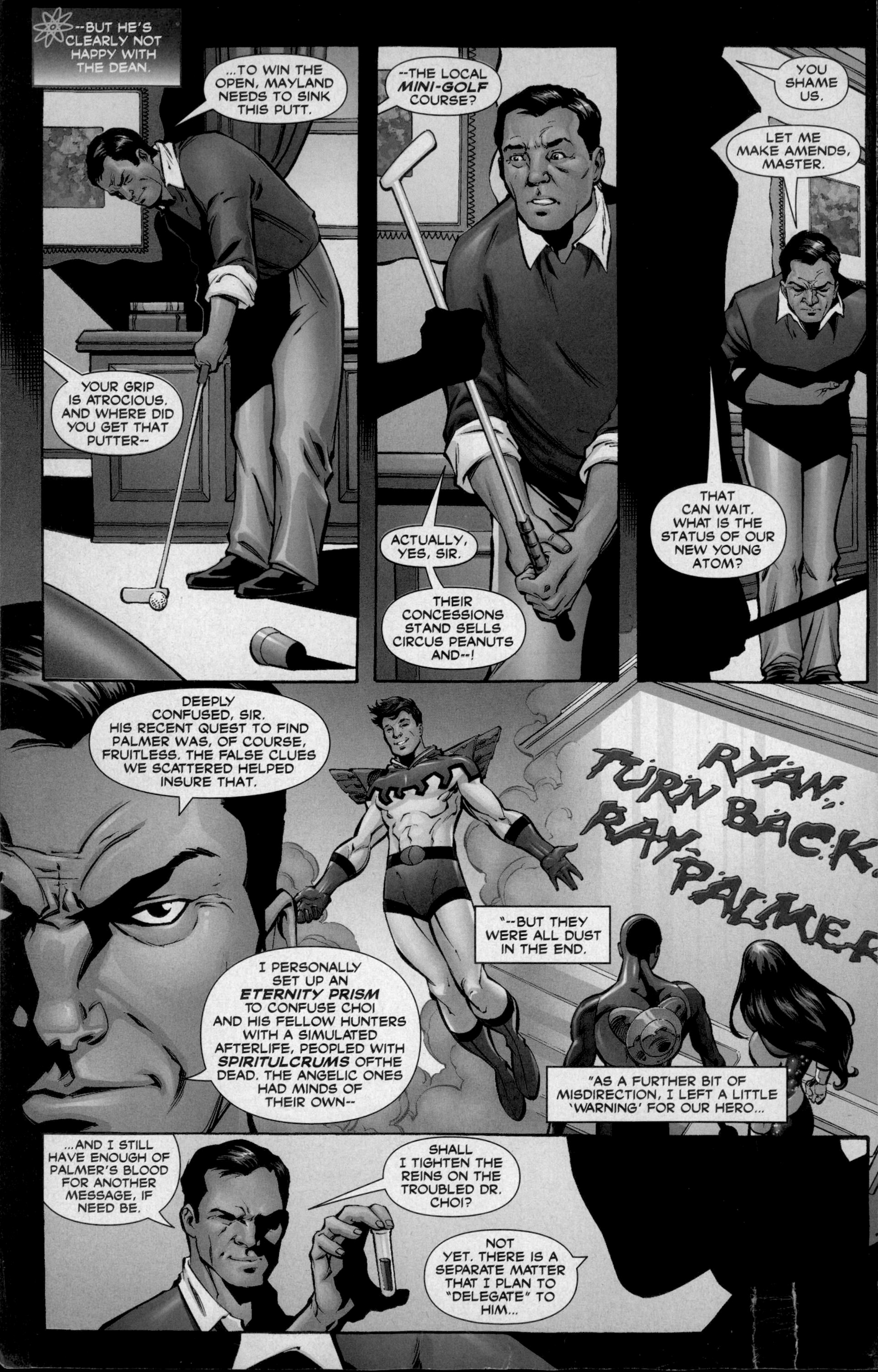
--BUT HE'S CLEARLY NOT HAPPY WITH THE DEAN.
...TO WIN THE OPEN, MAYLAND NEEDS TO SINK THIS PUTT.
YOUR GRIP IS ATROCIOUS. AND WHERE DID YOU GET THAT PUTTER--
--THE LOCAL MINI-GOLF COURSE?
ACTUALLY, YES, SIR.
THEIR CONCESSIONS STAND SELLS CIRCUS PEANUTS AND--!
YOU SHAME US.
LET ME MAKE AMENDS, MASTER.
THAT CAN WAIT. WHAT IS THE STATUS OF OUR NEW YOUNG ATOM?
DEEPLY CONFUSED, SIR. HIS RECENT QUEST TO FIND PALMER WAS, OF COURSE, FRUITLESS. THE FALSE CLUES WE SCATTERED HELPED INSURE THAT.
I PERSONALLY SET UP AN ETERNITY PRISM TO CONFUSE CHOI AND HIS FELLOW HUNTERS WITH A SIMULATED AFTERLIFE, PEOPLED WITH SPIRITULCRUMS OFTHE DEAD. THE ANGELIC ONES HAD MINDS OF THEIR OWN--
"--BUT THEY WERE ALL DUST IN THE END.
RYAN. TURN BACK. RAY PALMER
"AS A FURTHER BIT OF MISDIRECTION, I LEFT A LITTLE 'WARNING' FOR OUR HERO...
...AND I STILL HAVE ENOUGH OF PALMER'S BLOOD FOR ANOTHER MESSAGE, IF NEED BE.
SHALL I TIGHTEN THE REINS ON THE TROUBLED DR. CHOI?
NOT YET. THERE IS A SEPARATE MATTER THAT I PLAN TO "DELEGATE" TO HIM...

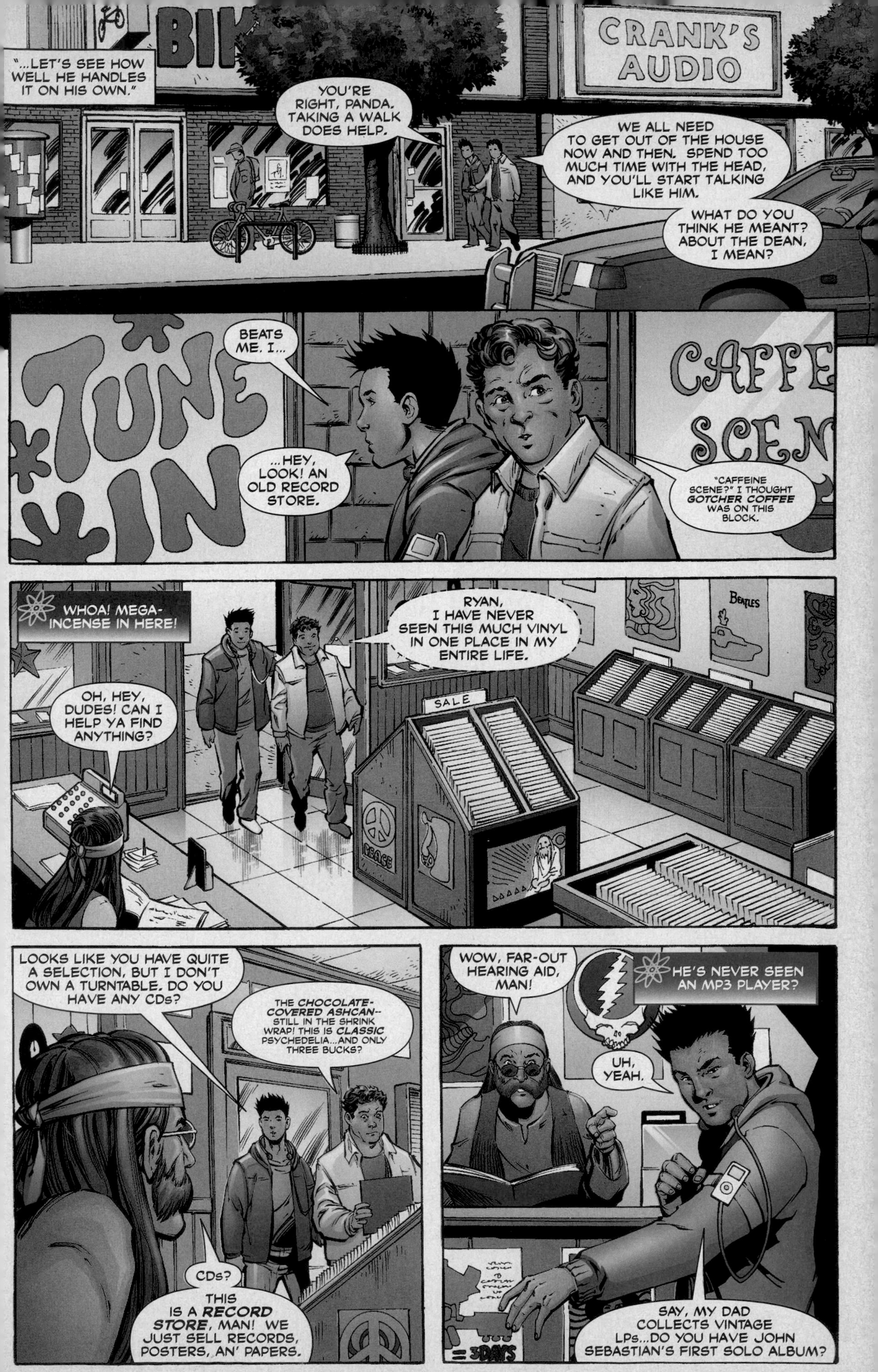
"...LET'S SEE HOW WELL HE HANDLES IT ON HIS OWN."
CRANK'S AUDIO
YOU'RE RIGHT, PANDA. TAKING A WALK DOES HELP.
WE ALL NEED TO GET OUT OF THE HOUSE NOW AND THEN. SPEND TOO MUCH TIME WITH THE HEAD, AND YOU'LL START TALKING LIKE HIM.
WHAT DO YOU THINK HE MEANT? ABOUT THE DEAN, I MEAN?
TUNE IN
BEATS ME. I...
...HEY, LOOK! AN OLD RECORD STORE.
"CAFFEINE SCENE?" I THOUGHT GOTCHER COFFEE WAS ON THIS BLOCK.
WHOA! MEGA-INCENSE IN HERE!
RYAN, I HAVE NEVER SEEN THIS MUCH VINYL IN ONE PLACE IN MY ENTIRE LIFE.
OH, HEY, DUDES! CAN I HELP YA FIND ANYTHING?
SALE
BEATLES
PEACE
LOOKS LIKE YOU HAVE QUITE A SELECTION, BUT I DON'T OWN A TURNTABLE. DO YOU HAVE ANY CDs?
THE CHOCOLATE-COVERED ASHCAN--STILL IN THE SHRINK WRAP! THIS IS CLASSIC PSYCHEDELIA...AND ONLY THREE BUCKS?
CDs?
THIS IS A RECORD STORE, MAN! WE JUST SELL RECORDS, POSTERS, AN' PAPERS.
WOW, FAR-OUT HEARING AID, MAN!
HE'S NEVER SEEN AN MP3 PLAYER?
UH, YEAH.
SAY, MY DAD COLLECTS VINTAGE LPs...DO YOU HAVE JOHN SEBASTIAN'S FIRST SOLO ALBUM?
3 DAYS

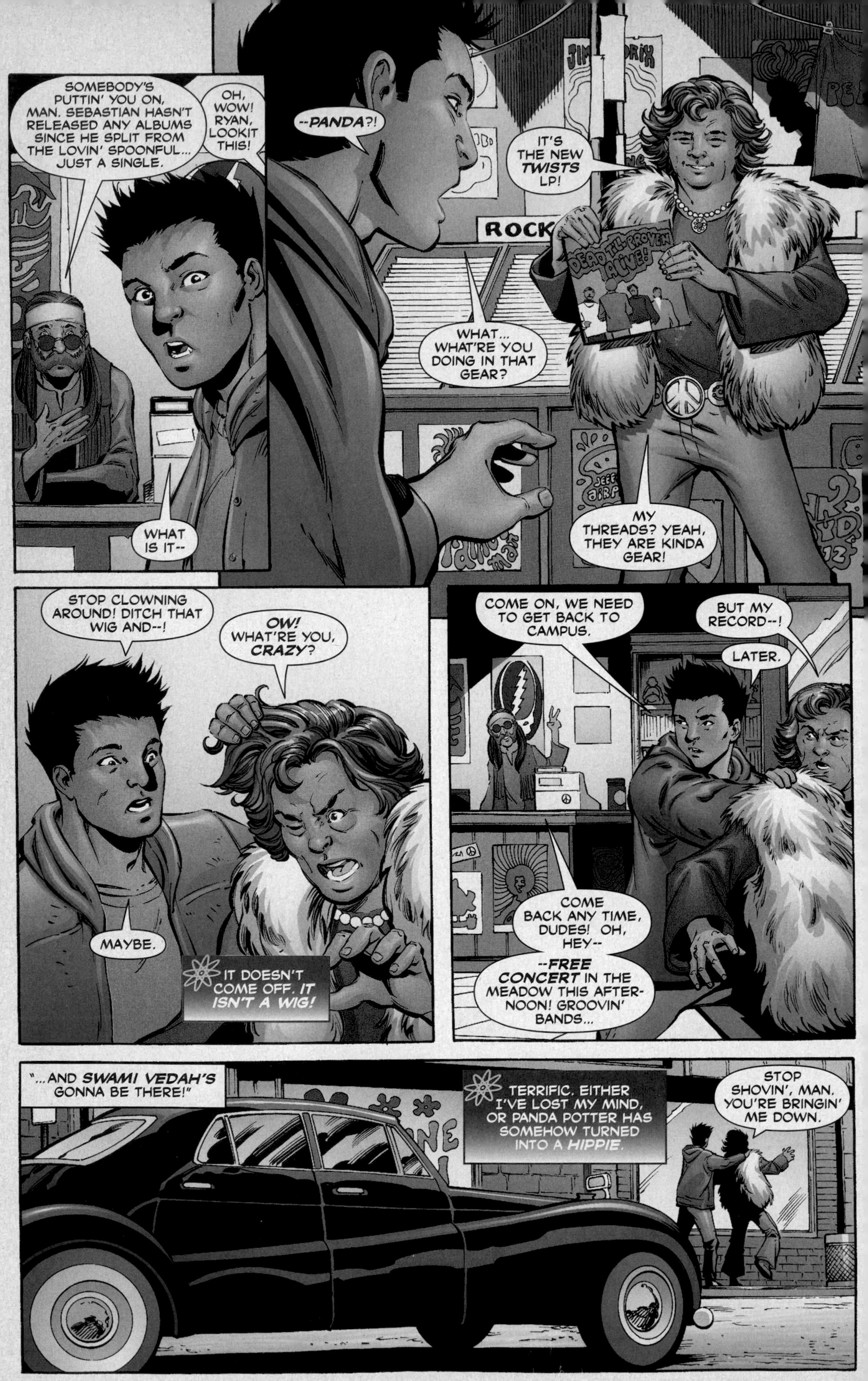
SOMEBODY'S PUTTIN' YOU ON, MAN. SEBASTIAN HASN'T RELEASED ANY ALBUMS SINCE HE SPLIT FROM THE LOVIN' SPOONFUL... JUST A SINGLE.
OH, WOW! RYAN, LOOKIT THIS!
WHAT IS IT--
--PANDA?!
WHAT... WHAT'RE YOU DOING IN THAT GEAR?
IT'S THE NEW TWISTS LP!
ROCK
DEAD TILL PROVEN ALIVE!
MY THREADS? YEAH, THEY ARE KINDA GEAR!
STOP CLOWNING AROUND! DITCH THAT WIG AND--!
OW! WHAT'RE YOU, CRAZY?
MAYBE.
IT DOESN'T COME OFF. IT ISN'T A WIG!
COME ON, WE NEED TO GET BACK TO CAMPUS.
BUT MY RECORD--!
LATER.
COME BACK ANY TIME, DUDES! OH, HEY--
--FREE CONCERT IN THE MEADOW THIS AFTER-NOON! GROOVIN' BANDS...
"...AND SWAMI VEDAH'S GONNA BE THERE!"
TERRIFIC. EITHER I'VE LOST MY MIND, OR PANDA POTTER HAS SOMEHOW TURNED INTO A HIPPIE.
STOP SHOVIN', MAN. YOU'RE BRINGIN' ME DOWN.

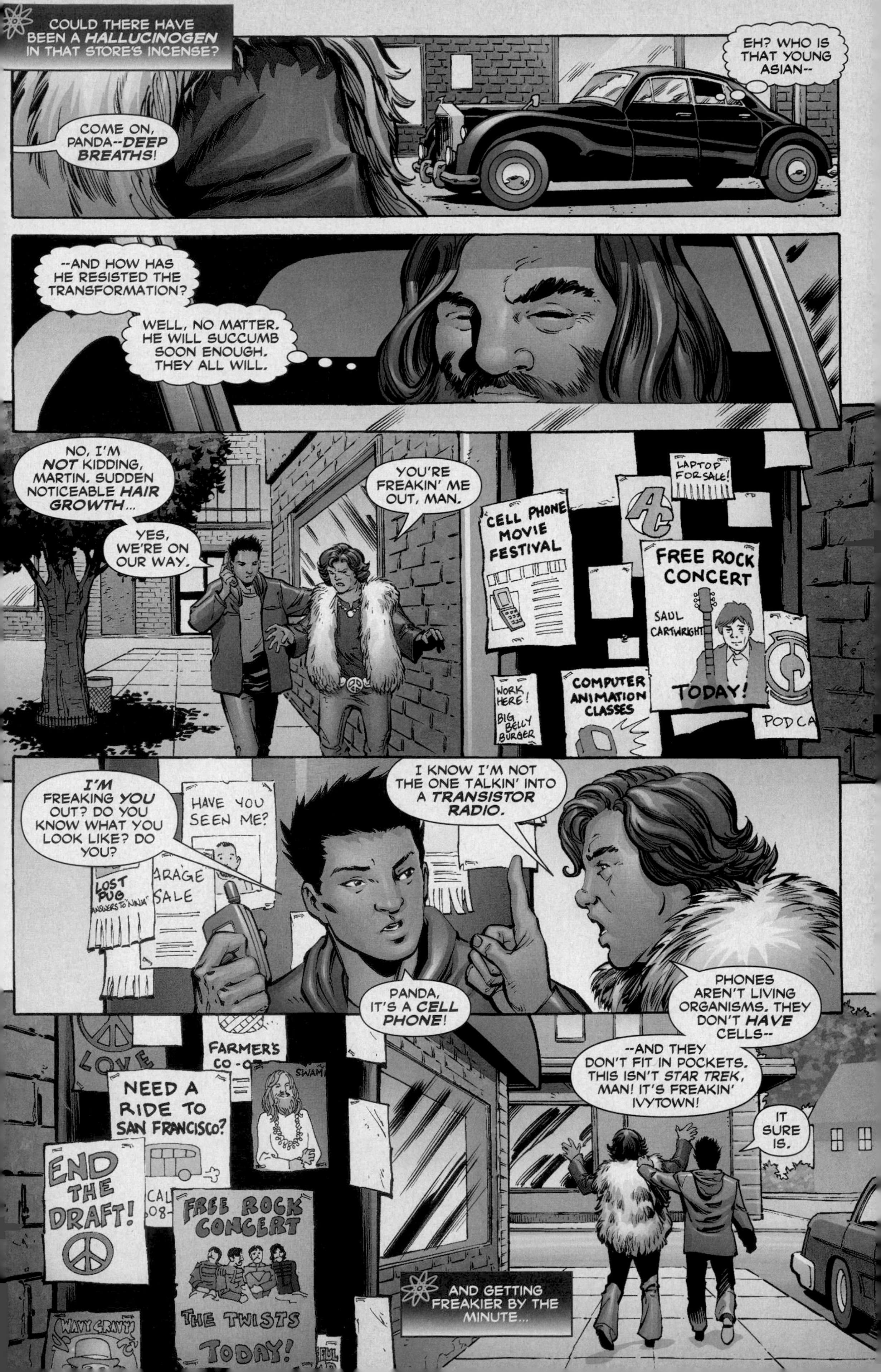
COULD THERE HAVE BEEN A HALLUCINOGEN IN THAT STORE'S INCENSE?
COME ON, PANDA--DEEP BREATHS!
EH? WHO IS THAT YOUNG ASIAN--
--AND HOW HAS HE RESISTED THE TRANSFORMATION?
WELL, NO MATTER. HE WILL SUCCUMB SOON ENOUGH. THEY ALL WILL.
NO, I'M NOT KIDDING, MARTIN. SUDDEN NOTICEABLE HAIR GROWTH...
YES, WE'RE ON OUR WAY.
YOU'RE FREAKIN' ME OUT, MAN.
CELL PHONE MOVIE FESTIVAL
LAPTOP FOR SALE!
FREE ROCK CONCERT
SAUL CARTWRIGHT
TODAY!
WORK HERE! BIG BELLY BURGER
COMPUTER ANIMATION CLASSES
POD CA
I'M FREAKING YOU OUT? DO YOU KNOW WHAT YOU LOOK LIKE? DO YOU?
HAVE YOU SEEN ME?
LOST PUG ANSWERS TO "NINJA"
ARAGE SALE
I KNOW I'M NOT THE ONE TALKIN' INTO A TRANSISTOR RADIO.
PANDA, IT'S A CELL PHONE!
PHONES AREN'T LIVING ORGANISMS. THEY DON'T HAVE CELLS--
--AND THEY DON'T FIT IN POCKETS. THIS ISN'T STAR TREK, MAN! IT'S FREAKIN' IVYTOWN!
IT SURE IS.
LOVE
FARMER'S CO-O
SWAMI
NEED A RIDE TO SAN FRANCISCO?
END THE DRAFT!
FREE ROCK CONCERT
THE TWISTS
TODAY!
WAVY GRAVY
AND GETTING FREAKIER BY THE MINUTE...

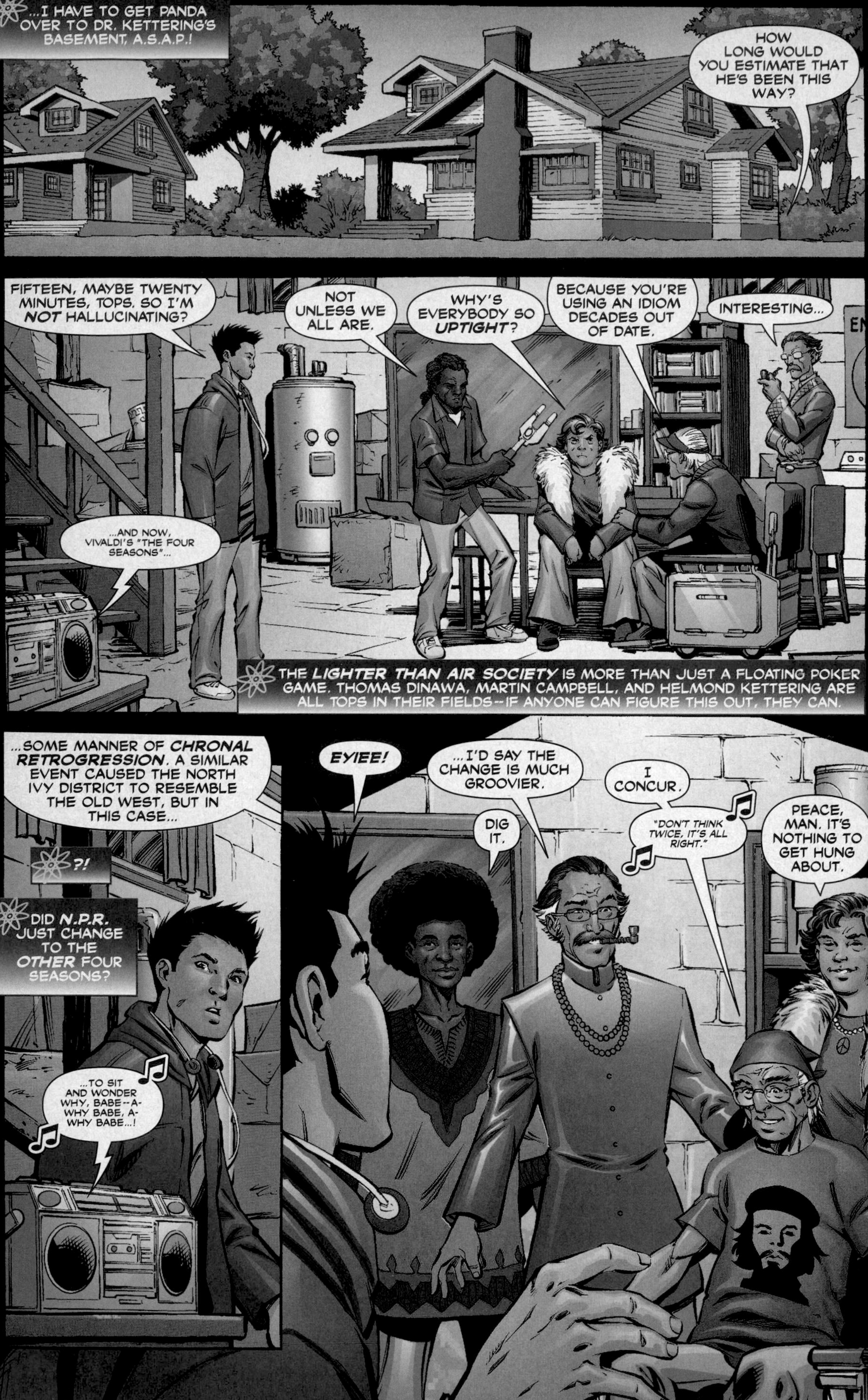

...I HAVE TO GET PANDA OVER TO DR. KETTERING'S BASEMENT, A.S.A.P.!
HOW LONG WOULD YOU ESTIMATE THAT HE'S BEEN THIS WAY?
FIFTEEN, MAYBE TWENTY MINUTES, TOPS. SO I'M NOT HALLUCINATING?
NOT UNLESS WE ALL ARE.
WHY'S EVERYBODY SO UPTIGHT?
BECAUSE YOU'RE USING AN IDIOM DECADES OUT OF DATE.
INTERESTING...
...AND NOW, VIVALDI'S "THE FOUR SEASONS"...
THE LIGHTER THAN AIR SOCIETY IS MORE THAN JUST A FLOATING POKER GAME. THOMAS DINAWA, MARTIN CAMPBELL, AND HELMOND KETTERING ARE ALL TOPS IN THEIR FIELDS--IF ANYONE CAN FIGURE THIS OUT, THEY CAN.
...SOME MANNER OF CHRONAL RETROGRESSION. A SIMILAR EVENT CAUSED THE NORTH IVY DISTRICT TO RESEMBLE THE OLD WEST, BUT IN THIS CASE...
EYIEE!
?!
...I'D SAY THE CHANGE IS MUCH GROOVIER.
DIG IT.
I CONCUR.
"DON'T THINK TWICE, IT'S ALL RIGHT."
PEACE, MAN. IT'S NOTHING TO GET HUNG ABOUT.
DID N.P.R. JUST CHANGE TO THE OTHER FOUR SEASONS?
...TO SIT AND WONDER WHY, BABE--A-WHY BABE, A-WHY BABE...!

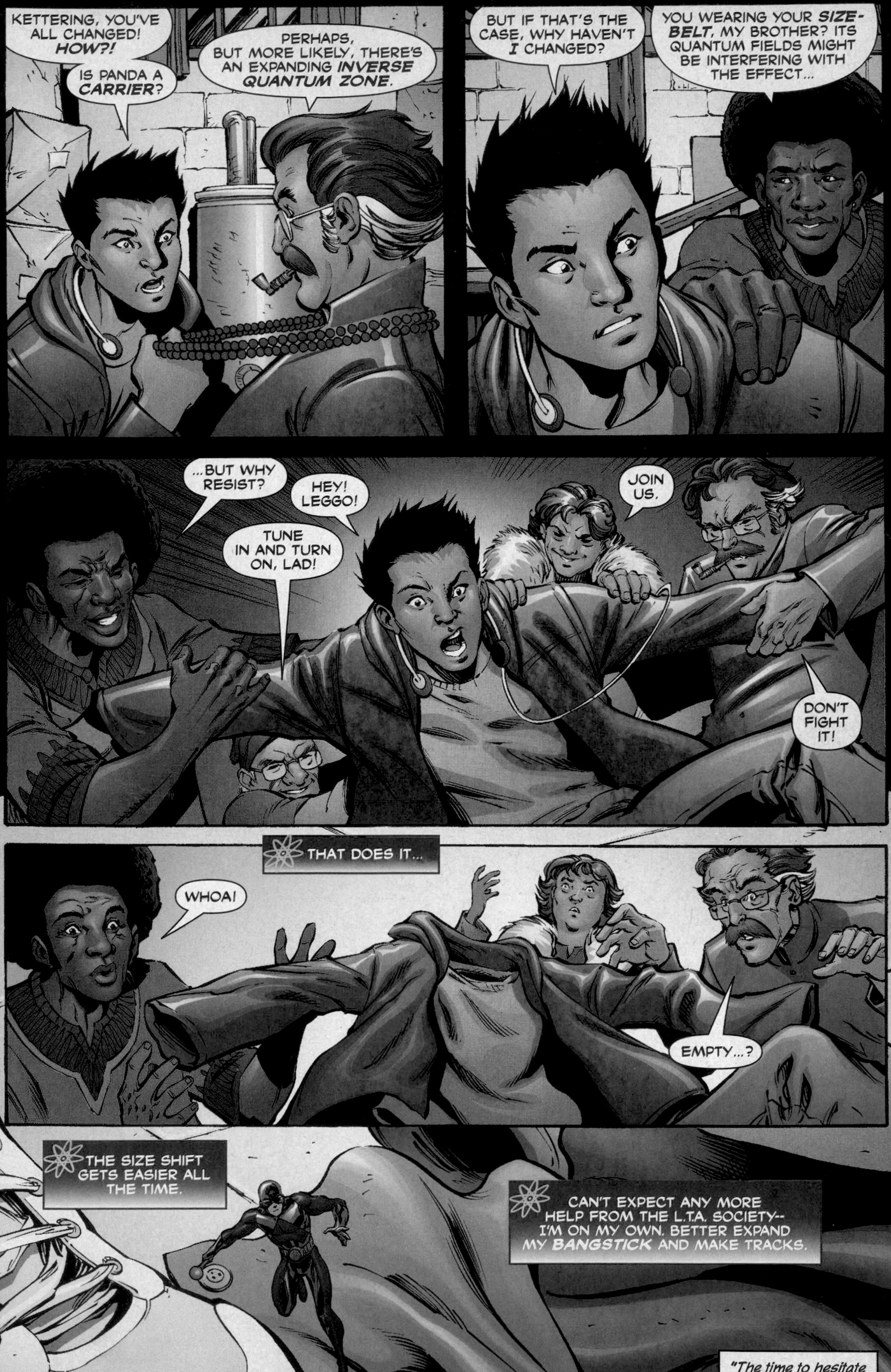
KETTERING, YOU'VE ALL CHANGED! HOW?!
IS PANDA A CARRIER?
PERHAPS, BUT MORE LIKELY, THERE'S AN EXPANDING INVERSE QUANTUM ZONE.
BUT IF THAT'S THE CASE, WHY HAVEN'T I CHANGED?
YOU WEARING YOUR SIZE-BELT, MY BROTHER? ITS QUANTUM FIELDS MIGHT BE INTERFERING WITH THE EFFECT...
...BUT WHY RESIST?
HEY! LEGGO!
TUNE IN AND TURN ON, LAD!
JOIN US.
DON'T FIGHT IT!
THAT DOES IT...
WHOA!
EMPTY...?
THE SIZE SHIFT GETS EASIER ALL THE TIME.
CAN'T EXPECT ANY MORE HELP FROM THE L.T.A. SOCIETY-- I'M ON MY OWN. BETTER EXPAND MY BANGSTICK AND MAKE TRACKS.
"The time to hesitate is through." --JIM MORRISON

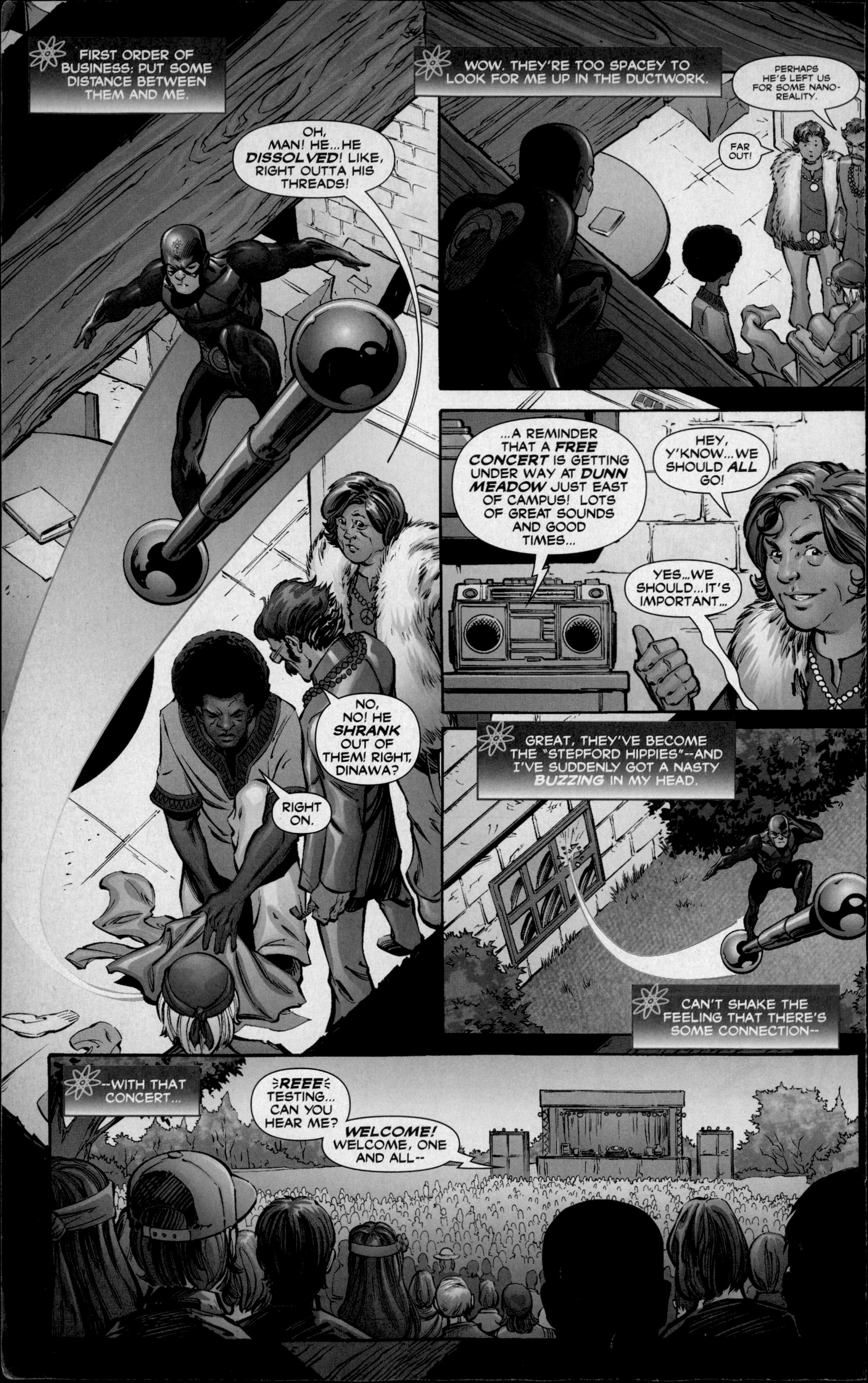

FIRST ORDER OF BUSINESS: PUT SOME DISTANCE BETWEEN THEM AND ME.
OH, MAN! HE...HE DISSOLVED! LIKE, RIGHT OUTTA HIS THREADS!
NO, NO! HE SHRANK OUT OF THEM! RIGHT, DINAWA?
RIGHT ON.
WOW. THEY'RE TOO SPACEY TO LOOK FOR ME UP IN THE DUCTWORK.
PERHAPS HE'S LEFT US FOR SOME NANO-REALITY.
FAR OUT!
...A REMINDER THAT A FREE CONCERT IS GETTING UNDER WAY AT DUNN MEADOW JUST EAST OF CAMPUS! LOTS OF GREAT SOUNDS AND GOOD TIMES...
HEY, Y'KNOW...WE SHOULD ALL GO!
YES...WE SHOULD...IT'S IMPORTANT...
GREAT, THEY'VE BECOME THE "STEPFORD HIPPIES"--AND I'VE SUDDENLY GOT A NASTY BUZZING IN MY HEAD.
CAN'T SHAKE THE FEELING THAT THERE'S SOME CONNECTION--
--WITH THAT CONCERT...
REEE TESTING... CAN YOU HEAR ME?
WELCOME! WELCOME, ONE AND ALL--

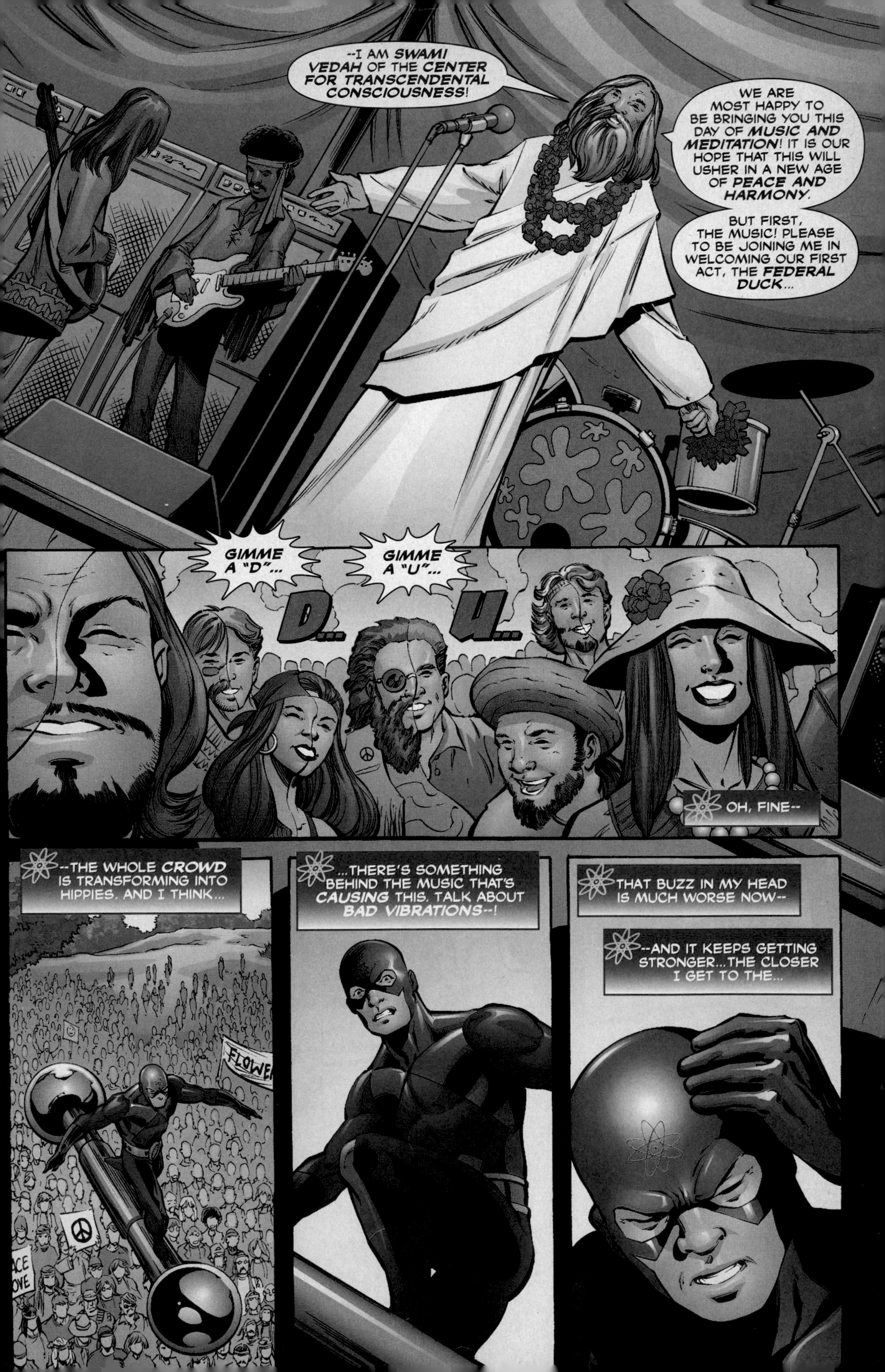
--I AM SWAMI VEDAH OF THE CENTER FOR TRANSCENDENTAL CONSCIOUSNESS!
WE ARE MOST HAPPY TO BE BRINGING YOU THIS DAY OF MUSIC AND MEDITATION! IT IS OUR HOPE THAT THIS WILL USHER IN A NEW AGE OF PEACE AND HARMONY.
BUT FIRST, THE MUSIC! PLEASE TO BE JOINING ME IN WELCOMING OUR FIRST ACT, THE FEDERAL DUCK...
GIMME A "D"...
GIMME A "U"...
D...
U...
OH, FINE--
--THE WHOLE CROWD IS TRANSFORMING INTO HIPPIES. AND I THINK...
FLOWER
...THERE'S SOMETHING BEHIND THE MUSIC THAT'S CAUSING THIS. TALK ABOUT BAD VIBRATIONS--!
THAT BUZZ IN MY HEAD IS MUCH WORSE NOW--
--AND IT KEEPS GETTING STRONGER...THE CLOSER I GET TO THE...

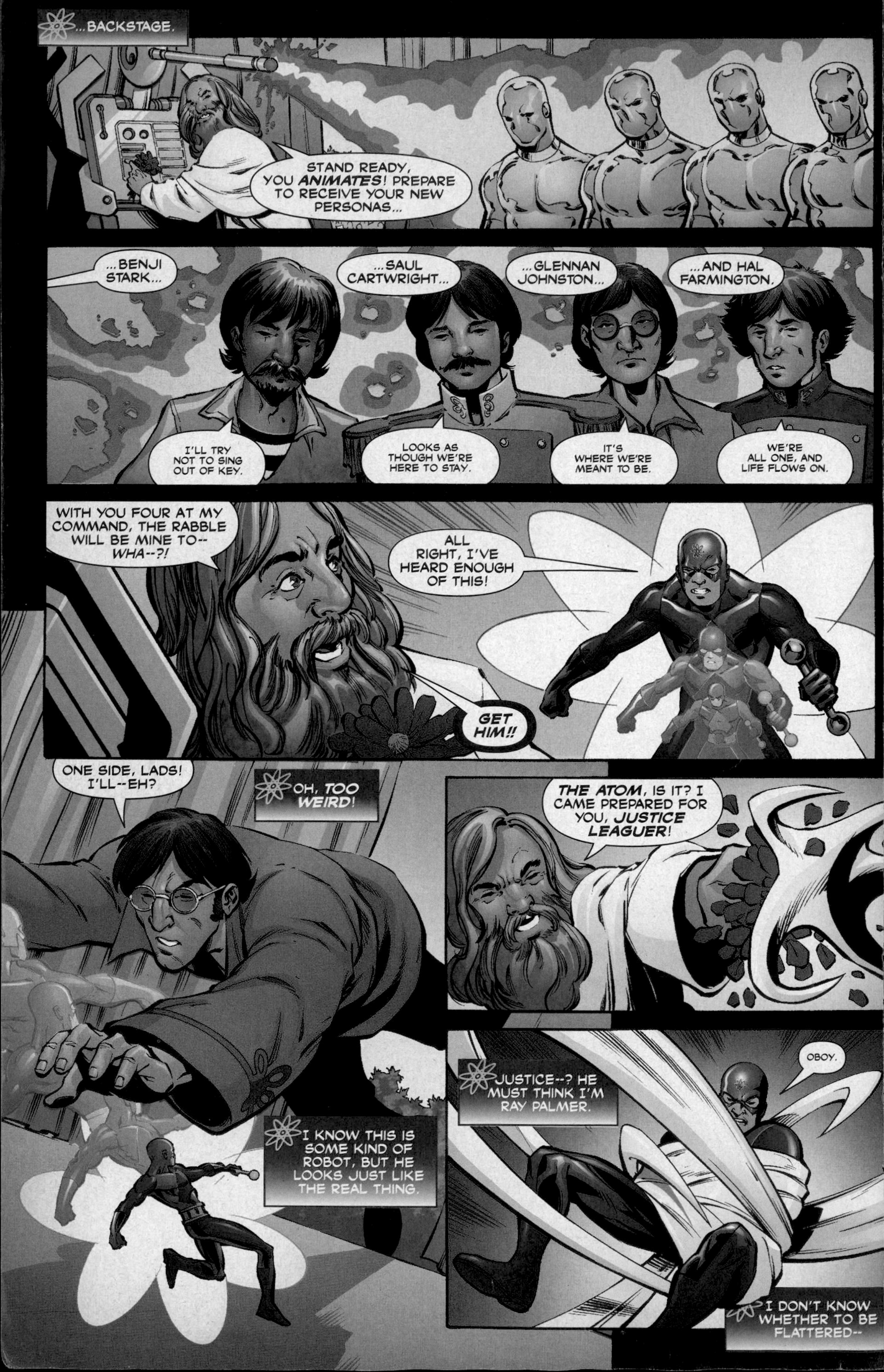
...BACKSTAGE.
STAND READY, YOU ANIMATES! PREPARE TO RECEIVE YOUR NEW PERSONAS...
...BENJI STARK...
...SAUL CARTWRIGHT...
...GLENNAN JOHNSTON...
...AND HAL FARMINGTON.
I'LL TRY NOT TO SING OUT OF KEY.
LOOKS AS THOUGH WE'RE HERE TO STAY.
IT'S WHERE WE'RE MEANT TO BE.
WE'RE ALL ONE, AND LIFE FLOWS ON.
WITH YOU FOUR AT MY COMMAND, THE RABBLE WILL BE MINE TO-- WHA--?!
ALL RIGHT, I'VE HEARD ENOUGH OF THIS!
GET HIM!!
ONE SIDE, LADS! I'LL--EH?
OH, TOO WEIRD!
I KNOW THIS IS SOME KIND OF ROBOT, BUT HE LOOKS JUST LIKE THE REAL THING.
THE ATOM, IS IT? I CAME PREPARED FOR YOU, JUSTICE LEAGUER!
JUSTICE--? HE MUST THINK I'M RAY PALMER.
OBOY.
I DON'T KNOW WHETHER TO BE FLATTERED--

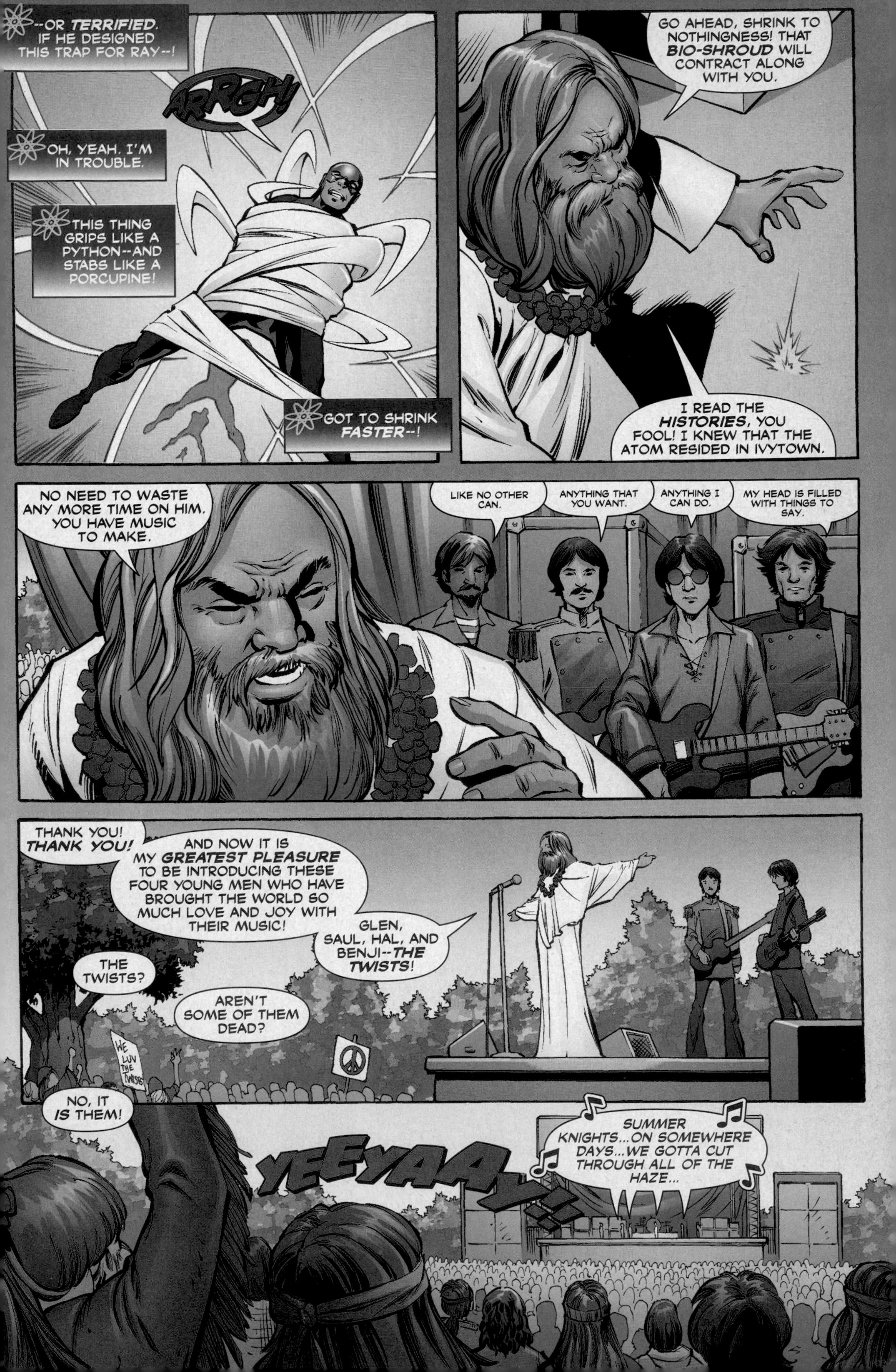
--OR TERRIFIED. IF HE DESIGNED THIS TRAP FOR RAY--!
ARRGH!
OH, YEAH. I'M IN TROUBLE.
THIS THING GRIPS LIKE A PYTHON--AND STABS LIKE A PORCUPINE!
GOT TO SHRINK FASTER--!
GO AHEAD, SHRINK TO NOTHINGNESS! THAT BIO-SHROUD WILL CONTRACT ALONG WITH YOU.
I READ THE HISTORIES, YOU FOOL! I KNEW THAT THE ATOM RESIDED IN IVYTOWN.
NO NEED TO WASTE ANY MORE TIME ON HIM. YOU HAVE MUSIC TO MAKE.
LIKE NO OTHER CAN.
ANYTHING THAT YOU WANT.
ANYTHING I CAN DO.
MY HEAD IS FILLED WITH THINGS TO SAY.
THANK YOU! THANK YOU!
AND NOW IT IS MY GREATEST PLEASURE TO BE INTRODUCING THESE FOUR YOUNG MEN WHO HAVE BROUGHT THE WORLD SO MUCH LOVE AND JOY WITH THEIR MUSIC!
GLEN, SAUL, HAL, AND BENJI--THE TWISTS!
THE TWISTS?
AREN'T SOME OF THEM DEAD?
WE LUV THE TWISTS
NO, IT IS THEM!
YEEYAAAY!!
SUMMER KNIGHTS...ON SOMEWHERE DAYS...WE GOTTA CUT THROUGH ALL OF THE HAZE...

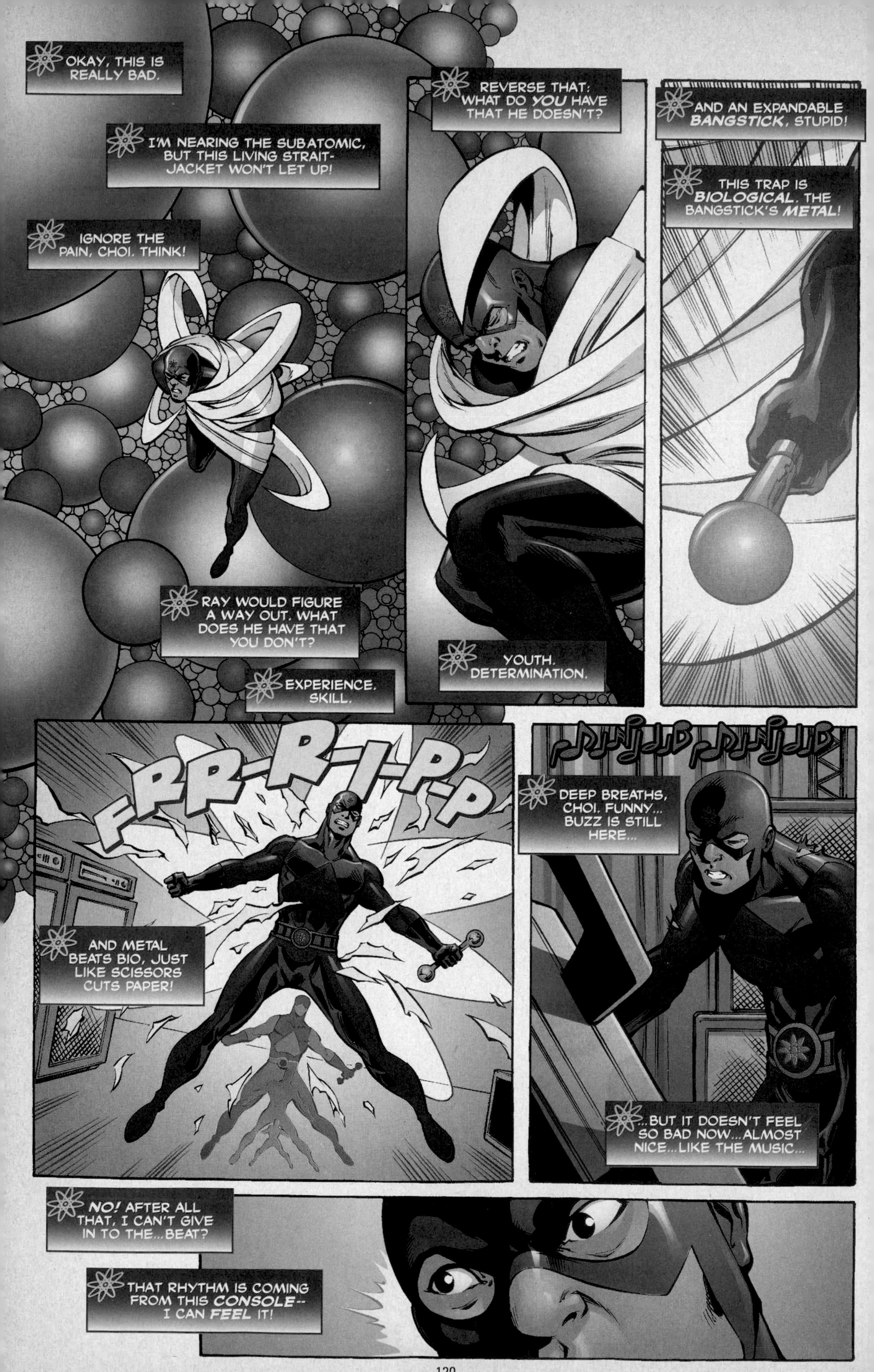

OKAY, THIS IS REALLY BAD.
I'M NEARING THE SUBATOMIC, BUT THIS LIVING STRAIT-JACKET WON'T LET UP!
IGNORE THE PAIN, CHOI. THINK!
RAY WOULD FIGURE A WAY OUT. WHAT DOES HE HAVE THAT YOU DON'T?
EXPERIENCE. SKILL.
REVERSE THAT: WHAT DO YOU HAVE THAT HE DOESN'T?
YOUTH. DETERMINATION.
AND AN EXPANDABLE BANGSTICK, STUPID!
THIS TRAP IS BIOLOGICAL. THE BANGSTICK'S METAL!
FRR-R-I-P-P
AND METAL BEATS BIO, JUST LIKE SCISSORS CUTS PAPER!
DEEP BREATHS, CHOI. FUNNY... BUZZ IS STILL HERE...
...BUT IT DOESN'T FEEL SO BAD NOW...ALMOST NICE...LIKE THE MUSIC...
NO! AFTER ALL THAT, I CAN'T GIVE IN TO THE...BEAT?
THAT RHYTHM IS COMING FROM THIS CONSOLE-- I CAN FEEL IT!

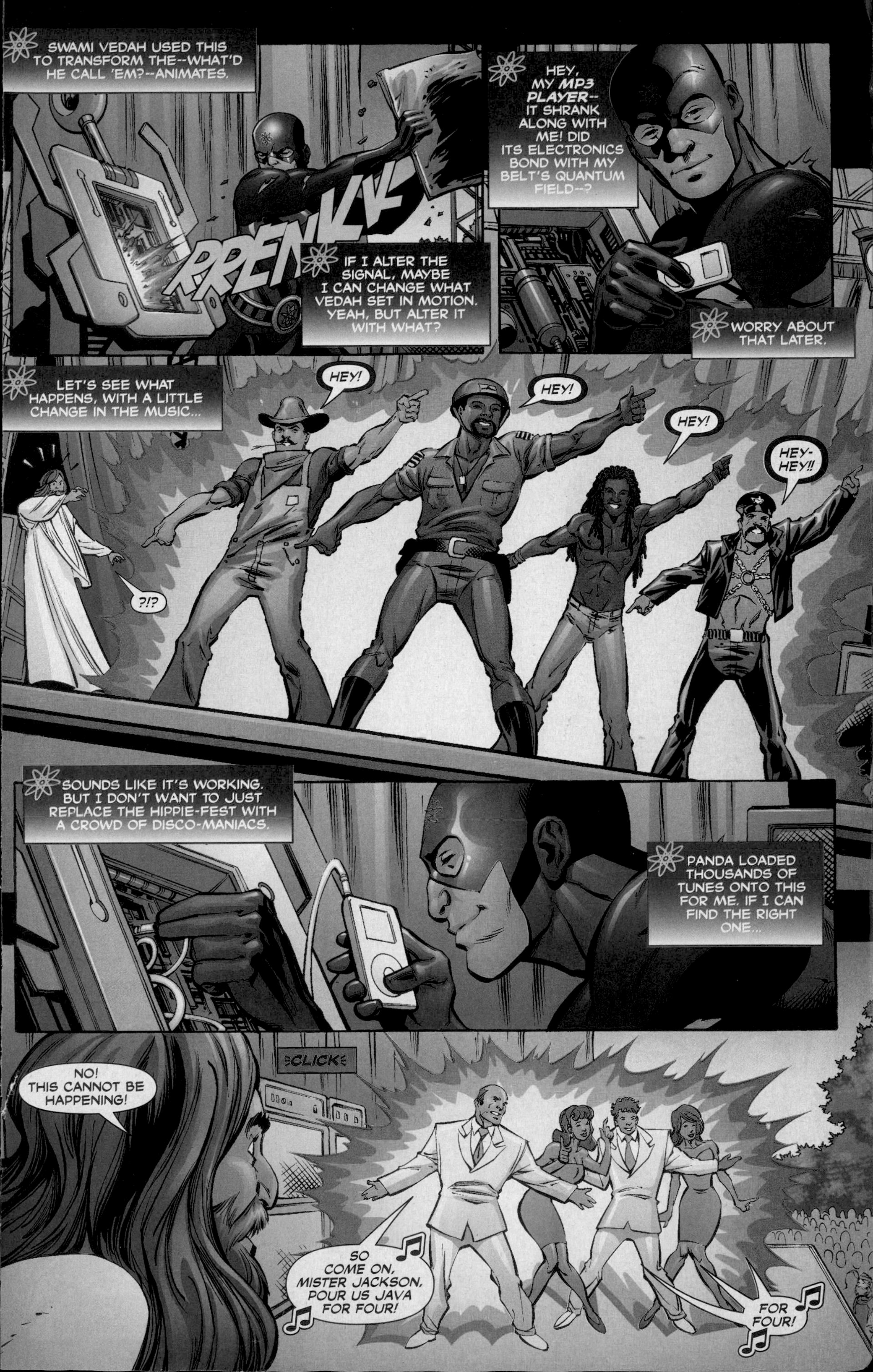
SWAMI VEDAH USED THIS TO TRANSFORM THE--WHAT'D HE CALL 'EM?--ANIMATES.
RRRENKK
IF I ALTER THE SIGNAL, MAYBE I CAN CHANGE WHAT VEDAH SET IN MOTION. YEAH, BUT ALTER IT WITH WHAT?
HEY, MY MP3 PLAYER-- IT SHRANK ALONG WITH ME! DID ITS ELECTRONICS BOND WITH MY BELT'S QUANTUM FIELD--?
WORRY ABOUT THAT LATER.
LET'S SEE WHAT HAPPENS, WITH A LITTLE CHANGE IN THE MUSIC...
HEY!
HEY!
HEY!
HEY-HEY!!
?!?
SOUNDS LIKE IT'S WORKING. BUT I DON'T WANT TO JUST REPLACE THE HIPPIE-FEST WITH A CROWD OF DISCO-MANIACS.
PANDA LOADED THOUSANDS OF TUNES ONTO THIS FOR ME. IF I CAN FIND THE RIGHT ONE...
CLICK
NO! THIS CANNOT BE HAPPENING!
SO COME ON, MISTER JACKSON, POUR US JAVA FOR FOUR!
FOR FOUR!

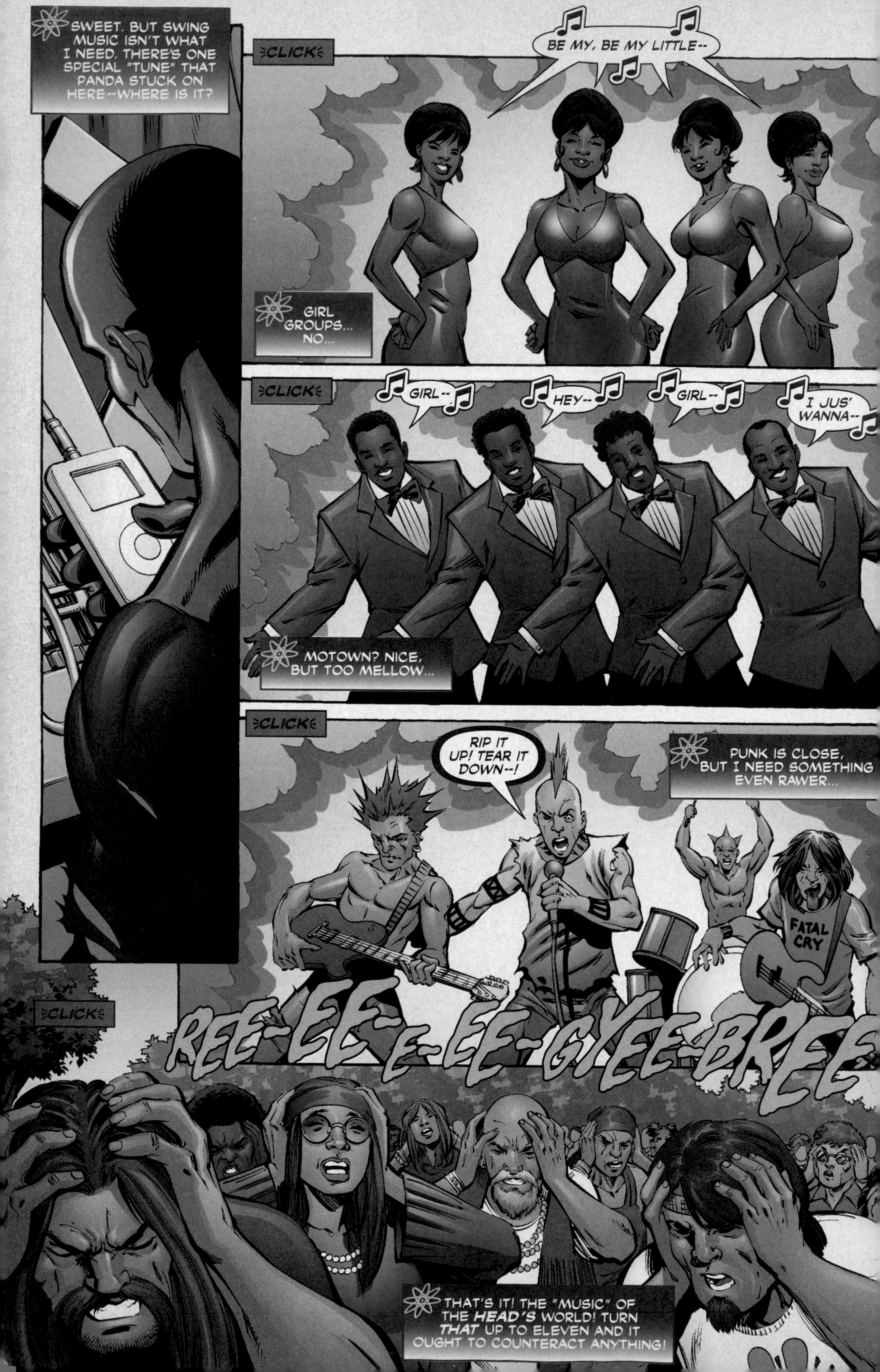
SWEET. BUT SWING MUSIC ISN'T WHAT I NEED. THERE'S ONE SPECIAL "TUNE" THAT PANDA STUCK ON HERE--WHERE IS IT?
CLICK
BE MY, BE MY LITTLE--
GIRL GROUPS... NO...
CLICK
GIRL--
HEY--
GIRL--
I JUS' WANNA--
MOTOWN? NICE, BUT TOO MELLOW...
CLICK
RIP IT UP! TEAR IT DOWN--!
PUNK IS CLOSE, BUT I NEED SOMETHING EVEN RAWER...
FATAL CRY
CLICK
REE-EE-E-EE-GYEE-BREE
THAT'S IT! THE "MUSIC" OF THE HEAD'S WORLD! TURN THAT UP TO ELEVEN AND IT OUGHT TO COUNTERACT ANYTHING!

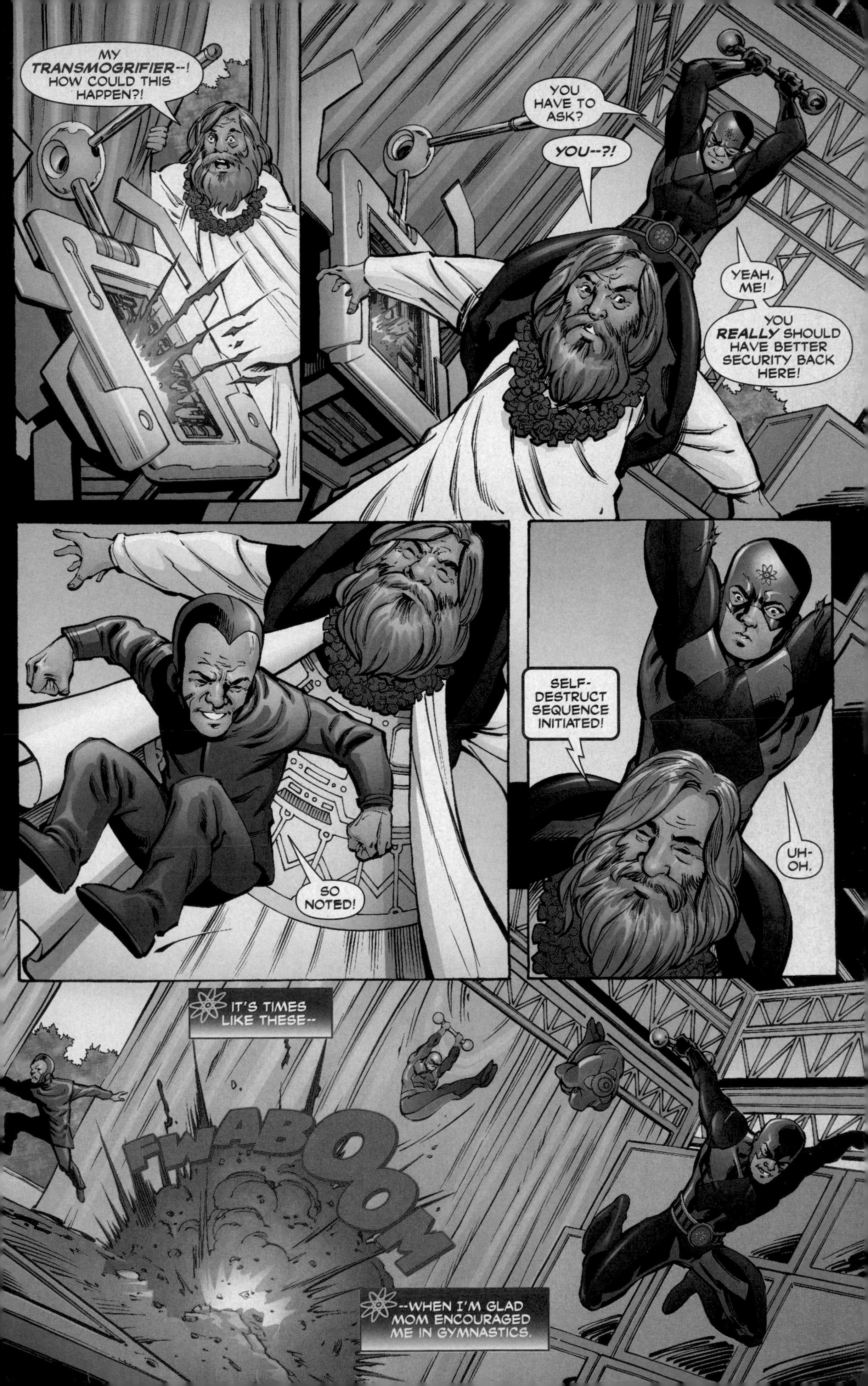

MY TRANSMOGRIFIER--! HOW COULD THIS HAPPEN?!
YOU HAVE TO ASK?
YOU--?!
YEAH, ME!
YOU REALLY SHOULD HAVE BETTER SECURITY BACK HERE!
SO NOTED!
SELF-DESTRUCT SEQUENCE INITIATED!
UH-OH.
IT'S TIMES LIKE THESE--
FWABOOOM
--WHEN I'M GLAD MOM ENCOURAGED ME IN GYMNASTICS.

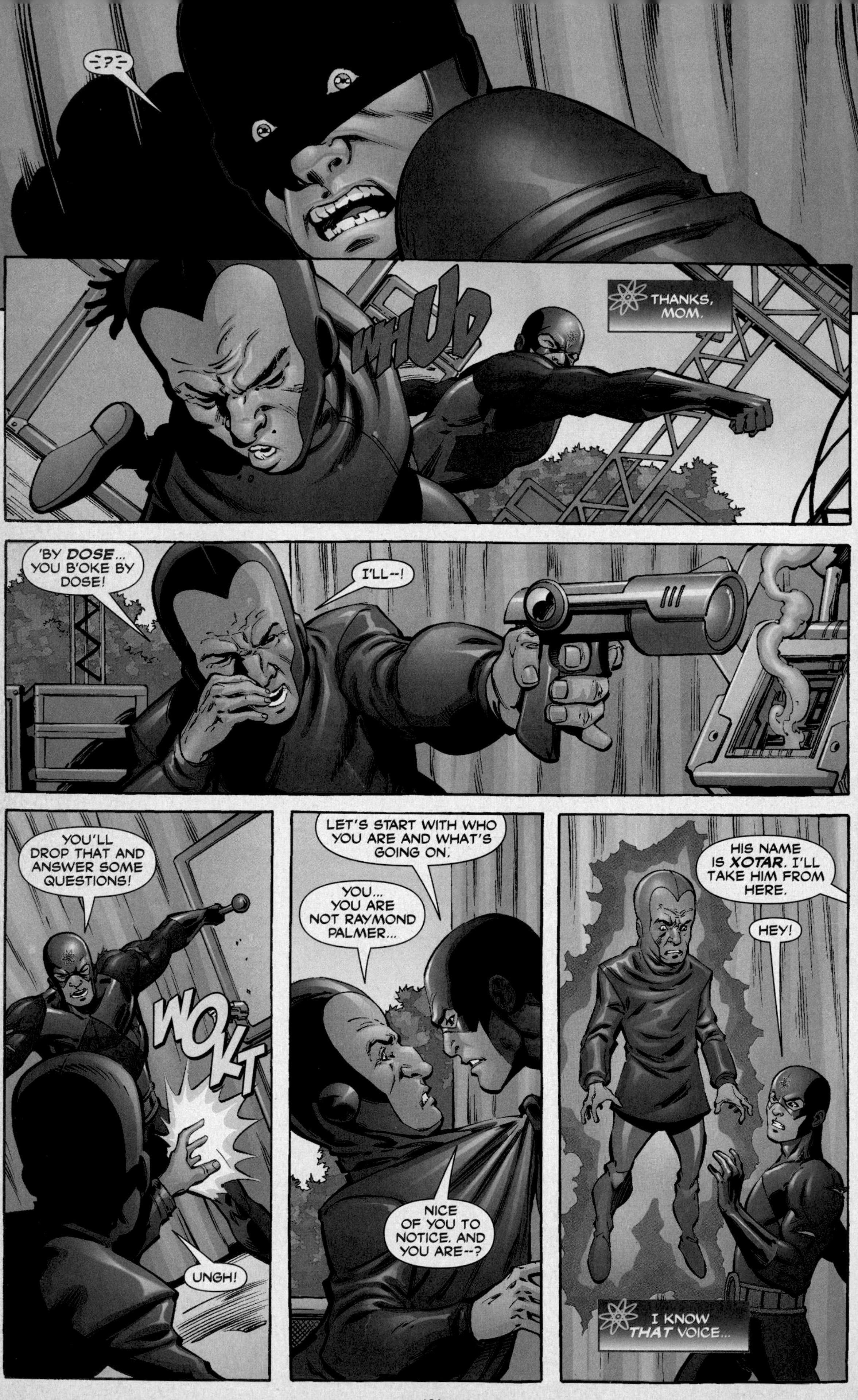
-?-
WHUD
THANKS, MOM.
'BY DOSE... YOU B'OKE BY DOSE!
I'LL--!
YOU'LL DROP THAT AND ANSWER SOME QUESTIONS!
WOKT
UNGH!
LET'S START WITH WHO YOU ARE AND WHAT'S GOING ON.
YOU... YOU ARE NOT RAYMOND PALMER...
NICE OF YOU TO NOTICE. AND YOU ARE--?
HIS NAME IS XOTAR. I'LL TAKE HIM FROM HERE.
HEY!
I KNOW THAT VOICE...

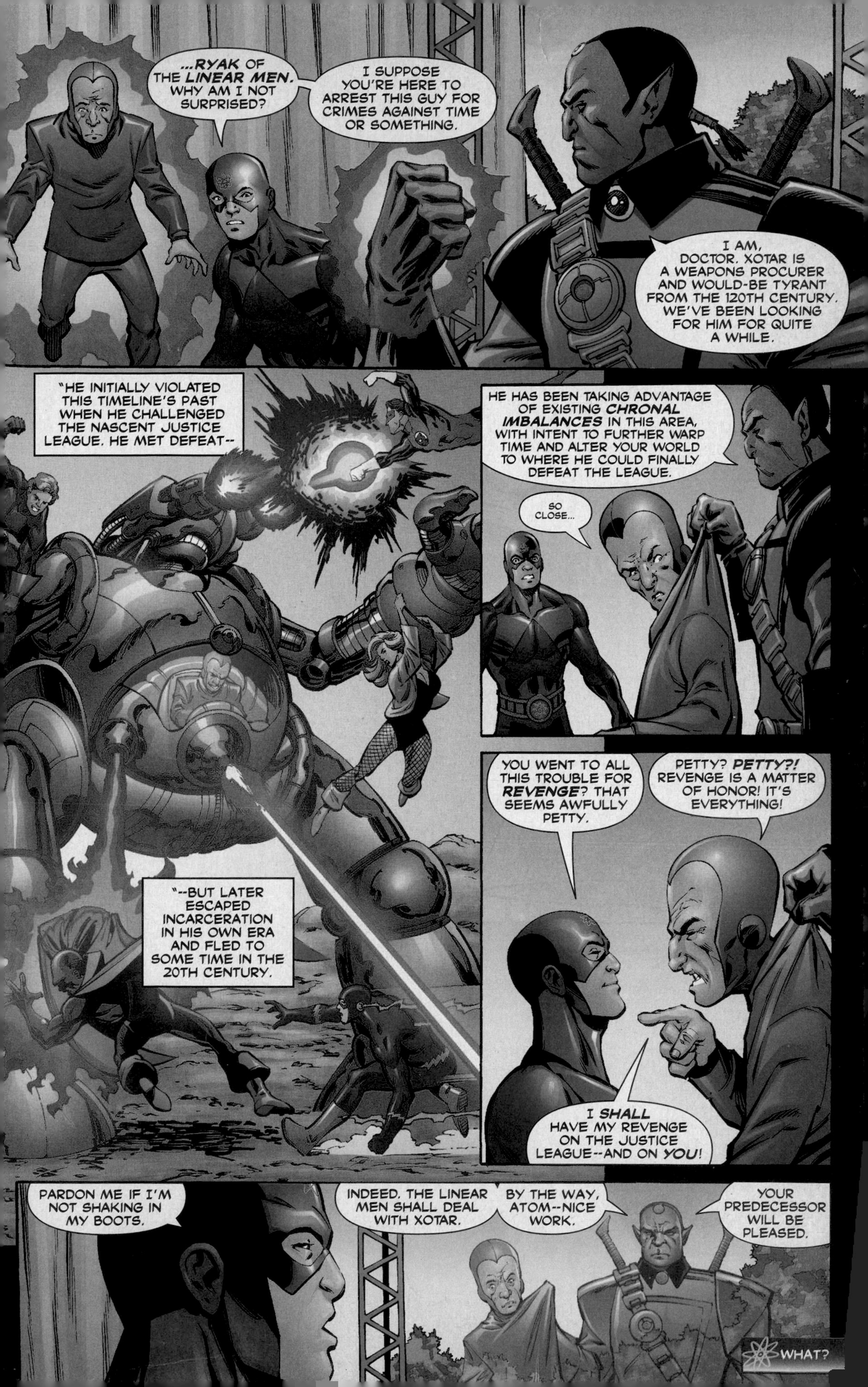
...RYAK OF THE LINEAR MEN. WHY AM I NOT SURPRISED?
I SUPPOSE YOU'RE HERE TO ARREST THIS GUY FOR CRIMES AGAINST TIME OR SOMETHING.
I AM, DOCTOR. XOTAR IS A WEAPONS PROCURER AND WOULD-BE TYRANT FROM THE 120TH CENTURY. WE'VE BEEN LOOKING FOR HIM FOR QUITE A WHILE.
"HE INITIALLY VIOLATED THIS TIMELINE'S PAST WHEN HE CHALLENGED THE NASCENT JUSTICE LEAGUE. HE MET DEFEAT--
"--BUT LATER ESCAPED INCARCERATION IN HIS OWN ERA AND FLED TO SOME TIME IN THE 20TH CENTURY.
HE HAS BEEN TAKING ADVANTAGE OF EXISTING CHRONAL IMBALANCES IN THIS AREA, WITH INTENT TO FURTHER WARP TIME AND ALTER YOUR WORLD TO WHERE HE COULD FINALLY DEFEAT THE LEAGUE.
SO CLOSE...
YOU WENT TO ALL THIS TROUBLE FOR REVENGE? THAT SEEMS AWFULLY PETTY.
PETTY? PETTY?! REVENGE IS A MATTER OF HONOR! IT'S EVERYTHING!
I SHALL HAVE MY REVENGE ON THE JUSTICE LEAGUE--AND ON YOU!
PARDON ME IF I'M NOT SHAKING IN MY BOOTS.
INDEED. THE LINEAR MEN SHALL DEAL WITH XOTAR.
BY THE WAY, ATOM--NICE WORK.
YOUR PREDECESSOR WILL BE PLEASED.
WHAT?

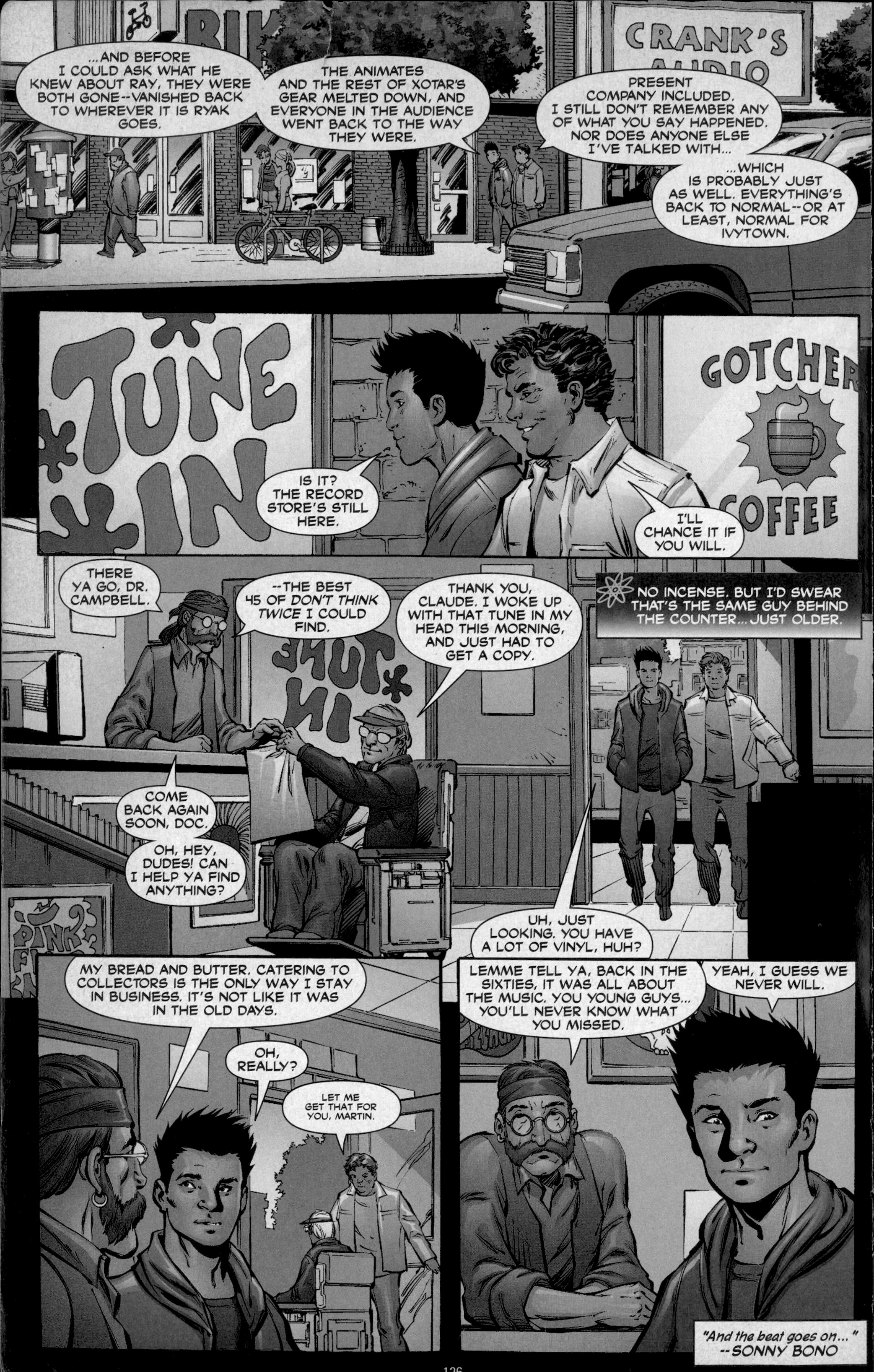
CRANK'S AUDIO
...AND BEFORE I COULD ASK WHAT HE KNEW ABOUT RAY, THEY WERE BOTH GONE--VANISHED BACK TO WHEREVER IT IS RYAK GOES.
THE ANIMATES AND THE REST OF XOTAR'S GEAR MELTED DOWN, AND EVERYONE IN THE AUDIENCE WENT BACK TO THE WAY THEY WERE.
PRESENT COMPANY INCLUDED. I STILL DON'T REMEMBER ANY OF WHAT YOU SAY HAPPENED. NOR DOES ANYONE ELSE I'VE TALKED WITH...
...WHICH IS PROBABLY JUST AS WELL. EVERYTHING'S BACK TO NORMAL--OR AT LEAST, NORMAL FOR IVYTOWN.
TUNE IN
GOTCHER COFFEE
IS IT? THE RECORD STORE'S STILL HERE.
I'LL CHANCE IT IF YOU WILL.
THERE YA GO, DR. CAMPBELL.
--THE BEST 45 OF *DON'T THINK TWICE* I COULD FIND.
THANK YOU, CLAUDE. I WOKE UP WITH THAT TUNE IN MY HEAD THIS MORNING, AND JUST HAD TO GET A COPY.
NO INCENSE. BUT I'D SWEAR THAT'S THE SAME GUY BEHIND THE COUNTER...JUST OLDER.
COME BACK AGAIN SOON, DOC.
OH, HEY, DUDES! CAN I HELP YA FIND ANYTHING?
UH, JUST LOOKING. YOU HAVE A LOT OF VINYL, HUH?
MY BREAD AND BUTTER. CATERING TO COLLECTORS IS THE ONLY WAY I STAY IN BUSINESS. IT'S NOT LIKE IT WAS IN THE OLD DAYS.
OH, REALLY?
LET ME GET THAT FOR YOU, MARTIN.
LEMME TELL YA, BACK IN THE SIXTIES, IT WAS ALL ABOUT THE MUSIC. YOU YOUNG GUYS... YOU'LL NEVER KNOW WHAT YOU MISSED.
YEAH, I GUESS WE NEVER WILL.
"And the beat goes on..." --SONNY BONO

READ MORE ADVENTURES OF YOUR FAVORITE HEROES IN THESE COLLECTIONS FROM DC COMICS:

KINGDOM COME

THE GREATEST SUPER-HERO EPIC OF TOMORROW!
ELSEWORLDS
KINGDOM COME
Mark WAID Alex ROSS

Mark Waid and **Alex Ross** deliver a grim tale of youth versus experience, tradition versus change and what defines a hero. KINGDOM COME is a riveting story pitting the old guard — Superman, Batman, Wonder Woman and their peers — against a new uncompromising generation.

WINNER OF FIVE EISNER AND HARVEY AWARDS, INCLUDING BEST LIMITED SERIES AND BEST ARTIST

IDENTITY CRISIS

NEW YORK TIMES BEST-SELLING AUTHOR OF THE ZERO GAME
BRAD MELTZER
RAGS MORALES MICHAEL BAIR
IDENTITY CRISIS
Introduction by JOSS WHEDON, creator of BUFFY THE VAMPIRE SLAYER and FIREFLY

BRAD MELTZER
RAGS MORALES
MICHAEL BAIR

CRISIS ON INFINITE EARTHS

CRISIS
ON INFINITE EARTHS
MARV WOLFMAN & GEORGE PÉREZ

MARV WOLFMAN
GEORGE PÉREZ

DC: THE NEW FRONTIER VOLUME 1

DC: The New Frontier
VOLUME ONE
BY DARWYN COOKE WITH DAVE STEWART

DARWYN COOKE
DAVE STEWART

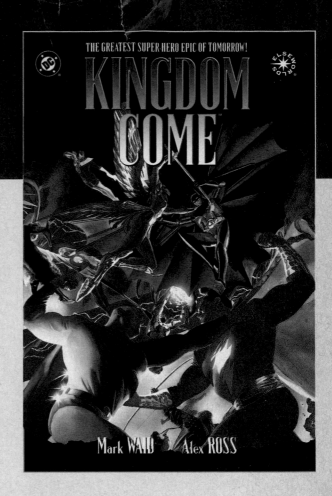

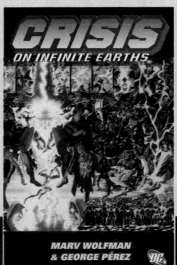

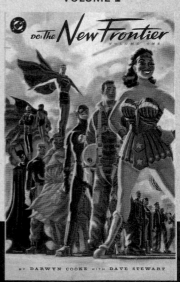

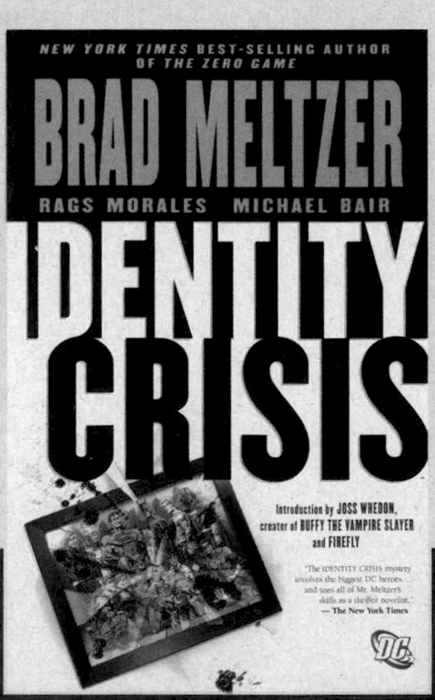

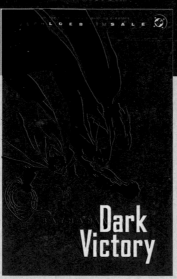